DOCUMENTS
IN BRITISH
HISTORY

VOLUME II

1688 TO THE PRESENT

DOCUMENTS IN BRITISH HISTORY

VOLUME II
1688 TO THE PRESENT

SECOND EDITION

Brian L. Blakeley
Jacquelin Collins

Department of History
Texas Tech University

McGRAW-HILL, INC.
New York   St. Louis   San Francisco   Auckland   Bogotá
Caracas   Lisbon   London   Madrid   Mexico   Milan   Montreal
New Delhi   Paris   San Juan   Singapore   Sydney   Tokyo   Toronto

This book was set in Times Roman by The Clarinda Company.
The editors were Pamela Gordon and Niels Aaboe;
the production supervisor was Louise Karam.
The cover was designed by Carla Bauer.
Project supervision was done by The Wheetley Company, Inc.
R. R. Donnelley & Sons Company was printer and binder.

Cover painting credit:
Victoria, 1863 after portrait of 1838, by Sir George Hayter.
National Portrait Gallery, London.

DOCUMENTS IN BRITISH HISTORY

Volume II: 1688 to the Present

1 2 3 4 5 6 7 8 9 0   DOC   DOC   9 0 9 8 7 6 5 4 3 2

ISBN 0-07-005702-8

Library of Congress Cataloging-in-Publication Data

Documents in British history / [compiled by] Brian L. Blakeley,
   Jacquelin Collins. — 2nd ed.
      p.   cm.
   Rev. ed. of: Documents in English history, 1974, c1975.
   Contents: v. 1. Early times to 1714 — v. 2. 1688 to the present.
   ISBN 0-07-005702-8 (vol. 2)
   1. Great Britain—History—Sources.   I. Blakeley, Brian L.
II. Collins, Jacquelin (date).   III. Blakeley, Brian L., comp.
Documents in English history.
DA26.D58   1993
942—dc20   92-31437

ABOUT THE AUTHORS

BRIAN L. BLAKFLEY is a professor of history at Texas Tech University. He has taught at Texas Tech since 1970. He received his M.A. and Ph.D. from Duke University in 1964 and 1966. He has published *The Colonial Office, 1868–1892* and several articles. His primary interests are in the history of modern Britain and of the British Empire.

JACQUELIN COLLINS is an associate professor of history and Associate Dean for Undergraduate Affairs in the College of Arts and Sciences at Texas Tech University. He received a B.A. and M.A. from Rice University in 1956 and 1959. He received a Ph.D. from the University of Illinois, Urbana-Champaign, in 1964 and a J.D. from Texas Tech University School of Law in 1984. His primary interests are in Tudor-Stuart England, constitutional and legal development, and Scotland.

CONTENTS

PREFACE

Welcome to the Study of British history. Having spent our adult lives teaching the history of the several peoples making up the British Isles—the English, the Scots, the Irish, and the Welsh—we are naturally impressed with the contributions they have collectively made to the development of European and world civilization. In constitutional usage, economic innovation, and literary, scientific, and artistic achievement, few, if any, peoples have equaled the British. These accomplishments were probably, in part, due to the melting-pot nature of the British Isles. The kingdom of England, an amalgam of Celtic, Anglo-Saxon, Danish, and Norman peoples and cultures, eventually combined with the Scots, Irish, and Welsh to create the United Kingdom. In more modern times, the British Empire aided in the spread of British institutions, language, and ideas around the world. In addition, British history has a value independent of its world impact. Filled with heroic achievements and epic failures, admirable heroes and despicable scoundrels, and profound ideas and transient fads, the history of the British Isles is a mirror of our own hopes and fears. We understand ourselves and our history only if we appreciate others and their experiences.

In attempting to understand the past, beginning students frequently assume that history, in this case British history, is a compilation of facts, the mere learning of which imparts knowledge. With experience, however, they will come to the realization that written history is essentially the answers to questions that various historians have arrived at and recorded for others. These conclusions vary according to the questions posed and the beliefs and prejudices of the historians who have asked the questions and searched for evidence to answer their queries. It is not surprising, therefore, that each generation must write its history anew—not only contemporary history but also that of earlier items. Definitive history is possible only for historians who have abandoned the arduous task of seeking new answers to questions both old and new.

There is, nevertheless, a constant factor in history, a factor essential if historians are not to wander off into the wilderness of their own imaginations. This ingredient is the evidence used in answering the questions they have raised. A historian's evidence is also a means by which other historians can judge the extent of the research and the validity of the answers presented. This evidence is often referred to as "documents." Originally, when the descipline of history was less sophisticated, it was assumed that documents were written and that only written records could reveal the secrets of the past. Without these written documents there was only "prehistory," a shadowy and mysterious age visited by lesser beings such as archeologists and anthropologists. More recently, historians have come to understand that evidence is where you find it and worth whatever you make of it. Written records remain valuable, but a discerning historian may be able to understand some questions by a careful examination of other evidence— political cartoons from *Punch,* the archeological evidence of the industrial revolution, or the games and toys of Victorian children. In using such evidence, the historian may have to ask more subtle questions and accept more tentative conclusions, but the historical process is essentially the same. Evidence of any kind, once recognized and appropriated by a historian, becomes a document to be used again and again by the historian and colleagues in the same field.

No historian, not even the beginning undergraduate, should remain a passive spectator. Each must ask questions and seek answers to them. At first, the student will be led to the written accounts of other historians. This approach, however, often results in confusion: historical accounts frequently differ from one another. Which is correct? At this point one should not become discouraged. Instead, the student should recognize in this confusion, frustration—and, yes, even anger—the maturing of a historian. Students who persevere will be led back first to the documents and evidence used by previous historians and then, hopefully, to new evidence. Along the way they ask their own questions and arrive at their own answers, with the same caution and confidence as other historians.

Each student of British history, who has now become a historian, needs the assistance of others; the task of historical research is too immense for a single person to investigate each aspect of the human experience. This collection of documents, as did our first edition, published in 1975, attempts to aid the beginning student in two ways.

1. We have included many of the documents generally agreed to be among the most important to an understanding of British history. To appreciate the British experience, you must know about the Bill of Rights, Adam Smith's *Wealth of Nations,* the Reform Bill of 1832, the National Petition, Darwin's *Origin of Species,* Kipling's *"Recessional,"* and the Beveridge Report. These documents provide evidence that has been used, and will continue to be used, to answer the hardest and most persistent questions in British history.

2. We have presented a wide variety of documents to illustrate the diversity of historical evidence. Some of this evidence cannot be presented in a book: for example, a film of a 1960s Beatles' concert used by a social historian seeking to understand the youth culture of the era. Nevertheless, nonwritten documents such as archeological sites of the industrial revolution, the paintings of the eighteenth-century artist, William Hogarth, and the artifacts found in the Victoria

and Albert Museum, can be included, and they reveal the variety of historical documents. Most of the book appropriately consists of written documents, since the majority of historians still rely almost entirely on this type of evidence. Even here, however, we have included a wide variety. Chronicles, speeches, diaries, poetry, nursery rhymes, song lyrics, cartoons, and governmental records and laws are examples of this variety. For a historian, imagination in both the framing of questions and the use of evidence is essential.

We have placed the documents in chronological order and have not attempted to group them topically. The division into two volumes has been done largely for reasons of cost and convenience of assignment. Each document in our volumes is a self-contained unit, sufficiently complete with its introduction to be understood and appreciated by itself. We have, however, been conscious of the place of each document in British history. The introductions provide a thread of continuity from one document to another, should you choose to read several documents in succession.

In this revised edition, we have added comtemporary documents, and we have sought to emphasize the British experience as opposed to that simply of England. We have included documents reflecting this broader British perspective, such as songs and poems of Robert Burns and *The Massacre of Glenco*. We have strengthened the social and cultural dimension, especially the contribution of women. The reader can now find not only the first Boy Scout manual, but Harriet Martineau's views on the proper education for young Victorian women and Marie Stopes's analysis of why marriage so frequently disappoints. We have included new types of historical evidence, that used by the industrial archaeologist and the museum curator. Finally, many of those who used the first edition, our wise and perceptive friends, have argued that some documents, most especially Orwell's *Road to Wigan Pier* and Macmillan's "Wind of Change" speech, required inclusion simply because of their importance to the concept of cultural literacy.

Many people have given us help in preparing *Documents in British History* as well as our 1975 *Documents in English History*. Patrick C. Lipscomb III, Brian C. Levack, and Stanford E. Lehmberg read the first manuscript and made recommendations for its improvement. C. Warren Hollister gave needed encouragement. For this edition, Joseph J. Mogan, Jr. and Marijane R. Davis provided valuable assistance. Derek Blakeley, our resourceful agent in London, was especially helpful. Wayne Anderson, history and political science editor at John Wiley & Sons, Inc., made preparation of our first edition more fun than it might have been. Sarah Touborg, Pamela Gordon, and Niels Aaboe, editors at McGraw-Hill, have done the same for this two-volume edition. John Beasley of The Wheetley Company, Inc., has taught us much about the craft of publishing. We also thank David Follmer. Finally, for their valuable suggestions, we are grateful to the readers of this second edition: Lois Margaret Barnett, the University of Southern Mississippi; Eugene J. Bourgeois, Southwest Texas State

University; David Cressy, California State University at Long Beach; John D. Fair, Auburn University at Montgomery; Thomas William Heyck, Northwestern University; Theodore Koditschek, the University of Missouri; Carol Martel, Arizona State University; and George B. Stow, LaSalle University. We give thanks to all of these folk, to our colleagues at Texas Tech University, and to our wives and families.

Again, we welcome each of you to the study of British history. Our prejudices, which led us to study this subject and now lead us to invite others to do the same, are apparent but unabashed. For the students who are about to discover Britain and its history this book was written; to them it is dedicated.

Brian L. Blakeley

Jacquelin Collins

DOCUMENTS IN BRITISH HISTORY

VOLUME II
1688 TO THE PRESENT

1
The Bill of Rights (1689)

The Glorious Revolution of 1688 to 1689 was both the culmination of a century-long constitutional struggle between Crown and Parliament and the consequence of specific actions of James II (1685–1688). Seldom have subjects been so quickly and thoroughly alienated from their king. At the beginning of his reign they were favorably inclined toward him, but three years later not even the Tories and Anglicans, who believed in nonresistance and indefeasible divine right, would lift a finger to save him. Increasingly the English people saw James's active Roman Catholicism and his inclination to tyranny as related dangers. These departures from English practice justified the abandonment of their sworn allegiance to their king.

The heart of the revolutionary settlement was the Bill of Rights, Parliament's official confirmation of the original Declaration of Rights written by the Convention Parliament of February 1689 and presented to William and Mary as the terms of their invitation to become king and queen. Like Magna Carta and the Petition of Right, the Bill of Rights was a settlement of specific violations of the law and the promise that in the future the law would be obeyed. This conservative pretense was, however, not always accurate. The statement on "raising or keeping a standing army" reflected more a fear than an established law or custom. Although the Revolution was accomplished by the cooperation of both political parties, the terms of the settlement were more Whig than Tory. Specifically, the throne was recognized as vacant, and it was then granted not to Mary, the sole legal heir (ignoring James's son, later called the Old Pretender, born in June 1688), but to William and Mary jointly. Also, limitations on the succession, specifically regarding religion, were firmly established. Parliament was not actually proclaimed sovereign, but by its actions there could be no doubt that it was. The Revolution was a wedding of Whig principles with Tory pragmatism, a triumph of English practicality more than of logic.

Source: Statutes of the Realm, VI, 142–144 (1 William and Mary, Sess. 2, c. 2).

AN ACT DECLARING THE RIGHTS AND LIBERTIES OF THE SUBJECT AND SETLEING THE SUCCESSION OF THE CROWNE

Whereas the Lords Spirituall and Temporall and Com̄ons assembled at Westminster lawfully fully and freely representing all the Estates of the People of this Realme did upon the thirteenth day of February in the yeare of our Lord one thousand six hundred eighty eight present unto their Majesties then called and known by the Names and Stile of William and Mary Prince and Princesse of Orange being present in their proper Persons a certaine Declaration in Writeing made by the said Lords and Com̄ons in the Words following viz

Whereas the late King James the Second by the Assistance of diverse evill Councellors Judges and Ministers imployed by him did endeavour to subvert and extirpate the Protestant Religion and the Lawes and Liberties of this Kingdome. . . .

All which are utterly and directly contrary to the knowne Lawes and Statutes and Freedome of this Realme.

And whereas the said late King James the Second haveing Abdicated the Government and the Throne being thereby Vacant His [Highnesse] the Prince of Orange (whome it hath pleased Almighty God to make the glorious Instrument of Delivering this Kingdome from Popery and Arbitrary Power) did (by the Advice of the Lords Spirituall and Temporall and diverse principall Persons of the Commons) cause Letters to be written to the Lords Spirituall and Temporall being Protestants and other Letters to the severall Countyes Cityes Universities Burroughs and Cinque Ports for the Choosing of such Persons to represent them as were of right to be sent to Parlyament to meete and sitt at Westminster upon the two and twentyeth day of January in this Yeare one thousand six hundred eighty and eight in order to such an Establishment as that their Religion Lawes and Liberties might not againe be in danger of being Subverted, Upon which Letters Elections haveing beene accordingly made.

And thereupon the said Lords Spirituall and Temporall and Commons pursuant to their respective Letters and Elections being now assembled in a full and free Representative of this Nation takeing into their most serious Consideration the best meanes for attaining the Ends aforesaid Doe in the first place (as their Auncestors in like Case have usually done) for the Vindicating and Asserting their auntient Rights and Liberties, Declare

That the pretended Power of Suspending of Laws or the Execution of Laws by Regall Authority without Consent of Parlyament is illegall.

That the pretended Power of Dispensing with Laws or the Execution of Laws by Regall Authoritie as it hath beene assumed and exercised of late is illegall.

That the Commission for erecting the late Court of Commissioners for Ecclesiasticall Causes and all other Commissions and Courts of like nature are Illegall and Pernicious.

That levying Money for or to the Use of the Crowne by pretence of

Prerogative without Grant of Parlyament for longer time or in other manner then the same is or shall be granted is Illegall.

That it is the Right of the Subjects to petition the King and all Commitments and Prosecutions for such Petitioning are Illegall.

That the raising or keeping a standing Army within the Kingdome in time of Peace unlesse it be with Consent of Parlyament is against Law.

That the Subjects which are Protestants may have Arms for their Defence suitable to their Conditions and as allowed by Law.

That Election of Members of Parlyament ought to be free.

That the Freedome of Speech and Debates or Proceedings in Parlyament ought not to be impeached or questioned in any Court or Place out of Parlyament.

That excessive Baile ought not to be required nor excessive Fines imposed nor cruell and unusuall Punishments inflicted.

That Jurors ought to be duely impannelled and returned and Jurors which passe upon Men in Trialls for High Treason ought to be Freeholders.

That all Grants and Promises of Fines and Forfeitures of particular persons before Conviction are illegall and void.

And that for Redresse of all Grievances and for the amending strengthening and preserveing of the Lawes Parlyaments ought to be held frequently.

And they doe Claime Demand and Insist upon all and singular the Premises as their undoubted Rights and Liberties and that noe Declarations Judgements Doeings or Proceedings to the Prejudice of the People in any of the said Premisses ought in any wise to be drawne hereafter into Consequence or Example. To which Demand of their Rights they are particularly encouraged by the Declaration of his Highnesse the Prince of Orange as being the onely meanes for obtaining a full Redresse and Remedy therein. Haveing therefore an intire Confidence That his said Highnesse the Prince of Orange will perfect the Deliverance soe farr advanced by him and will still preserve them from the Violation of their Rights which they have here asserted and from all other Attempts upon their Religion Rights and Liberties, The said Lords Spirituall and Temporall and Commons assembled at Westminster doe Resolve That William and Mary Prince and Princesse of Orange be and be declared King and Queene of England France and Ireland and the Dominions thereunto belonging to hold the Crowne and Royall Dignity of the said Kingdomes and Dominions to them the said Prince and Princesse dureing their Lives and the Life of the Survivour of them And that the sole and full Exercise of the Regall Power to be onely in and executed by the said Prince of Orange in the Names of the said Prince and Princesse dureing their joynt Lives And after their Deceases the said Crowne and Royall Dignitie of the said Kingdomes and Dominions to be to the Heires of the Body of the said Princesse And for default of such Issue to the Princesse Anne of Denmarke and the Heires of her Body And for default of such Issue to the Heires of the Body of the said Prince of Orange. And the Lords Spirituall

and Temporall and Commons doe pray the said Prince and Princesse to accept
the same accordingly. . . . And whereas it hath beene found by Experience that
it is inconsistent with the Safety and Welfare of this Protestant Kingdome to be
governed by a Popish Prince or by any King or Queene marrying a Papist the
said Lords Spirituall and Temporall and Commons doe further pray that it may
be enacted That all and every person and persons that is are or shall be reconciled to or shall hold Communion with the See or Church of Rome or shall pro-
fesse the Popish Religion or shall marry a Papist shall be excluded and be for
ever uncapeable to inherit possesse or enjoy the Crowne and Government of this
Realme and Ireland and the Dominions thereunto belonging or any part of the
same or to have use or exercise any Regall Power Authoritie or Jurisdiction
within the same [And in all and every such Case or Cases the People of these
Realmes shall be and are hereby absolved of their Allegiance] And the said
Crowne and Government shall from time to time descend to and be enjoyed by
such person or persons being Protestants as should have inherited and enjoyed
the same in case the said person or persons soe reconciled holding Communion
or Professing or Marrying as aforesaid were naturally dead.

2
John Locke, *Two Treatises of Government* (1690)

The Glorious Revolution was vindicated not only by the solid facts of its immediate success and of England's ensuing prosperity, but by the commonsense arguments of England's most influential political essay. In 1690 appeared anonymously John Locke's *Two Treatises of Government: In the Former, the False Principles and Foundations of Sir Robert Filmer, And His Followers, are Detected and Overthrown. The Latter is an Essay concerning The True Original, Extent, and End of Civil-Government.* The first treatise, seldom read today, is a refutation of Filmer's Biblical justification of the patriarchal authority of absolute monarchs. In the second treatise, a passage of which is reproduced below, Locke gives his own understanding of the basis of government. It is a contract between the people and their government, the people retaining the right to recall the legislature and the executive if they violate the trust given them. All people are subject to the law of nature, which they can discern by their reason. They are understood to enter society and to set up a government—a legislature and an executive—to avoid certain inconveniences inherent in an otherwise felicitous state of nature. Their chief concern "is the preservation of property," which is understood to be not only lands and material goods but more widely "the Lives, Liberties, and Estates of the People." Despite Locke, however, it has remained a concern whether lives and liberties should take primacy over estates, or indeed whether they can be separated.

The *Two Treatises* is in reality a single work. Locke wrote in his preface, "Thou hast here the Beginning and End of a Discourse," "the Papers that should have filled up the middle, and were more than all the rest," having been lost. Although published in 1690, it was probably written between 1679 and 1681, and certainly before 1683. Thus, Locke wrote during the Exclusion Crisis, to justify what the earl of Shaftesbury, his friend and patron, was attempting, and not in 1689 and 1690, to justify what had already been accomplished. As such, Locke's ideas were potentially dangerous.

Source: John Locke, *Two Treatises of Government: A Critical Edition with an Introduction and Apparatus Criticus,* by Peter Laslett, Second Edition, Cambridge: At the University Press, 1967, pp. 430–432. Reprinted by permission of Cambridge University Press.

5

This helps to explain his exile from 1683 till 1689 and his extreme care in not acknowledging his authorship of the *Two Treatises* until a few days before his death.

It was Locke's genius to combine the radical ideas of the Puritan revolution and the Exclusion Crisis with tradition and common sense, making them palatable and useful, even if not always consistent and logical. In all respects, the *Two Treatises* was the intellectual counterpart of the Glorious Revolution, owing its success to the Revolution more than the Revolution owed its justification to the *Two Treatises*. Its primary importance in the long run was to put English ideas and practice in a packaged form available for export. In the eighteenth century England began to eclipse the once-mighty France, and French thinkers and politicians looked to England, and preeminently to Locke, for an alternative to absolute monarchy.

The Reason why Men enter into Society, is the preservation of their Property; and the end why they chuse and authorize a Legislative, is, that there may be Laws made, and Rules set as Guards and Fences to the Properties of all the Members of the Society, to limit the Power, and moderate the Dominion of every Part and Member of the Society. For since it can never be supposed to be the Will of the Society, that the Legislative should have a Power to destroy that, which every one designs to secure, by entering into Society, and for which the People submitted themselves to the Legislators of their own making; whenever the *Legislators endeavour to take away, and destroy the Property of the People*, or to reduce them to Slavery under Arbitrary Power, they put themselves into a state of War with the People, who are thereupon absolved from any farther Obedience, and are left to the common Refuge, which God hath provided for all Men, against Force and Violence. Whensoever therefore the *Legislative* shall transgress this fundamental Rule of Society; and either by Ambition, Fear, Folly or Corruption, *endeavour to grasp* themselves, *or put into the hands of any other an Absolute Power* over the Lives, Liberties, and Estates of the People; By this breach of Trust they *forfeit the Power,* the People had put into their hands, for quite contrary ends, and it devolves to the People, who have a Right to resume their original Liberty, and, by the Establishment of a new Legislative (such as they shall think fit) provide for their own Safety and Security, which is the end for which they are in Society. What I have said here, concerning the Legislative, in general, holds true also concerning the *supreame Executor,* who having a double trust put in him, both to have a part in the Legislative, and the supreme Execution of the Law, Acts against both, when he goes about to set up his own Arbitrary Will, as the Law of the Society. He *acts* also *contrary to his Trust,* when he either imploys the Force, Treasure, and Offices of the Society, to corrupt the *Representatives,* and gain them to his purposes: or openly pre-ingages the *Electors,* and prescribes to their choice, such, whom he has by Sollicitations, Threats, Promises, or otherwise won to his designs; and imploys them to bring in such, who have promised before-hand, what to Vote, and what to Enact. Thus to regulate Candidates and *Electors,* and new model the ways of *Election,* what is it but to cut up the Government by the Roots, and poison the very Fountain of publick Security? For the People having reserved to themselves the Choice of their *Representatives,* as the Fence to their Properties, could do it for no other end, but that they might always be freely chosen, and so chosen, freely act and advise, as the necessity of the Commonwealth, and the publick Good should, upon examination, and mature debate, be judged to require. . . . What Power they ought to have in the Society, who thus imploy it contrary to the trust went along with it in its first Institution, is easie to determine; and one cannot but see, that he, who has once attempted any such thing as this, cannot any longer be trusted.

To this perhaps it will be said, that the People being ignorant, and always discontented, to lay the Foundation of Government in the unsteady Opinion, and uncertain Humour of the People, is to expose it to certain ruine; And *no Government will be able long to subsist,* if the People may set up a new Legislative, whenever they take offence at the old one. To this, I Answer: Quite the contrary. People are not so easily got out of their old Forms, as some are apt to suggest. They are hardly to be prevailed with to amend the acknowledg'd Faults, in the Frame they have been accustom'd to. And if there be any Original defects, or adventitious ones introduced by time, or corruption; 'tis not an easie thing to get them changed, even when all the World sees there is an opportunity for it. This slowness and aversion in the People to quit their old Constitutions, has, in the many Revolutions which have been seen in this Kingdom, in this and former Ages, still kept us to, or, after some interval of fruitless attempts, still brought us back again to our old Legislative of King, Lords and Commons: And whatever provocations have made the Crown be taken from some of our Princes Heads, they never carried the People so far, as to place it in another Line.

3
The Massacre of Glenco (1703).
Scotland in the Glorious
Revolution, 1692

The political events of 1688–1689 came, in England, to be called the "Glorious Revolution." Unlike the Puritan Revolution of 1640–1660, it was brief, bloodless, and successful, as subsequent history was to demonstrate. In Scotland the revolution was at most half-glorious—in Ireland it was not glorious at all.

The Scots Parliament, dominated by Protestant Lowlanders, followed England's lead in 1689 and with its Claim of Right declared the abdication of James VII and the accession of William and Mary. But the Highland clans, remembering their Gaelic and Catholic traditions, inclined to Jacobitism. At Killiecrankie in July 1689, Viscount Dundee led the wild charge of half-naked Highlanders, scattering the government forces sent against them. But Dundee was killed, and, without his leadership, the clans drifted back to their glens and took up again their traditional pastimes of stealing nolt (cattle) and fighting among themselves. The government set out to subdue them piecemeal.

The passage below is taken from the report of the government commission which in 1695 investigated the massacre which took place in Glencoe in February 1692. The chief of the MacDonalds of Glencoe, a lesser but notorious branch of the great MacDonald clan, was slow to swear allegiance to William. Going to the wrong place and then being delayed by bad weather, he made his submission on January 6, almost a week after the deadline. The Scottish officials of William's government, having lost patience with the Highlands and with Glencoe most of all, seem already to have marked the Glencoe MacDonalds for savage retribution.

The brutality of the attack and even the death toll of some 38 killed at the time and many more killed by a winter snowstorm as they attempted to escape over the hills, were not outside the tradition of Highland violence. What made this massacre noteworthy was the meditated calculation with which it was carried out and

Source: The Massacre of Glenco. Being a True Narrative of the Barbarous Murther of the Glenco-men, in the Highlands of Scotland, by way of Military Execution, on the 13th of Feb. 1692. London: Printed, and Sold by B. Bragg, at the Blue-Ball in Ave-Mary-Lane, 1703, pp. 11–18.

the government sanction, perhaps even from William himself, which it seemed to have. It clashed with a growing European and British sense of acceptable government and human behavior. More than anything else, it intensified the Highlanders' hatred for the governments of Edinburgh and London, and it confirmed the clans in their Jacobite loyalties. Though the Scots Parliament, representing principally the Lowlands, accepted union with England in 1707, the Highlands, in the Jacobite uprisings of 1715 and 1745, had twice more to be subdued. After Bonnie Prince Charlie and his Highland forces were finally destroyed at Culloden in 1746, the repression of the clans was resolute and thoroughgoing. The Highland clearances destroyed a way of life, but they made available a hardy and enterprising people for the conquering and populating of an overseas empire.

His Majesty's Proclamation of Indemnity was publish'd in Aug. 1691, offering a free Indemnity and Pardon to all the Highlanders who had been in Arms, upon their coming in and taking the Oath of Allegiance betwixt and the first of January thereafter: And in compliance with the Proclamation, the deceas'd Glenco goes about the end of Decemb. 1691 to Col. Hill, Governor of Fort-William at Inverlochie, and desir'd the Colonel to minister to him the Oath of Allegiance, that he might have the King's Indemnity: But Col. Hill in his Deposition . . . doth farther depone, That he hasten'd him away all he could, and gave him a Letter to Ardkinlas to receive him as a lost Sheep, and the Colonel produces Ardkinlas's Answer to that Letter, dated the 9th of January 1691, bearing, that he had indeavoured to receive the great lost Sheep Glenco, and that Glenco had undertaken to bring in all his Friends and Followers as the Privy-Council should order, and Ardkinlas farther writes, that he was sending to Edinburgh that Glenco, tho' he had mistaken in coming to Colonel Hill to take the Oath of Allegiance, might yet be welcome, and that thereafter the Col. should take care that Glenco's Friends and Followers may not suffer, till the King and Councils Pleasure be known. . . .

After that Glenco had taken the Oath of Allegiance as is said, he went home to his own House, and as his own two Sons above name'd depone, He not only liv'd there for some Days quietly and securely, but call'd his People together, and told them he had taken the Oath of Allegiance, and made his Peace, and therefore desir'd and engag'd them to live peaceably under King William's Government. . . .

These things having preceeded the Slaughter, which happen'd not to be committed until the 13th of February 1692, six Weeks after the deceas'd Glenco had taken the Oath of Allegiance at Inverary. The Slaughter of the Glenco Men was in this manner, viz. John and Alexander Mac-Donald, Sons to the deceas'd

Glenco, depone, That . . . Glenlyon, a Captain of the Earl of Argyle's Regiment, with Lieutenant Lindsay and Ensign Lindsay, and six score Soldiers, return'd to Glenco about the 1st of February 1692, where, at their Entry, the elder Brother John met them with about 20 Men, and demanded the reason of their coming, and Lieutenant Lindsey shew'd him his Orders for quartering there under Colonel Hill's Hand, and gave assurance that they were only come to Quarter; whereupon they were billeted in the Country, and had free Quarters and kind Entertainment, living familiarly with the People until the 13th Day of Feb. and Alexander farther depones, That Glenlyon being his Wive's Uncle came almost every Day and took his Morning Drink at his House, and that the very Night before the Slaughter, Glenlyon did play at Cards in his own Quarters with both the Brothers, and John depones, That old Glenco his Father had invited Glenlyon, Lieutenant Lindsay, and Ensign Lindsay, to dine with him upon the very day the Slaughter happen'd. But on the 13th day of February, being Saturday, about four or five in the Morning, Lieutenant Lindsay, with a party of the foresaid Soldiers, came to old Glenco's House, where, having call'd in a Friendly manner, and got in, they shot his Father dead with several Shots as he was rising out of his Bed; and the Mother having got up and put on her Clothes, the Soldiers stripp'd her naked and drew the Rings off her Fingers with their Teeth. . . .

The said John Macdonald, eldest Son to the deceas'd Glenco depones, the same morning that his Father was kill'd there came Soldiers to his House before Day, and call'd at his Window, which gave him the Alarm, and made him go to Innerriggen, where Glenlyon was quarter'd, and that he found Glenlyon and his Men preparing their Arms, which made the Deponent ask the Cause; but Glenlyon gave him only good Words, and said they were to march against some of Glengaries Men, and if there were Ill intended, would not he have told Sandy and his Neice? meaning the Deponents Brother and his Wife; which made the Deponent go home and go again to his Bed, untill his Servant, who hindred him to sleep, rais'd him; and when he rose and went out, he perceiv'd about 20 Men coming towards his House with their Bayonets fix'd to their Muskets; whereupon he fled to the Hill, and having Auchnaion, a little Village in Glenco, in view, he heard the Shots wherewith Auchintriaten and four more were kill'd; and that he heard also the Shots at Innerriggen, where Glenlyon had caus'd to kill nine more, as shall be hereafter declar'd and this is confirm'd by the concurring Deposition of Alexander Macdonald his Brother, whom a Servant wak'd out of sleep, saying, It is not time for you to be sleeping, when they are killing your Brother at the Door; which made Alexander to flee with his Brother to the Hill, where both of them heard the foresaid Shots at Auchnaion and Innerriggin: And the said John, Alexander and Archibald Macdonald's do all depone, That the same Morning there was one Serjeant Barber and a Party at Auchnaion, and that Auchintriaten being there in his Brother's House with eight more sitting about the Fire, the Soldiers discharg'd upon them about 18 Shot, which kill'd

Auchintriaten and four more; but the other four, whereof some were wounded, falling down as dead, Serjeant Barber laid hold on Auchintriaten's Brother, one of the four, and ask'd him if he were alive? He answer'd, That he was, and that he desir'd to die without rather than within: Barber said, That for his Meat that he had eaten, he would do him the Favour to kill him without; but when the Man was brought out, and Soldiers brought up to shoot him, he having his Plaid loose flung it over their Faces and so escap'd; and the other three broke through the back of the House and escap'd: And this Account the Deponents had from the Men that escap'd. And at Innerriggin, where Glenlyon was quartered, the Soldiers took other nine Men and did bind them Hand and Foot, kill'd them one by one with Shot; and when Glenlyon inclin'd to save a young Man of about 20 Years of Age, one Captain Drummond came and ask'd how he came to be sav'd, in respect of the Orders that were given, and shot him dead; and another young Boy of about 13 Years ran to Glenlyon to be sav'd, he was likewise shot dead. . . . And another Witness of the same declares, That upon the same 13th of February, Glenlyon and Lieutenant Lindsay, and their Soldiers, did in the Morning before Day fall upon the People of Glenco when they were secure in their Beds and kill'd them, and he being at Innerriggin fled with the first, but heard Shots and had two Brothers killed there, with three Men more and a Woman, who were all buried before he came back. And all these five Witnesses concur, That the foresaid Slaughter was made by Glenlyon and his Soldiers, after they had been quarter'd, and liv'd peaceably and friendly with the Glenco-Men about 13 Days, and that the Number of those whom they knew to be slain were about 25, and that the Soldiers after the Slaughter did burn the Houses, Barns and Goods, and carried away a great Spoil of Horse, Nolt and Sheep, above a 1000. . . .

4

The Riot Act (1715). The Maintenance of Law and Order

The Act of Settlement (1701) confirmed the exclusion of the Catholic Stuarts from the throne and designated Electress Sophia of Hanover and her heirs as the royal successors to William III and Princess Anne. Although most English accepted the Revolution, some Roman Catholics and diehard legitimists remained Jacobites, drinking toasts to the king over the water (James, the Old Pretender, who was in France). Sophia's son, George I (1714–1727), peacefully succeeded Queen Anne. Jacobites and others soon found George and his Hanoverian retinue unattractive and very German. Tumultuous assemblies and riots occurred in several parts of England, and an invasion by the Pretender was anticipated. The Whig government, firmly in control of Parliament but not confident of its control of the kingdom, passed the Riot Act of 1715.

The lapse in 1603 of the Tudor riot acts and the abolition of Star Chamber in 1641 left no settled means of dealing with crowds that either threatened to get out of control or actually did. Toward the end of the Stuart period, efforts, largely unsuccessful, were made to include riot within the scope of treason. The Riot Act of 1715, reviving the terms of the Tudor acts, gave magistrates greater authority to enforce order. One hour after the "reading of the Riot Act" the mere presence of twelve or more people became a felony, and those acting to suppress it were indemnified against charges that might be brought against them by injured rioters. Some doubt remained, however, regarding the enforcement of the law in the intervening hour and the extent of the force that might be used thereafter. The act illustrates both the tumultuous condition of England in the eighteenth century and the absence of an effective system of law enforcement.

AN ACT FOR PREVENTING TUMULTS AND RIOTOUS ASSEMBLIES AND FOR THE MORE SPEEDY AND EFFECTUAL PUNISHING THE RIOTERS

I. Whereas *of late many rebellious riots and tumults have been in divers parts of this kingdom, to the disturbance of the publick peace, and the endangering of his*

Source: The Statutes At Large, XIII, 142–144 (1 George I. c. 5).

Majesty's person and government, and the same are yet continued and fomented by persons disaffected to his Majesty, presuming so to do, for that the punishments provided by the laws now in being are not adequate to such heinous offences; and by such rioters his Majesty and his administration have been most maliciously and falsly traduced, with an intent to raise divisions, and to alienate the affections of the people from his Majesty: therefore for the preventing and suppressing of such riots and tumults, and for the more speedy and effectual punishing the offenders therein; be it enacted . . . That if any persons to the number of twelve or more, being unlawfully, riotously, and tumultously assembled together, to the disturbance of the publick peace . . . and being required or commanded by any one or more justice or justices of the peace, or by the sheriff of the county, or his under-sheriff, or by the mayor, bailiff or bailiffs, or other head-officer, or justice of the peace of any city or town corporate . . . by proclamation to be made in the King's name, in the form herein after directed, to disperse themselves, and peaceably to depart to their habitations, or to their lawful business, shall . . . unlawfully, riotously, and tumultuously remain or continue together by the space of one hour after such command or request . . . that then such continuing together . . . shall be adjudged felony without benefit of clergy, and the offenders therein shall be adjudged felons, and shall suffer death as in case of felony without benefit of clergy.

II. And be it further enacted by the authority aforesaid, That the order and form of the proclamation . . . shall be as hereafter followeth (that is to say) the justice of the peace, or other person authorized by this act to make the said proclamation shall, among the said rioters, or as near to them as he can safely come, with a loud voice command, or cause to be commanded silence to be, while proclamation is making, and after that, shall openly and with loud voice make or cause to be made proclamation in these words, or like in effect:

OUR *sovereign Lord the King chargeth and commandeth all persons, being assembled, immediately to disperse themselves, and peaceably to depart to their habitations, or to their lawful business, upon the pains contained in the act made in the first year of King* George, *for preventing tumults and riotous assemblies.*

God save the King.

III. And be it further enacted by the authority aforesaid, That if such persons . . . shall continue together and not disperse themselves within one hour, That then it shall and may be lawful to and for every justice of the peace . . . and other peace-officer . . . and for such other . . . persons as shall be commanded to be assisting unto any such justice of the peace . . . or other head-officer aforesaid . . . to seize and apprehend, and they are hereby required to seize and apprehend such persons so unlawfully, riotously and tumultuously continuing together after proclamation made, as aforesaid, and forthwith to carry the persons so apprehended before one or more of his Majesty's justices of the peace . . . in order to their being proceeded against for such their offences according to law; and that if the persons so unlawfully, riotously and tumultuously assembled, or any of them, shall happen to be killed, maimed or hurt . . . by reason of their resisting the persons so dispersing, seizing or apprehending, or endeavouring to disperse, seize or apprehend them, that then every such justice of the peace . . . or other peace-officer, and all and singular persons, being aiding and assisting to them . . . shall be free, discharged and indemnified . . . of, for, or concerning the killing, maiming, or hurting of any such person or persons.

5
Jonathan Swift, *A Modest Proposal* (1729). A Radical Solution to the Problems of Ireland

Jonathan Swift (1667–1745) is known primarily for one book, *Gulliver's Travels,* a satire on the period of Robert Walpole but erroneously regarded by many today as a children's story. Swift was, to his contemporaries, one of a small group of eminent essayists and satirists, including Richard Steele, Joseph Addison, and Daniel Defoe. These men wielded their pens alternately to promote and to subvert the governments of the early eighteenth century. Historians use their pamphlets and essays, still widely read today because of their style, to study the major problems of late Stuart and Hanoverian England and to understand the attitudes of the educated class to which they were addressed.

Swift, an ambitious and arrogant man, never achieved the political prominence and influence he so desperately sought. Because he used his literary talents to support the Tories and their antiwar policies during the reign of Queen Anne (1702–1714), the accession of George I (1714–1727) and the resulting ascendancy of the Whigs forced him to retire to Dublin, where he served until his death in 1745 as the dean of St. Patrick's Cathedral.

Swift's mission in later life was to expose the harshness and injustice of British rule in Ireland, specifically the political, religious,

Source: Carl Van Doren, ed., *The Portable Swift,* New York: The Viking Press, 1948, pp. 549, 551–553, 555–556, 559.

and economic plight of the Roman Catholic peasantry. To this end he published a number of pamphlets, the most famous being *A Modest Proposal for Preventing the Children of Poor People from Being a Burthen to Their Parents or Country, and for Making Them Beneficial to the Public.* Although Swift was a member of the Protestant establishment, his pamphlet earned him the freedom of the city of Dublin and recognition as one of the ablest defenders of Irish liberties. The savageness of his satire reflects the intensity both of his personal frustrations and of his abhorrence of England's policies in Ireland.

A *Modest Proposal* first appeared in Dublin in October 1729. It was immediately reprinted several times, achieving a popularity lasting to the present time.

It is a melancholy object to those who walk through this great town, or travel in the country, when they see the streets, the roads, and cabin-doors crowded with beggars of the female sex, followed by three, four, or six children, *all in rags,* and importuning every passenger for an alms. These mothers, instead of being able to work for their honest livelihood, are forced to employ all their time in strolling, to beg sustenance for their helpless infants, who, as they grow up, either turn thieves for want of work, or leave their dear Native Country to fight for the Pretender in Spain, or sell themselves to the Barbadoes.

I think it is agreed by all parties that this prodigious number of children, in the arms, or on the backs, or at the heels of their mothers, and frequently of their fathers, is in the present deplorable state of the kingdom a very great additional grievance; and therefore whoever could find out a fair, cheap, and easy method of making these children sound useful members of the commonwealth would deserve so well of the public as to have his statue set up for a preserver of the nation. . . .

I shall now therefore humbly propose my own thoughts, which I hope will not be liable to the least objection.

I have been assured by a very knowing American of my acquaintance in London, that a young healthy child well nursed is at a year old a most delicious, nourishing, and wholesome food, whether stewed, roasted, baked, or broiled, and I make no doubt that it will equally serve in a fricassee, or a ragout.

I do therefore humbly offer it to public consideration, that of the hundred and twenty thousand children already computed, twenty thousand may be reserved for breed, whereof only one fourth part to be males, which is more than we allow to sheep, black-cattle, or swine, and my reason is that these children are seldom the fruits of marriage, a circumstance not much regarded by our savages, therefore one male will be sufficient to serve four females. That the remaining hundred thousand may at a year old be offered in sale to the persons of quality, and fortune, through the kingdom, always advising the mother to let them suck plentifully in the last month, so as to render them plump, and fat for a good table. A child will make two dishes at an entertainment for friends, and when the family dines alone, the fore or hind quarter will make a reasonable dish, and seasoned with a little pepper or salt will be very good boiled on the fourth day, especially in winter.

I have reckoned upon a medium, that a child just born will weigh 12 pounds, and in a solar year if tolerably nursed increaseth to 28 pounds.

I grant this food will be somewhat dear, and therefore very proper for landlords, who, as they have already devoured most of the parents, seem to have the best title to the children. . . .

I have already computed the charge of nursing a beggar's child (in which list I reckon all cottagers, labourers, and four-fifths of the farmers) to be about two shillings *per annum,* rags included, and I believe no gentleman would repine to give ten shillings for the carcass of a good fat child, which, as I have said, will make four dishes of excellent nutritive meat, when he hath only some particular friend or his own family to dine with him. Thus the Squire will learn to be a good landlord, and grow popular among his tenants, the mother will have eight shillings net profit, and be fit for work till she produces another child.

Those who are more thrifty (as I must confess the times require) may flay the carcass; the skin of which, artificially dressed, will make admirable gloves for ladies, and summer boots for fine gentlemen. . . . I think the advantages by the proposal which I have made are obvious and many, as well as of the highest importance.

For first, as I have already observed, it would greatly lessen the number of Papists, with whom we are yearly over-run, being the principal breeders of the nation, as well as our most dangerous enemies. . . .

Secondly, The poorer tenants will have something valuable of their own, which by law be made liable to distress, and help to pay their landlord's rent, their corn and cattle being already seized, and *money a thing unknown.* . . .

Sixthly, This would be a great inducement to marriage, which all wise nations have either encouraged by rewards, or enforced by laws and penalties. It would increase the care and tenderness of mothers toward their children, when they were sure of a settlement for life, to the poor babes, provided in some sort by the public to their annual profit instead of expense. We should see an honest emulation among the married women, which of them could bring the fattest child to the market, men would become as fond of their wives, during the time of their pregnancy, as they are now of their mares in foal, their cows in calf, or sows when they are ready to farrow, nor offer to beat or kick them (as it is too frequent a practice) for fear of a miscarriage. . . .

I profess in the sincerity of my heart that I have not the least personal interest in endeavouring to promote this necessary work, having no other motive than the *public good of my country, by advancing our trade, providing for infants, re-*

lieving the poor, and giving some pleasure to the rich. I have no children by which I can propose to get a single penny; the youngest being nine years old, and my wife past child-bearing.

6

The Hat Act (1732) and the Iron Act (1750). Mercantilistic Regulation of Trade

To the mercantilist of the eighteenth century, it was self-evident that political units were not created with equal economic rights. Colonies had been founded, and were now defended, because of their economic value to the "mother country," meaning among other things that they were to provide a market for manufactured goods. The British naturally attempted to restrict manufacturing in the colonies, particularly when it competed with established industries in Britain. Skilled artisans were discouraged from going to America. Colonial legislation favorable to manufacturing interests was often vetoed. Finally, and most visibly, Parliament at Westminster passed legislation restricting certain colonial industries, the most famous being the Hat Act (1732) and the Iron Act (1750). Although both acts are restrictive, there was an important difference between them. The Hat Act prohibited the export of all hats made in the plantations, but the Iron Act actually encouraged the production and export of iron, as long as it was in pig or bar form.

The effectiveness of this legislation in obstructing the growth of American industry has often been debated. Most historians now argue that its importance has been exaggerated. Much of this legislation, including the Iron Act, was ignored by the colonists and the British officials. In addition, other industries, including shipbuilding and shoe and paper manufacturing, were never regulated even in theory. Still others, such as the production of naval stores (turpentine, tar, and pitch), were actively encouraged. In most instances, when an industry failed to develop in the colonies, it was

Source: The Statutes At Large, XVI, 304–305, 307 (5 George II. c. 22); XX, 97, 99–100 (23 George II. c. 29).

due to its inefficiency and its inability to compete with the more mature British industry. The lack of capital and the high cost of labor probably did more to retard American industrial growth than all of Britain's mercantilistic legislation combined. Perhaps the most significant consequence of the Hat Act and the Iron Act was their exploitation after 1763 as political grievances.

AN ACT TO PREVENT THE EXPORTATION OF HATS OUT OF ANY OF HIS MAJESTY'S COLONIES OR PLANTATIONS IN AMERICA AND TO RESTRAIN THE NUMBER OF APPRENTICES TAKEN BY THE HAT-MAKERS IN THE SAID COLONIES OR PLANTATIONS, AND FOR THE BETTER ENCOURAGING THE MAKING HATS IN GREAT BRITAIN

Whereas *the art and mystery of making hats in* Great Britain *hath arrived to great perfection, and considerable quantities of hats manufactured in this kingdom have heretofore been exported to his Majesty's plantations or colonies in* America, *who have been wholly supplied with hats from Great Britain; and whereas great quantities of hats have of late years been made, and the said manufacture is daily increasing in the* British *plantations in* America, *and is from thence exported to foreign markets, which were heretofore supplied from Great Britain, and the hat-makers in the said plantations take many apprentices for very small terms, to the discouragement of the said trade, and debasing the said manufacture:* wherefore for preventing the said ill practices for the future, and for promoting and encouraging the trade of making hats in *Great Britain,* be it enacted . . . That . . . no hats or felts whatsoever, dyed or undyed, finished or unfinished, shall be shipt, loaden or put on board any ship or vessel in any place or parts within any of the *British* plantations . . . and also that no hats or felts, either dyed or undyed, finished or unfinished, shall be loaden upon any horse, cart or other carriage, to the intent or purpose to be exported, transported, shipped off, carried or conveyed out of any of the said *British* plantations to any other of the *British* plantations, or to any other place whatsoever, by any person or persons whatsoever.

VII. And it is hereby further enacted by the authority aforesaid, That no person residing in any of his Majesty's plantations in *America* shall . . . make or cause to be made, any felt or hat of or with any wool or stuff whatsoever, unless he shall have first served as an apprentice in the trade or art of felt-making during the space of seven years at the least; neither shall any felt-maker or hat-maker in any of the said plantations imploy, retain or set to work, in the said art or trade, any person as a journeyman or hired servant, other than such as shall have lawfully served an apprenticeship in the said trade for the space of seven years; nor shall any felt-maker or hat-maker in any of the said plantations have, take or keep above the number of two apprentices at one time, or take any apprentice for any less term than seven years, upon pain to forfeit and pay the sum of five pounds for every month that he shall continue offending in the premisses contrary to the true meaning of this act. . . .

VIII. And be it further enacted by the authority aforesaid, That no person or persons inhabiting in the said plantations . . . shall retain or set on work, in the said art of hat or felt making, any black or negro, upon pain to forfeit and pay the sum of five pounds for every month wherein such person or persons shall so offend, contrary to the meaning of this act.

AN ACT TO ENCOURAGE THE IMPORTATION OF PIG AND BAR IRON FROM HIS MAJESTY'S COLONIES IN AMERICA; AND TO PREVENT THE ERECTION OF ANY MILL OR OTHER ENGINE FOR SLITTING OR ROLLING OF IRON; OR ANY PLATEING FORGE TO WORK WITH A TILT HAMMER; OR ANY FURNACE FOR MAKING STEEL IN ANY OF THE SAID COLONIES

Whereas *the importation of bar iron from his Majesty's colonies in* America, *into the port of* London, *and the importation of pig iron from the said colonies, into any port of* Great Britain, *and the manufacture of such bar and pig iron in* Great Britain, *will be a great advantage not only to the said colonies, but also to this kingdom, by furnishing the manufacturers of iron with a supply of that useful and necessary commodity, and by means thereof large sums of money, now annually paid for iron to foreigners, will be saved to this kingdom, and a greater quantity of the woollen, and other manufactures of* Great Britain, *will be exported to* America, *in exchange for such iron so imported;* be it therefore enacted . . . That . . . the several and respective subsidies, customs, impositions, rates, and duties, now payable on pig iron, made in and imported from his Majesty's colonies in *America,* into any port of *Great Britain,* shall cease . . . and that . . . no subsidy, custom, imposition, rate, or duty whatsoever, shall be payable upon bar iron made in and imported from the said colonies into the port of *London;* any law, statute, or usage to the contrary thereof in any wise notwithstanding.

IX. And, that pig and bar iron made in his Majesty's colonies in *America* may be further manufactured in this kingdom, be it further enacted . . . That . . . no mill or other engine for slitting or rolling of iron, or any plateing-forge to work with a tilt hammer, or any furnace for making steel, shall be erected, or after such erection, continued, in any of his Majesty's colonies in *America;* and if any person or persons shall erect, or cause to be erected, or after such erection, continue, or cause to be continued, in any of the said colonies, any such mill, engine, forge, or furnace, every person or persons so offending, shall, for every such mill, engine, forge, or furnace, forfeit the sum of two hundred pounds of lawful money of *Great Britain.*

7
John Wesley, *Journal* (1738).
The Methodist Revival

John Wesley (1703–1791) was a reluctant revolutionary, forced against his will to take action against an established church. Anglicanism, he felt, had become overly intellectual and callous to the needs of the general population, specifically the residents of the new industrial cities. While at Oxford, Wesley and his younger brother, Charles, formed the Holy Club. Ignoring charges of being "enthusiasts" and "methodists," because of their disciplined and purposeful study of religion, they devoted much of their time to social work. In 1738, after two frustrating years in James Oglethorpe's debtor colony of Georgia, Wesley experienced a spiritual crisis. His failures in Georgia undoubtedly contributed to his fear that, by emphasizing "good works," he was also failing God. His Aldersgate experience, reproduced below from his *Journal,* finally brought him peace of mind. His acceptance of salvation by faith alone, by a "true trust and confidence in the mercy of God through our Lord Jesus Christ," launched his great career as an evangelist.

During the next 50 years, Wesley traveled approximately 250,000 miles, mostly on horseback, and delivered an estimated 40,000 sermons. He was a strange revivalist, however. His university training made him uncomfortable with the enthusiasm generated at some of his outdoor meetings. He was also reluctant to break with the Church of England, remaining an Anglican priest until his death in 1791. Only gradually did "Pope John" come to exercise control over a de facto religious denomination, Methodism. Unlike some revolutionaries, he lived to see his movement become socially respectable. He accepted this rationally although, one senses, with some regret. "I do not see how it is possible in the nature of things for a religious revival to last long. For religion must necessarily produce industry and frugality. And these cannot but produce riches. But as Riches increase, so will Pride and love of the world in all of its branches."

Another interesting aspect of the Wesleyan movement was its relationship to the other reform movements of the eighteenth cen-

Source: The Journal of John Wesley, edited by Nehemiah Curnock, New York: Capricorn Books, 1963, pp. 49–52.

tury. Although Wesley's early career confirms Methodism's social dimension, secular reform was never his primary concern. Politically he was a Tory, opposed to the ideas of John Wilkes and of the Continental Congresses; religiously he was intolerant, averse to Roman Catholic emancipation; socially he disliked government regulation of business, preferring child labor to the idleness of play. His career illustrates the conflict of priorities present in many religions: to stress the spiritual salvation of one's own soul or to show concern for the material welfare of one's neighbor.

Nowhere was Wesley's concern for salvation more evident than in the hundreds of hymns he and Charles wrote. Hymns were a means of communication with God, especially if, as he stipulated in his 1761 "Directions for Singing," they were sung "lustily," "modestly," "spiritually," and "exactly as they were printed." As early as 1737 in Georgia he produced what was both the first American and the first Anglican hymnal. Over the years other versions appeared, culminating in *A Collection of Hymns for the Use of the People called Methodists* (1780), the basis for all future Methodist hymnals. "O for a Thousand Tongues to Sing," the first hymn in this and all later editions, reflects Wesley's recognition of human failings and of the salvation that comes from God:

> O for a thousand tongues to sing
> My dear Redeemer's praise!
> The glories of my God and King,
> The triumphs of his grace!
>
> . . .
>
> He breaks the power of cancelled sin,
> He sets the prisoner free;
> His blood can make the foulest clean—
> His blood availed for me.

Hymns are important historical documents, reflecting over time the varying approaches to salvation. Later hymns such as Julia Ward Howe's "The Battle Hymn of the Republic" and the Salvation Army's "Onward Christian Soldiers" reveal changing attitudes toward the role of the church in promoting political, social, and economic justice.

The *Journal of John Wesley* consists of almost daily comments written during most of his adult life. Most entries, briefer than those below, describe simply a sermon preached and the congregation's response. The standard edition, in eight volumes, was edited by Nehemiah Curnock in 1909.

24 May 1738. . . . . All the time I was at Savannah I was thus beating the air.
Being ignorant of the righteousness of Christ, which, by a living faith in Him,
bringeth salvation "to every one that believeth," I sought to establish my own
righteousness; and so laboured in the fire all my days. I was now properly
"under the law"; I knew that "the law" of God was "spiritual; I consented to it,
that it was good." Yea, "I delighted in it, after the inner man." Yet was I "carnal,
sold under sin." Every day was I constrained to cry out, "What I do, I allow not:
for what I would, I do not; but what I hate, that I do. . . ."

In this vile, abject state of bondage to sin, I was indeed fighting continually,
but not conquering. Before, I had willingly served sin; now it was unwillingly;
but I still served it. I fell, and rose, and fell again. Sometimes I was overcome,
and in heaviness: sometimes I overcame, and was in joy. For as in the former
state I had some foretastes of the terrors of the law, so had I in this, of the comforts of the gospel. . . .

On my return to England, January 1738, being in imminent danger of death,
and very uneasy on that account, I was strongly convinced that the cause of that
uneasiness was unbelief; and that the gaining a true, living faith was the "one
thing needful" for me. But still I fixed not this faith on its right object: I meant
only faith in God, not faith in or through Christ. Again, I knew not that I was
wholly void of this faith; but only thought I had not enough of it. So that when
Peter Böhler, whom God prepared for me as soon as I came to London, affirmed
of true faith in Christ (which is but one), that it had those two fruits
inseparably attending it, "dominion over sin, and constant peace from a sense
of forgiveness," I was quite amazed, and looked upon it as a new gospel. If
this was so, it was clear I had not faith. But I was not willing to be convinced of
this. . . .

When I met Peter Böhler again, he consented to put the dispute upon the
issue which I desired, namely, Scripture and experience. I first consulted the
Scripture. But when I set aside the glosses of men, and simply considered the
words of God, comparing them together, endeavouring to illustrate the obscure
by the plainer passages; I found they all made against me, and was forced to retreat to my last hold, "that experience would never agree with the literal interpretation of those scriptures. Nor could I therefore allow it to be true, till I found
some living witnesses of it." He replied, he could show me such any time; if I
desired it, the next day. And accordingly, the next day he came again with three
others, all of whom testified, of their own personal experience, that a true, living
faith in Christ is inseparable from a sense of pardon for all past, and freedom
from all present, sins. They added with one mouth, that this faith was the gift,
the free gift, of God; and that He would surely bestow it upon every soul who
earnestly and perseveringly sought it. I was now thoroughly convinced; and by
the grace of God, I resolved to seek it unto the end: 1. By absolutely renouncing
all dependence, in whole or in part, upon my own works or righteousness; on
which I had really grounded my hope of salvation, though I knew it not, from

my youth up. 2. By adding to the constant use of all the other means of grace, continual prayer for this very thing, justifying, saving faith, a full reliance on the blood of Christ shed for me; a trust in Him as my Christ, as my sole justification, sanctification, and redemption.

I continued thus to seek it (though with stranger indifference, dulness, and coldness, and unusually frequent relapses into sin), till Wednesday, May 24. . . .

In the evening I went very unwillingly to a society in Aldersgate Street, where one was reading Luther's preface to the Epistle to the Romans. About a quarter before nine, while he was describing the change which God works in the heart through faith in Christ, I felt my heart strangely warmed. I felt I did trust in Christ, Christ alone, for salvation: and an assurance was given me, that He had taken away my sins, even mine, and saved me from the law of sin and death.

I began to pray with all my might for those who had in a more especial manner despitefully used me and persecuted me. I then testified openly to all there, what I now first felt in my heart. But it was not long before the enemy suggested, "This cannot be faith; for where is thy joy?" Then was I taught, that peace and victory over sin are essential to faith in the Captain of our salvation; but that, as to the transports of joy that usually attend the beginning of it, especially in those who have mourned deeply, God sometimes giveth, sometimes withholdeth them, according to the counsels of His own will.

After my return home, I was much buffeted with temptations; but cried out, and they fled away. They returned again and again. I as often lifted up my eyes, and he "sent me help from His holy place." And herein I found the difference between this and my former state chiefly consisted. I was striving, yea, fighting with all my might under the law, as well as under grace. But then I was sometimes, if not often, conquered; now I was always conqueror.

8

Samuel Sandys and Sir Robert Walpole, Debate in the House of Commons (1741). The Office of Prime Minister

Despite Parliament's preeminence after 1688, the king remained the chief executive and possessed vast areas of independence in the day-to-day running of the government. His most important prerogative was the power to appoint his own advisers. Parliament could remove these ministers through impeachment or by refusing to vote the funds necessary for the implementation of their policies. It lacked, however, the practical ability to influence their routine activities on behalf of the king's government. The ultimate solution to the problem of controlling the executive was the development of the office of prime minister, the head of a cabinet, all of whose members were jointly responsible to the House of Commons and capable of removal by a simple majority vote. This system of responsible government, worked out during the eighteenth and nineteenth centuries, seems today so natural and obvious that it is difficult not to see some constitutional architect plotting its development from the beginning.

Although kings throughout England's history had chief, or prime ministers, the evolution of the present office began in the early eighteenth century. This was due first to the weakness of Queen Anne (1702–1714) and then to the disinclination of George I (1714–1727) and George II (1727–1760) to attend the meetings of their ministers. The first modern prime minister—who presided over and dominated the cabinet, who through his personality or other influence managed the House of Commons, and who was the king's "prime minister"—was Sir Robert Walpole, who held this position from 1721 to 1742. The debate in Commons below reveals the frustration and outrage felt by opposition members at the extended dominance of Walpole. The charges of Sandys and the reply of Walpole show that their understanding of the office of prime minister was at best embryonic.

William Cobbett (1762–1835), who began publishing the *Parliamentary Debates* in 1803, complemented his project by re-

Source: William Cobbett, *Parliamentary History of England*, 36 vols., London, 1806–1820, XI, 1223–1224, 1229–1230, 1232, 1241–1242, 1284, 1287, 1295–1296.

constructing the debates for the period prior to 1803. The 36 large volumes he produced between 1806 and 1820 provide the historian with a ready source of evidence on the workings of Parliament, evidence that previously had to be gleaned from many different sources.

DEBATE IN THE COMMONS ON
MR. SANDYS'S MOTION FOR THE REMOVAL
OF SIR ROBERT WALPOLE

Mr. Sandys: Sir . . . I believe, there is not a gentleman of this House, who is not sensible, that both the foreign and domestic measures of our government, for several years past, have been dissatisfactory to a great majority of the nation, I may say to almost every man in the nation, who has not been concerned in advising or carrying them on. I believe, there is not a gentleman in this House, if he will freely declare his sentiments, who is not sensible, that one single person in the administration has not only been thought to be, but has actually been the chief, if not the sole adviser and promoter of all those measures. . . . As I am only to propose an Address to remove him from his majesty's counsels, I have no occasion to accuse him of any crime; the people's being generally dissatisfied with him and suspicious of his conduct, is a sufficient foundation for such an Address, and a sufficient cause for his majesty's removing him from his counsels; because, no sovereign of these kingdoms ought to employ a minister, who is become disagreeable to the generality of the people; and when any minister happens to become so, it is our duty to inform his majesty of it, that he may give satisfaction to his people, by the removal of such a minister. . . .

According to our constitution, we can have no sole and prime minister: we ought always to have several prime ministers or officers of state: every such officer has his own proper department; and no officer ought to meddle in the affairs belonging to the department of another. But it is publicly known, that this minister, having obtained a sole influence over all our public counsels, has not only assumed the sole direction of all public affairs, but has got every officer of state removed that would not follow his direction, even in the affairs belonging to his own proper department. By this means he hath monopolized all the favours of the crown, and engrossed the sole disposal of all places, pensions, titles, and ribbons, as well as of all preferments, civil, military, or ecclesiastical.

This, Sir, is of itself a most heinous offence against our constitution: but he has greatly aggravated the heinousness of his crime; for, having thus monopolized all the favours of the crown, he has made a blind submission to his direction at elections and in parliament, the only ground to hope for any honours or preferments, and the only tenure by which any gentleman could preserve what he had. This is so notoriously known, that it can stand in need of no proof. . . .

But farther, Sir, suppose this minister had never been guilty of any crime, error, or oversight in his public conduct; suppose the people had all along been perfectly pleased with his administration, yet the very length of it is, in a free country, sufficient cause for removing him. It is a most dangerous thing in a free government, to allow any man to continue too long in the possession of great power: most common-wealths have been overturned by this very oversight; and in this country, we know how difficult it has often proved, for our parliament to draw an old favourite from behind the throne, even when he has been guilty of the most heinous crimes. I wish this may not be our case at present; for though I shall not say, nor have I at present any occasion for shewing, that the favourite I am now complaining of has been guilty of heinous crimes, yet I will say, that there is a very general suspicion against him, that this suspicion is justified by the present situation of our affairs both at home and abroad, and that it is ridiculous to expect, that any proper discovery should be made, as long as he is in possession of all the proofs, and has the distribution of all the penalties the crown can inflict, as well as of all the favours the crown can bestow. Remove him from the king's counsels and presence; remove him from those high offices and power he is now possessed of; if he has been guilty of any crimes, the proof may then be come at, and the witnesses against him will not be afraid to appear: till you do this, it is impossible to determine, whether he is guilty or innocent; and, considering the universal clamour against him, it is high time to reduce him to such a condition, as that he may be brought to a fair, an impartial, and a strict account. If he were conscious of his being entirely innocent, and had a due regard to the security and glory of his master and sovereign, he would have chose to have put himself into this condition long before this time: since he has not thought fit to do so, it is our duty to endeavour to do it for him; and therefore I shall conclude with moving,

> "That an humble address be presented to his majesty, that he will be graciously pleased to remove the right hon. sir Robert Walpole, knight of the most noble order of the garter, first commissioner for executing the office of treasurer of the exchequer, chancellor and under-treasurer of the exchequer, and one of his majesty's most honourable privy council, from his majesty's presence and counsels for ever."

Sir *Robert Walpole:* Sir, it has been observed by several gentlemen in vindication of this motion, that if it should be carried, neither my life, liberty, or estate will be affected. But do the honourable gentlemen consider my character and reputation as of no moment? . . . . As I am conscious of no crime, my own experience convinces me, that none can be justly imputed. I must therefore ask the gentlemen, from whence does this attack proceed? From the passions and prejudices of the parties combined against me. . . . .

I am called repeatedly and insidiously prime and sole minister. . . . .

Have gentlemen produced one instance of this exorbitant power, of the influence which I extend to all parts of the nation, of the tyranny with which I oppress those who oppose, and the liberality with which I reward those who support me? But having first invested me with a kind of mock dignity, and styled me a prime minister, they impute to me an unpardonable abuse of that chimerical authority which they only have created and conferred. If they are really persuaded that the army is annually established by me, that I have the sole disposal of posts and honours, that I employ this power in the destruction of liberty, and the diminution of commerce, let me awaken them from their delusion. Let me expose to their view the real condition of the public weal; let me shew them that the crown has made no encroachments, that all supplies have been granted by parliament, that all questions have been debated with the same freedom as before the fatal period, in which my counsels are said to have gained the ascen–dancy. . . .

But while I unequivocally deny that I am sole and prime minister, and that to my influence and direction all the measures of government must be attributed, yet I will not shrink from the responsibility which attaches to the post I have the honour to hold; and should, during the long period in which I have sat upon this bench, any one step taken by government be proved to be either disgraceful or disadvantageous to the nation, I am ready to hold myself accountable.

To conclude, Sir, though I shall always be proud of the honour of any trust or confidence from his majesty, yet I shall always be ready to remove from his counsels and presence, when he thinks fit; and therefore I should think myself very little concerned in the event of the present question, if it were not for the encroachment that will thereby be made upon the prerogatives of the crown. But I must think, that an address to his majesty to remove one of his servants, without so much as alleging any particular crime against him, is one of the greatest encroachments that was ever made upon the prerogatives of the crown; and therefore, for the sake of my master, without any regard for my own, I hope all those that have a due regard for our constitution, and for the rights and prerogatives of the crown, without which our constitution cannot be preserved, will be against this motion.

9
William Hogarth, Prints (1725–1763).
The Artist as Social Critic

William Hogarth (1697–1764) is recognized as one of England's greatest artists. His art, unique for the eighteenth century, reflected what he saw in everyday life. This explains why his paintings and prints never appealed to the wealthy English connoisseurs, who, Hogarth complained, preferred "shiploads of dead Christs, Madonnas, and Holy Families." He disliked this pretentious art of the continent and agreed with Dr. Samuel Johnson, who once stated: "I had rather see the portrait of a dog I know than all the allegories you can show me." Hogarth gloried in his Englishness, visiting France only once in his lifetime and disliking the experience. He was a social critic and a moralist. He felt that art should do more than entertain; it should "improve the mind" and be "of public utility." Hogarth's sense of morality, which was that of the rising middle class, was best expressed in his famous progresses: "The Harlot's Progress" (1732), "The Rake's Progress" (1735), "Marriage-à-la-Mode" (1745), and "Industry and Idleness" (1747). Because these paintings were later engraved, the prints being sold to subscribers, Hogarth's work reached a far wider audience than that of any other eighteenth-century artist.

Hogarth's social criticism is clearly visible in the prints below. "The Sleeping Congregation" (Plate A) was a jab at the lethargy of the Church of England. Plate B, "Chairing the Members," the fourth and final of his "Election" prints, ridiculed the process by which members were elected to Parliament. Plate C, "Inhabitants of the Moon," pointed an accusing finger at the corruption of the establishment—the monarchy, the church, and the law. "Gin Lane" (Plate D), Hogarth's most famous print, illustrated the evils of the unregulated traffic in cheap gin, which beggared society but profited the pawnbroker. Hogarth's simple solution in Plate E, "Beer Street," was to encourage people to consume beer.

> Beer, happy Produce of our Isle
> Can sinewy Strength impart,
> And wearied with Fatigue and Toil
> Can chear each manly Heart.

Finally, Hogarth's talent at caricature, evident in "John Wilkes, Esquire" (Plate F), served as an example for such later political cartoonists and satirists as James Gillray and Thomas Rowlandson.

The art of any era can provide insight into the tastes and general attitudes of the people. Hogarth's prints, by dealing largely with social problems and by appealing to a large audience, are more valuable in this regard than the works of any other English artist. His paintings and etchings are widely scattered, the most complete collection being in the British Museum.

28

PLATE A
"The Sleeping Congregation" (by courtesy of the Trustees of the British Museum).

PLATE B
"Chairing the Members" (by courtesy of the Trustees of the British Museum).

PLATE C
"Inhabitants of the Moon" (by courtesy of the Trustees of the British Museum).

PLATE D
"Gin Lane" (by courtesy of the Trustees of the British Museum).

PLATE E
"Beer Street" (by courtesy of the Trustees of the British Museum).

PLATE F
"John Wilkes, Esquire" (by courtesy of the Trustees of the British Museum).

10
Horace Walpole, Letters.
The 1745 Jacobite Rebellion

Horace Walpole (1717–1797), the fourth son of prime minister Sir Robert Walpole, was a member of Parliament from 1741 to 1767. His life revolved, however, around Strawberry Hill, his house at Twickenham, which had the appearance of a small castle and contained his private printing press, from which he produced, among other things, his own Gothic novel, *The Castle of Otranto* (1764). He was a scholar and a gentleman. He was a member of society, he traveled abroad, he was acquainted with everyone, he knew everything that was happening. His thousands of letters were filled with his astute, witty, and scandalous observations on people and events. Although often an annoyance to his contemporaries, Walpole is through his letters one of the historian's brightest windows into the eighteenth century.

In the letters below he describes to Horace Mann, one of his chief correspondents and the British envoy to Florence from 1740 to 1784, the Jacobite uprising of 1745. They detail the attempt of Bonnie Prince Charlie to gain the throne for his father, the Old Pretender —his routing of General Sir John Cope's forces at Prestonpans on September 21, his march into England as far as Derby, a mere 80 miles from London, his turning back on December 6, when England did not rise on his behalf, his retreat into the Highlands but not before defeating another English army at Falkirk on January 17, 1746, and, finally, his utter defeat by the duke of Cumberland and the demise of the Jacobite threat at Culloden on April 16. It must be remembered that Walpole's account is no better than the source from which he obtained it, which is uncertain. On the other hand, his keen observations of feelings and reactions in England were his own and should be taken seriously. He is at his reportorial and entertaining best when giving his impression of Parliament's reception of the news that Hessian mercenaries had been hired and when he observes that

Source: Horace Walpole's *Correspondence with Sir Horace Mann,* Vol. III, edited by W. S. Lewis, Warren Hunting Smith, and George L. Lam *(The Yale Edition of Horace Walpole's Correspondence,* edited by W. S. Lewis, Vol. XIX), New Haven: Yale University Press, 1954, pp. 101–103, 116–118, 178–180, 185, 188–189, 246–249. Copyright 1954 by Yale University Press.

London has been reduced "to a state of Presbyterian dullness," relieved only by the marriage of the duchess of Bridgwater.

A volume of Walpole's letters was included in his works published in 1798, the year after his death. Since then, longer and
fuller editions have succeeded one after another, the latest complete edition, not yet finished, being projected to run to about fifty
volumes.

September 6, 1745

The confusion that I have found, and the danger we are in, prevent my talking
of anything else. The young Pretender, at the head of three thousand men, has
got a march on General Cope, who is not eighteen hundred strong; and when the
last accounts came away, was fifty miles nearer Edinburgh than Cope; and by
this time is there. The clans will not rise for the government: the Dukes of Argyle and Athol are come post to town, not having been able to raise a man. . . .

I look upon Scotland as gone! I think of what King William said to Duke
Hamilton, when he was extolling Scotland; "My Lord, I only wish it was an
hundred thousand miles off, and that you was king of it."

There are two manifestos published, signed Charles Prince, Regent for his father, King of Scotland, England, France, and Ireland. By one, he promises to
preserve everybody in their just rights; and orders all persons who have public
moneys in their hands to bring it to him; and by the other dissolves the Union
between England and Scotland. —But all this is not the worst! Notice came yesterday, that there are ten thousand men, thirty transports and ten men of war at
Dunkirk. Against this force, we have—I don't know what—scarce fears! Three
thousand Dutch we hope are by this time landed in Scotland; three more are
coming hither: we have sent for ten regiments from Flanders, which may be here
in a week, and we have fifteen men of war in the Downs.

September 27, 1745

I can't doubt but the joy of the Jacobites has reached Florence before this letter—Your two or three Irish priests, I forget their names, will have set out to
take possession of abbey lands here. I feel for what you will feel, and for the insulting things that will be said to you upon the battle we have lost in Scotland—
but all this is nothing to what it prefaces. The express came hither on Tuesday
morning, but the Papists knew it on Sunday night. Cope lay in face of the rebels
all Friday, he scarce two thousand strong; they vastly superior, though we don't
know their numbers. The military people say that he should have attacked them.
However we are sadly convinced that they are not such raw ragamuffins as they
were represented. . . . One does not hear the boy's personal valour cried up, by
which, I conclude he was not in the action. Our dragoons most shamefully fled

without striking a blow, and are with Cope, who escaped in a boat to Berwick.
. . . This defeat has frightened everybody, but those it rejoices, and those it
should frighten most; but my Lord Granville still buoys up the King's spirits,
and persuades him it is nothing. He uses his ministers as ill as possible, and dis-
courages everybody that would risk their lives and fortunes with him. Marshal
Wade is marching against the rebels; but the King will not let him take above
eight thousand men; so that if they come into England, another battle, with no
advantage on our side, may determine our fate. . . .

Prince Charles has called a Parliament in Scotland for the 7th of October;
ours does not meet till the 17th so that even in the show of liberty and laws, they
are beforehand with us. With all this, we hear of no men of quality or fortune
having joined him, but Lord Elcho, whom you have seen at Florence; and the
Duke of Perth, a silly racehorsing boy, who is said to be killed in this battle. But
I gather no confidence from hence: my father always said, "If you see them
come again, they will begin by their lowest people; their chiefs will not appear
till the end." His prophecies verify every day!

December 9th 1745

I am glad I did not write to you last post as I intended; I should have sent you
an account that would have alarmed you; and the danger would have been over
before the letter had crossed the sea. The Duke, from some strange want of intelligence, lay last week for four and twenty hours under arms at Stone in
Staffordshire, expecting the rebels every moment, while they were marching in
all haste to Derby. The news of this threw the town into great consternation; but
his Royal Highness repaired his mistake, and got to Northampton between the
Highlanders and London. . . . They must either go to North Wales, where they
will probably all perish, or to Scotland, with great loss. We dread them no
longer. We are threatened with great preparations for a French invasion, but the
coast is exceedingly guarded; and for the people, the spirit against the rebels increases every day: though they have marched thus into the heart of the kingdom,
there has not been the least symptom of a rising, not even in the great towns of
which they possessed themselves. They have got no recruits since their first
entry into England, except one gentleman in Lancashire, one hundred and fifty
common men and two parsons at Manchester, and a physician from York. But
here in London the aversion to them is amazing: on some thoughts of the King's
going to an encampment at Finchley, the weavers not only offered him a thousand men, but the whole body of the law formed themselves into a little army
under the command of Lord Chief Justice Willes, and were to have done duty at
St. James's, to guard the royal family in the King's absence.

December 20, 1745

We have at last got a springtide of good luck. The rebels turned back from
Derby; and have ever since been flying with the greatest precipitation. . . . Into

England I scarce believe the Highlanders will be drawn again—To have come as far as Derby; to have found no rising in their favour, and to find themselves not strong enough to fight either army, will make lasting impressions! . . .

We had yesterday a very remarkable day in the House: the King notified his having sent for six thousand Hessians into Scotland. Mr Pelham for an address of thanks. Lord Cornbury (indeed an exceedingly honest man) was for thanking for the notice, not for the sending for the troops; and proposed to add a representation of the national being the only constitutional troops; and to hope we should be exonerated of these foreigners as soon as possible. Pitt, and that clan joined him; but the voice of the House, and the desires of the whole kingdom for all the troops we can get, were so strong, that on the division we were 190 to 44: I think and hope this will produce some Hanoverians too. . . .

In the midst of our political distresses, which I assure you have reduced the town to a state of Presbyterian dullness, we have been entertained with the marriage of the Duchess of Bridgwater and Dick Lyttelton: she, forty, plain, very rich, and with five children; he, six and twenty, handsome, poor, and proper to get her five more.

April 25th 1746

You have bid me for some time send you good news—well! I think, I will. . . .

On the 16th the Duke by forced marches came up with the rebels a little on this side Inverness—by the way, the battle is not christened yet; I only know that neither Prestonpans nor Falkirk are to be godfathers. The rebels, who fled from him after their victory, and durst not attack him when so much exposed to them at his passage of the Spay, now stood him, they seven thousand, he ten. They broke through Barril's regiment, and killed Lord Robert Kerr, a handsome young gentleman, who was cut to pieces with above thirty wounds; but they were soon repulsed and fled; the whole engagement not lasting above a quarter of an hour. The young Pretender escaped; Mr Conway says, he hears, wounded; he certainly was in the rear. They have lost above a thousand men in the engagement and pursuit; and six hundred were already taken. . . . The defeat is reckoned total, and the dispersion general; and all their artillery is taken. 'Tis a brave young Duke! The town is all blazing round me, as I write, with fireworks and illuminations: I have some inclination to lap up half a dozen skyrockets to make you drink the Duke's health. Mr Doddington, on the first report, came out with a very pretty illumination; so pretty, that I believe he had it by him, ready for *any* occasion.

11
Earl of Chesterfield, Letters (1748).
The Education of a Gentleman

Like many historical figures, Philip Dormer Stanhope, fourth earl of Chesterfield (1694–1773), has today a different significance than when he was alive. To the eighteenth century, he was an ambassador, a lord-lieutenant of Ireland, and a politician of considerable importance. Today his reputation rests on his letters; from a man of politics he has been transformed into a man of literature.

The writing of letters was then considered an art. Chesterfield, Horace Walpole, Samuel Johnson, and many others exercised great care to ensure that their correspondence was informative, coherent, and even entertaining. Much private correspondence has survived, aiding the historian in the study of all aspects of English life. Today, the telephone has replaced the letter, destroying a traditional and valuable form of historical evidence.

Chesterfield's most famous letters were written to his illegitimate son, Philip, to teach him the graces necessary for social and political advancement. Collectively, these letters constitute a gentleman's book of etiquette. One, reproduced below, details the proper conduct toward women. These letters have always been controversial. To Chesterfield's numerous critics, the letters are wicked, because they substitute manners for morality; one need not be a gentleman, he only need appear to be one. To prove their point, critics never fail to stress that the letters were addressed to a product of one of his numerous social indiscretions. Chesterfield, with his biting wit and arrogance, was unable to profit from his own advice on winning friends and influencing people. George II (1727–1760) looked upon him as nothing more than "a little tea-table scoundrel."

The originals of Chesterfield's letters, almost all of which have been published, are scattered among various local repositories, the British Library, and the Public Record Office. The first edition of his letters was published in 1774, the year following his death.

Source: The Letters of Philip Dormer Stanhope, 4th Earl of Chesterfield, edited by Bonamy Dobrée, 6 vols., New York: AMS Reprint, 1968, IV, 1205–1211. Reprinted with permission of AMS Press, Inc.

London, 5 September O.S. 1748

Dear Boy,

St. Thomas's day now draws near, when you are to leave Saxony and go to Berlin; and I take it for granted, that if anything is yet wanting to complete your knowledge of the state of that Electorate, you will not fail to procure it before you go away. . . . You will there be in more company than you have yet been; manners and attentions will therefore be more necessary. Pleasing in company is the only way of being pleased in it yourself. Sense and knowledge are the first and necessary foundations for pleasing in company; but they will by no means do alone, and they will never be perfectly welcome if they are not accompanied with manners and attentions. You will best acquire these by frequenting the companies of people of fashion; but then you must resolve to acquire them in those companies by proper care and observation; for I have known people who, though they have frequented good company all their lifetime, have done it in so inattentive and unobserving a manner as to be never the better for it, and to remain as disagreeable, as awkward, and as vulgar, as if they had never seen any person of fashion. When you go into good company (by good company is meant the people of the first fashion of the place) observe carefully their turn, their manners, their address, and conform your own to them. But this is not all, neither; go deeper still; observe their characters, and pry, as far as you can, into both their hearts and their heads. Seek for their particular merit, their predominant passion, or their prevailing weakness; and you will then know what to bait your hook with to catch them. . . .

As women are a considerable, or at least a pretty numerous part, of company; and as their suffrages go a great way towards establishing a man's character in the fashionable part of the world (which is of great importance to the fortune and figure he proposes to make in it), it is necessary to please them. I will therefore, upon this subject, let you into certain *arcana,* that will be very useful for you to know, but which you must with the utmost care, conceal, and never seem to know. Women, then, are only children of a larger growth; they have an entertaining tattle and sometimes wit; but for solid, reasoning good-sense, I never in my life knew one that had it, or who reasoned or acted consequentially for four-and-twenty hours together. . . . A man of sense only trifles with them, plays with them, humours and flatters them, as he does with a sprightly, forward child; but he neither consults them about, nor trusts them with, serious matters; though he often makes them believe that he does both; which is the thing in the world that they are proud of; for they love mightily to be dabbling in business (which, by the way, they always spoil); and being justly distrustful that men in general look upon them in a trifling light, they almost adore that man who talks more seriously to them, and who seems to consult and trust them; I say, who seems, for weak men really do, but wise ones only seem to do it. No flattery is either too high or too low for them. They will greedily swallow the highest, and gratefully accept of the lowest; and you may safely flatter any woman, from her understanding down to the exquisite taste of her fan. Women, who are either indisputably beautiful, or indisputably ugly, are best flattered upon the score of their understandings; but those who are in a state of mediocrity, are best flattered upon their beauty, or at least their graces; for every woman who is not absolutely ugly, thinks herself handsome; but, not hearing often that she is so, is the more grateful and the more obliged to the few who tell her so; whereas a decided and conscious beauty looks upon every tribute paid to her beauty, only as her due; but wants to shine, and to be considered on the side of her understanding; and a woman who is ugly enough to know that she is so, knows that she has nothing left for her but her understanding, which is consequently (and probably in more senses than one) her weak side. . . . It is, therefore, absolutely necessary to manage, please, and flatter them; and never to discover the least marks of contempt, which is what they never forgive; but in this they are not singular, for it is the same with men; who will much sooner forgive an injustice than an insult. Every man is not ambitious, or covetous, or passionate; but every man has pride enough in his composition to feel and resent the least slight and contempt. Remember, therefore, most carefully to conceal your contempt, however just, wherever you would not make an implacable enemy. Men are much more unwilling to have their weaknesses and their imperfections known, than their crimes; and, if you hint to a man that you think him silly, ignorant, or even illbred or awkward, he will hate you more, and longer, than if you tell him plainly that you think him a rogue. . . .

These are some of the hints which my long experience in the great world enables me to give you; and which, if you attend to them, may prove useful to you in your journey through it. I wish it may be a prosperous one; at least, I am sure that it must be your own fault if it is not. . . .

Adieu!

12

Samuel Johnson, *A Dictionary of the English Language* (1755)

Samuel Johnson (1709–1784) was in the eighteenth century England's dominant literary personality. He spent years as an anonymous denizen of Grub Street (see definition below), writing for various journals and sometimes reporting illegally the debates of the House of Commons, where he was careful to see that "the Whig dogs should not have the best of it." His *Dictionary*, published in 1755, suddenly made him famous. This plus his founding of the Literary Club in 1764, his edition of Shakespeare's plays in 1765, and his honorary degrees from Dublin and Oxford in 1765 and 1775 made him the respected Dr. Johnson, the literary lion and archcritic who ruled the kingdom of letters throughout the remainder of his lifetime and beyond. James Boswell (1740–1795), an enterprising Scot who initiated his long association with Johnson in 1763, produced in 1791 a massive *Life of Samuel Johnson*. He described Johnson's endearing foibles as well as his genius, confirming his reputation and establishing him as a figure somewhat larger than life.

Although English dictionaries had appeared before that of Johnson, none was very satisfactory. The widely varying spellings in the earlier documents in this book illustrate the writers' freedom and lack of direction. Johnson's two large folio volumes in 1755 and an abridgment a year later changed all this, raising the lexicographer's art to new levels of excellence and producing a practical guide to spelling and usage that was not superseded for nearly a century. The short passage from Johnson's preface and the definition of lexicographer, reproduced below, reveal his insight into his task. Though at first thinking that he might be able to "fix our language," to make it standard for all time, he soon concluded it was folly for anyone to "imagine that his dictionary can enbalm his language." The definitions below, besides their individual interest, reveal something of Johnson's character. Although obviously a Tory and in many respects a conservative, he was not afraid of

Source: Johnson's Dictionary: A Modern Selection, edited by E. L. McAdam, Jr., and George Milne, New York: Pantheon Books, A Division of Random House, 1963, pp. 4, 24, 71, 73, 74, 85, 103, 131, 158, 176, 193, 199, 202, 222, 225, 233, 268, 303, 304, 420, 449. Copyright (c) 1963 by E. L. McAdam, Jr. Reprinted by permission of Pantheon Books, a division of Random House, Inc.

using words or of making honest and forthright judgments. Little of the blunt Anglo-Saxon of popular speech found its way into his dictionary, but what did, along with the frankness of his definitions and comments, reveals in him, and in the eighteenth century in general, a lack of inhibition and an earthy sense of humor.

When I took the first survey of my undertaking, I found our speech copious without order, and energetick without rules: wherever I turned my view, there was perplexity to be disentangled, and confusion to be regulated; choice was to be made out of boundless variety, without any established principle of selection; adulterations were to be detected, without a settled test of purity; and modes of expressions to be rejected or received, without the suffrages of any writers of classical reputation or acknowledged authority. . . .

Of the event of this work, for which, having laboured it with so much application, I cannot but have some degree of parental fondness, it is natural to form conjectures. Those who have been persuaded to think well of my design, require that it should fix our language, and put a stop to those alterations which time and chance have hitherto been suffered to make in it without opposition. With this consequence I will confess that I flattered myself for a while; but now begin to fear that I have indulged expectation which neither reason nor experience can justify. When we see men grow old and die at a certain time one after another, from century to century, we laugh at the elixir that promises to prolong life to a thousand years; and with equal justice may the lexicographer be derided, who being able to produce no example of a nation that has preserved their words and phrases from mutability, shall imagine that his dictionary can embalm his language, and secure it from corruption and decay, that it is in his power to change sublunary nature, or clear the world at once from folly, vanity, and affectation.

assie′nto.   (In Spanish a contract or bargain.) A contract or convention between the king of Spain and other powers, for furnishing the Spanish dominions in America with negro slaves. This contract was transferred from the French to the English South-Sea company, by the treaty of 1713, for thirty years; who were likewise permitted to send a register ship, of 500 tuns, yearly to the Spanish settlements, with European goods. Chambers.

athle′tick.   (2) Strong of body; vigorous; lusty; robust. Science distinguishes a man of honour from one of those *athletick* brutes, whom undeservedly we call heroes. Dryden.

a′tom.   (1) Such a small particle as cannot be physically divided: and these are the first rudiments, or the component parts of all bodies. Quincy.

to ba′rbecue.   A term used in the West-Indies for dressing a hog whole; which, being split to the backbone, is laid flat upon a large gridiron, raised about two foot above a charcoal fire, with which it is surrounded.

> Oldfield, with more than harpy throat endu'd,
> Cries, send me, gods, a whole hog *barbecu'd*. Pope.

bo′oby.   (A word of no certain etymology; Henshaw thinks it a corruption of *bull-beef* ridiculously; Skinner imagines it to be derived from *bobo,* foolish, Span. Junius finds *bowbard* to be an old Scottish word for a *coward,* a con-*temptible fellow;* from which he naturally deduces *booby;* but the original of *bowbard* is not known.) A dull, heavy, stupid fellow; a lubber.

> Young master next must rise to fill him wine,
> And starve himself to see the *booby* dine. King.

corn.   (1) The seeds which grow in ears, not in pods; such as are made into bread. (4) An excrescence on the feet, hard and painful; probably so called from its form, though by some supposed to be denominated from its *corneous* or horny substance.

> Even in men, aches and hurts and *corns* do engrieve
> either towards rain or towards frost. Bacon's *Natural*
> *History.*

dri′nkmoney.   Money given to buy liquor. Peg's servants were always asking for *drinkmoney.* Arbuthnot.

to fart.   To break wind behind.

> As when we a gun discharge,
> Although the bore be ne'er so large,
> Before the flame from muzzle burst,
> Just at the breech it flashes first;
> So from my lord his passion broke,
> He *farted* first, and then he spoke. Swift.

gaol.   A prison; a place of confinement. It is always pronounced and too often written *jail,* and sometimes *goal.*

gas.   (A word invented by the chymists.) It is used by Van Helmont, and seems designed to signify, in general, a spirit not capable of being coagulated: but he uses it loosely in many senses, and very unintelligibly and inconsistently. Harris.

go'speller.   A name of the followers of Wicklif, who first attempted a reformation from popery, given them by the Papists in reproach, from their professing to follow and preach only the gospel.

go'ssip.   (1) One who answers for the child in baptism. (2) A tippling companion. (3) One who runs about tattling like women at a lying-in.

gru'bstreet.   Originally the name of a street in Moorfields in London, much inhabited by writers of small histories, dictionaries, and temporary poems; whence any mean production is called grubstreet.

jail.   A gaol; a prison; a place where criminals are confined. See *gaol.* It is written either way; but commonly by latter writers *jail.*

to ke'elhale.   To punish in the seamans way, by dragging the criminal under water on one side of the ship and up again on the other.

lexico'grapher.   A writer of dictionaries; a harmless drudge, that busies himself in tracing the original, and detailing the signification of words.

oats.   A grain, which in England is generally given to horses, but in Scotland supports the people.

pota'to.   (I suppose an American word.) An esculent root.

> Leek to the Welch, to Dutchmen butter's dear,
> Of Irish swains *potatoe* is the chear;
> Oats for their feasts the Scottish shepherds grind,
> Sweet turnips are the food of Blouzelind;
> While she loves turnips, butter I'll despise,
> Nor leeks, nor oatmeal nor *potatoe* prize. Gay.

potva'liant.   Heated with courage by strong drink.

pou'ndage.   (1) A certain sum deducted from a pound; a sum paid by the trader to the servant that pays the money, or to the person who procures him customers.

to'ry.   (A cant term, derived, I suppose, from an Irish word signifying a savage.) One who adheres to the antient constitution of the state, and the apostolical hierarchy of the church of England, opposed to a whig.

> The knight is more a *tory* in the country than the town,
> because it more advances his interest. Addison.

whig.   (2) The name of a faction.
The southwest counties of Scotland have seldom corn enough to serve them round the year; and the northern parts producing more than they need, those

in the west come in the summer to buy at Leith the stores that come from the north; and from a word, whiggam, used in driving their horses, all that drove were called the whiggamors, and shorter the *whiggs.* Now in that year before the news came down of duke Hamilton's defeat, the ministers animated their people to rise and march to Edinburgh; and they came up marching on the head of their parishes with an unheard-of fury, praying and preaching all the way as they came. The marquis of Argyle and his party came and headed them, they being about six thousand. This was called the whiggamor's in-road; and ever after that, all that opposed the court came in contempt to be called *whigs:* and from Scotland the word was brought into England, where it is now one of our unhappy terms of disunion. Burnet.

Whoever has a true value for church and state, should avoid the extremes of *whig* for the sake of the former, and the extremes of tory on the account of the latter. Swift.

13
Wilkes v. *Wood* (1763) and *Leach* v. *Money* (1765). John Wilkes and General Warrants

The English judiciary, intimidated and dominated by the Stuart kings, became independent in 1701, when the Act of Settlement confirmed and established William III's practice of appointing judges for life. Henceforth, judges could not be influenced by threats to alter their salaries or be removed except by an address of both houses of Parliament. The eighteenth century was characterized by outstanding justices, who used this independence to extend the rights of individuals and thereby added luster to the common law. Their decisions affirmed what William Blackstone wrote in his *Commentaries* (1765–1769) that in an independent judiciary "consists one main preservative of the public liberty."

One of the most famous and important issues was the legality of general warrants, ordering the arrest of unnamed persons and authorizing the seizure of private papers. The general warrant below

Source: T. B. Howell, ed., *A Complete Collection of State Trials and Proceedings for High Treason and Other Crimes and Misdemeanors,* Vol. XIX, London, 1816, pp. 881, 1167–1168, 1026–1027.

was issued on April 30, 1763, for the arrest of "the authors, printers and publishers" of *The North Briton,* No. 45, "together with
their papers," thus satisfying both conditions. One of the 49 men
arrested by the warrant was John Wilkes (1727–1797), a wild and
wealthy young man, a member of Parliament as well as of the Hell
Fire Club, and a founder of *The North Briton.* Number 45 had
been especially harsh in its criticism of the king and his ministers.
Wilkes quickly obtained his release on the grounds that he was a
member of Parliament, and then in a suit against Robert Wood, an
undersecretary of state, he was awarded damages for the rifling of
his papers. Lord Chief Justice of Common Pleas Sir Charles Pratt
declared that such seizures were "totally subversive of the liberty
of the subject." Two years later, in the case of *Leach* v. *Money,*
Lord Chief Justice Mansfield joined with other judges in declaring
the invalidity of a warrant, "upon the single objection of the incertainty of the person, being neither named or described." The illegality of general warrants was confirmed by Justice Pratt (now Lord
Camden) in the case of *Entick* v. *Carrington* in 1765 and by parliamentary resolution in 1766.

Wilkes's career was a curious but significant one. Besides his
wealth and his keen sense of the ridiculous, he had little to support
the fame that he attained as a champion of liberty, first in the matter of general warrants, then in his bid for election to Parliament in
1768 and 1769, and finally in 1771 for championing the right to
publish the debates of Parliament. His entering these struggles
demonstrated his flair for publicity and his intrepidity in the face of
restrictions on his liberty. When he grew older he became conservative and respectable, but for a decade "Wilkes and Liberty" (see
Plate F, doc. 9) was a popular cry among the common people. His
career as a radical illustrates both the dilapidation of the political
system of the 1760s and the dawning realization that repairs needed to be made.

The General Warrant, April 30, 1763

George Montague Dunk, earl of Halifax, viscount Sunbury and baron
Halifax, one of the lords of his majesty's most honourable privy council, lieutenant general of his majesty's forces, and principal secretary of state: these are
in his majesty's name to authorize and require you (taking a constable to your
assistance) to make strict and diligent search for the authors, printers and publishers of a seditious and treasonable paper, intitled, The North Briton, N° 45,
Saturday April 23, 1763, printed for G. Kearsley in Ludgate-street, London, and

them, or any of them, having found, to apprehend and seize, together with their papers, and to bring in safe custody before me, to be examined concerning the premises, and further dealt with according to law: and in the due execution thereof, all mayors, sheriffs, justices of the peace, constables, and all other his majesty's officers civil and military, and loving subjects whom it may concern, are to be aiding and assisting to you, as there shall be occasion; and for so doing this shall be your warrant. Given at St. James's the 26th day of April, in the third year of his majesty's reign.

DUNK HALIFAX

To Nathan Carrington, John Money, James Watson, and Robert Blackmore, four of his majesty's messengers in ordinary.

Wilkes v. *Wood,* December 6, 1763

His lordship then went upon the warrant, which he declared was a point of the greatest consequence he had ever met with in his whole practice. The defendants claimed a right, under precedents, to force persons' houses, break open escrutores, seize their papers, &c. upon a general warrant, where no inventory is made of the things thus taken away, and where no offenders' names are specified in the warrant, and therefore a discretionary power given to messengers to search wherever their suspicions may chance to fall. If such a power is truly invested in a secretary of state, and he can delegate this power, it certainly may affect the person and property of every man in this kingdom, and is totally subversive of the liberty of the subject.

And as for the precedents, will that be esteemed law in a secretary of state which is not law in any other magistrate of this kingdom? If they should be found to be legal, they are certainly of the most dangerous consequences; if not legal, must aggravate damages. Notwithstanding what Mr. Solicitor General has said, I have formerly delivered it as my opinion on another occasion, and I still continue of the same mind, that a jury have it in their power to give damages for more than the injury received. Damages are designed not only as a satisfaction to the injured person, but likewise as a punishment to the guilty, to deter from any such proceeding for the future, and as a proof of the detestation of the jury to the action itself.

As to the proof of what papers were taken away, the plaintiff could have no account of them; and those who were able to have given an account (which might have been an extenuation of their guilt) have produced none. It lays upon the jury to allow what weight they think proper to that part of the evidence. It is my opinion the office precedents, which had been produced since the Revolution, are no justification of a practice in itself illegal, and contrary to the fundamental principles of the constitution; though its having been the constant practice of the office, might fairly be pleaded in mitigation of damages.

The Jury, after withdrawing for near half an hour, returned, and found a general verdict upon both issues for the plaintiff, with a thousand pounds damages.

Leach v. Money, June 18, 1765

Lord *Mansfield* . . . At present—as to the validity of the warrant, upon the single objection of the incertainty of the person, being neither named nor described—the common law, in many cases, gives authority to arrest without warrant; more especially, where taken in the very act: and there are many cases where particular acts of parliament have given authority to apprehend, under general warrants; as in the case of writs of assistance, or warrants to take up loose, idle, and disorderly people. But here, it is not contended, that the common law gave the officer authority to apprehend; nor that there is any act of parliament which warrants this case.

Therefore it must stand upon principles of common law.

It is not fit, that the receiving or judging of the information should be left to the discretion of the officer. The magistrate ought to judge; and should give certain directions to the officer. This is so, upon reason and convenience.

Then as to authorities—Hale and all others hold such an uncertain warrant void: and there is no case or book to the contrary. . . .

Mr. Justice *Wilmot* declared, that he had no doubt, nor ever had, upon these warrants: he thought them illegal and void.

Neither had the two other judges, Mr. Justice Yates, and Mr. Justice Aston, any doubt (upon this first argument) of the illegality of them: for no degree of antiquity can give sanction to a usage bad in itself. And they esteemed this usage to be so. They were clear and unanimous in opinion, that this warrant was illegal and bad.

14
William Pitt, Speech in Commons (1766). American Taxation

Britain's victory in the Seven Years' War (1756–1763) established her preeminence as a world power, but it left her with serious problems: a heavy burden of debt; political unrest as evidenced by the commotions caused by John Wilkes; and, not least, increasingly difficult relations with her American colonies. After decades of benign neglect, the colonies began to attract the attention of the British government. To mitigate the Indian problem on the western frontier, the Proclamation of 1763 forbade settlement west of the Appalachians. To enforce a coherent economic policy within the empire, the Sugar Act of 1764 reduced colonial tariffs but provided the machinery for their collection. And to relieve the British taxpayer of a portion of the cost of defense and administration, the Stamp Act of 1765 imposed on the American colonies a tax on newspapers, advertisements, and legal documents. The British government viewed these actions as parts of a unified and rational imperial policy. The American colonists, however, regarded them as infringements of their lawful rights and liberties.

The colonists' successful resistance, especially in getting the Stamp Act repealed in 1766, was due in part to the support that they received from members of the British Parliament, especially those Whigs who felt that the Americans' problems were related to the general complaints they themselves had against the government of George III (1760–1820). One of the most outspoken champions of the Americans' right to resist "taxation without representation" was William Pitt the Elder (1708–1778), later the earl of Chatham. Today, Pitt is recognized as England's premier statesman of the mid-eighteenth century and, with the possible exception of Winston Churchill, her greatest wartime leader of the modern era. In a crisis he was a superb leader, as in the Seven Years' War when he saved the British Empire. On issues requiring insight and forthright judgment, he spoke out for the interests of Britain and for the principles of the Glorious Revolution. In Pitt's speech of January 14, 1766, one senses the power and the passion of his

Source: William Cobbett, *Parliamentary History of England,* 36 vols., London, 1806–1820, XVI, 98–100, 103–104, 107.

oratory and appreciates the similarity of arguments for political reform on both sides of the Atlantic.

I hope a day may be soon appointed to consider the state of the nation with
respect to America. . . . A subject of greater importance than ever engaged the
attention of this House! that subject only excepted, when near a century ago, it
was the question whether you yourselves were to be bound, or free. . . . It is
my opinion, that this kingdom has no right to lay a tax upon the colonies. At the
same time, I assert the authority of this kingdom over the colonies, to be sovereign and supreme, in every circumstance of government and legislation whatsoever. They are the subjects of this kingdom, equally entitled with yourselves to
all the natural rights of mankind and the peculiar privileges of Englishmen.
Equally bound by its laws, and equally participating of the constitution of this
free country. The Americans are the sons, not the bastards, of England.
Taxation is no part of the governing or legislative power. The taxes are a voluntary gift and grant of the Commons alone. In legislation the three estates of the
realm are alike concerned, but the concurrence of the peers and the crown to a
tax, is only necessary to close with the form of a law. The gift and grant is of the
Commons alone. In ancient days, the crown, the barons, and the clergy possessed the lands. In those days, the barons and the clergy gave and granted to the
crown. They gave and granted what was their own. At present, since the discovery of America, and other circumstances permitting, the Commons are become
the proprietors of the land. The crown has divested itself of its great estates. The
church (God bless it) has but a pittance. The property of the Lords, compared
with that of the Commons, is as a drop of water in the ocean: and this House
represents those Commons, the proprietors of the lands; and those proprietors
virtually represent the rest of the inhabitants. When, therefore, in this House we
give and grant, we give and grant what is our own. But in an American tax, what
do we do? We, your Majesty's Commons of Great Britain, give and grant to
your Majesty, what? Our own property? No. We give and grant to your Majesty,
the property of your Majesty's commons of America. It is an absurdity in terms.
    The distinction between legislation and taxation is essentially necessary to
liberty. The Crown, the Peers, are equally legislative powers with the Commons.
If taxation be a part of simple legislation, the Crown, the Peers, have rights in
taxation as well as yourselves: rights which they will claim, which they will exercise, whenever the principle can be supported by power.
    There is an idea in some, that the colonies are virtually represented in this
House. I would fain know by whom an American is represented here? Is he represented by any knight of the shire, in any county in this kingdom? Would to
God that respectable representation was augmented to a greater number! Or will
you tell him, that he is represented by any representative of a borough—a bor-

ough, which perhaps, its own representative never saw. This is what is called, "the rotten part of the constitution." It cannot continue the century; if it does not drop, it must be amputated. The idea of a virtual representation of America in this House, is the most contemptible idea that ever entered into the head of a man; it does not deserve a serious refutation.

The Commons of America, represented in their several assemblies, have ever been in possession of the exercise of this, their constitutional right, of giving and granting their own money. They would have been slaves if they had not enjoyed it. At the same time, this kingdom, as the supreme governing and legislative power, has always bound the colonies by her laws, by her regulations, and restrictions in trade, in navigation, in manufactures, in every thing, except that of taking their money out of their pockets without their consent.

Here I would draw the line. . . .

I have been charged with giving birth to sedition in America. They have spoken their sentiments with freedom, against this unhappy act, and that freedom has become their crime. . . . The gentleman tells us, America is obstinate; America is almost in open rebellion. I rejoice that America has resisted. Three millions of people, so dead to all the feelings of liberty, as voluntarily to submit to be slaves, would have been fit instruments to make slaves of the rest. . . .

A great deal has been said without doors, of the power, of the strength of America. It is a topic that ought to be cautiously meddled with. In a good cause, on a sound bottom, the force of this country can crush America to atoms. . . . But on this ground, on the Stamp Act, when so many here will think it a crying injustice, I am one who will lift up my hands against it.

In such a cause, your success would be hazardous. America, if she fell, would fall like a strong man. She would embrace the pillars of the state, and pull down the constitution along with her. Is this your boasted peace? Not to sheath the sword in its scabbard, but to sheath it in the bowels of your countrymen?

15
Oliver Goldsmith, "The Deserted Village" (1770)

Oliver Goldsmith (c. 1730–1774) was one of England's most versatile writers. He was an essayist (*The Citizen of the World*, 1762), a novelist (*The Vicar of Wakefield*, 1766), a poet ("The Deserted Village," 1770), and a playwright (*She Stoops to Conquer*, 1773).

Goldsmith's early life was not directed toward a career in literature. Born in a small Irish village, the fifth child of a poor rector, he spent his youth searching for a profession. While a student at Trinity College, Dublin, he was once forced to flee because of his participation in a student riot, and on another occasion he was imprisoned on suspicion of recruiting Scots for the French army. After considering several careers, including the church, law, and medicine, in 1756 he arrived destitute in London. There, befriended by Samuel Johnson, he became an original member of the Literary Club and found his calling.

In much of Goldsmith's writing there is a personal element, as is obvious in "The Deserted Village." In describing the misfortunes of the small farmer forced off the land because of enclosure, he is recalling the plight of the cottagers in his boyhood village. He also deplores the blatant materialism of the mercantile London he observed in later life. His portrayal of the effects of enclosure are, however, open to criticism. Some scholars argue that the individual misery resulting from enclosure was necessary to increase agricultural production and, in the long run, to raise the general standard of living. Also, was the pleasant rural life an accurate description or was it something existing only in Goldsmith's imagination, a reflection of the anti-urban bias so prevalent in England and later in the United States?

> Sweet smiling village, loveliest of the lawn,
> Thy sports are fled, and all thy charms withdrawn;
> Amidst thy bowers the tyrant's hand is seen,
> And desolation saddens all thy green:

Source: The Complete Poetical Works of Oliver Goldsmith, edited by Austin Dobson, London: Oxford University Press, 1906, pp. 24–25, 33, 36–37. Reprinted by the permission of Oxford University Press.

One only master grasps the whole domain,
And half a tillage stints thy smiling plain:
No more thy glassy brook reflects the day,
But chok'd with sedges, works its weedy way.
Along thy glades, a solitary guest,
The hollow-sounding bittern guards its nest;
Amidst thy desert walks the lapwing flies,
And tires their echoes with unvaried cries.
Sunk are thy bowers in shapeless ruin all,
And the long grass o'ertops the mould'ring wall;
And trembling, shrinking from the spoiler's hand,
Far, far away, thy children leave the land.

Ill fares the land, to hast'ning ills a prey,
Where wealth accumulates, and men decay:
Princes and lords may flourish, or may fade;
A breath can make them, as a breath has made;
But a bold peasantry, their country's pride,
When once destroy'd, can never be supplied.

A time there was, ere England's griefs began,
When every rood of ground maintain'd its man;
For him light labour spread her wholesome store,
Just gave what life requir'd, but gave no more:
His best companions, innocence and health;
And his best riches, ignorance of wealth.

But times are alter'd; trade's unfeeling train
Usurp the land and dispossess the swain;
Along the lawn, where scatter'd hamlets rose,
Unwieldy wealth, and cumbrous pomp repose;
And every want to opulence allied,
And every pang that folly pays to pride.
Those gentle hours that plenty bade to bloom,
Those calm desires that ask'd but little room,
Those healthful sports that grac'd the peaceful scene,
Liv'd in each look, and brighten'd all the green;
These, far departing, seek a kinder shore,
And rural mirth and manners are no more.

                        · · ·

Where then, ah! where, shall poverty reside,
To 'scape the pressure of contiguous pride?
If to some common's fenceless limits stray'd,
He drives his flock to pick the scanty blade,

Those fenceless fields the sons of wealth divide,
And e'en the bare-worn common is denied.

    If to the city sped—What waits him there?
To see profusion that he must not share;
To see ten thousand baneful arts combin'd
To pamper luxury, and thin mankind;
To see those joys the sons of pleasure know
Extorted from his fellow creature's woe.
Here, while the courtier glitters in brocade,
There the pale artist plies the sickly trade;
Here, while the proud their long-drawn pomps display,
There the black gibbet glooms beside the way.

            .   .   .

E'en now the devastation is begun,
And half the business of destruction done;
E'en now, methinks, as pond'ring here I stand,
I see the rural virtues leave the land:
Down where yon anchoring vessel spreads the sail,
That idly waiting flaps with ev'ry gale,
Downward they move, a melancholy band,
Pass from the shore, and darken all the strand.

            .   .   .

Teach erring man to spurn the rage of gain;
Teach him, that states of native strength possess'd,
Though very poor, may still be very bless'd;
That trade's proud empire hastes to swift decay,
As ocean sweeps the labour'd mole away;
While self-dependent power can time defy,
As rocks resist the billows and the sky.

16

The Unanimous Declaration of the Thirteen United States of America (1776)

The British government learned little from the failure of the Stamp Act; it simply devised subtler means to tax and more overt means to control. The Americans learned that protest did produce results and that their liberties were respected by many who sat in the parliament at Westminster. The mounting confrontation moved closer and closer to violence, developing a momentum of its own. Events such as the Boston Massacre in 1770 and the Boston Tea Party in 1773 produced the Coersive or Intolerable Acts of 1774, which in turn provoked the first and second Continental Congresses. The final stage, open warfare and independence, was begun at Lexington and Concord in 1775 and was confirmed by a declaration of independence in 1776.

Although not a part of the English constitution, the Unanimous Declaration of the Thirteen United States of America, as the title appears on the parchment copy, is most assuredly a product of it. It is in the tradition of Magna Carta, the Petition of Right, and the Bill of Rights, from an American point of view the fourth in a series of assertions of individual liberties. As in the first three, there is a statement of grievances against an English king and his government for violating the people's rights. George III, like James II in 1688, has "abdicated Government." And the British people, having not heard the cries of their brethren overseas, now become like "the rest of mankind, Enemies in War, in Peace Friends."

Besides the example of English practice and experience, one discerns the influence of John Locke's *Two Treatises of Government.* The rights claimed were not those of Englishmen alone: "they are endowed by their Creator with certain unalienable Rights . . . Life, Liberty and the pursuit of Happiness." As a result of the Declaration of Independence, English ideas of limited government were made universal in their application. Through Locke and the success of the American Revolution, England's constitutional experience was given to the world.

Source: Carl L. Becker, *The Declaration of Independence: A Study in the History of Political Ideas,* New York: Alfred A. Knopf, Inc., 1962, pp. 185–192.

THE UNANIMOUS DECLARATION OF THE THIRTEEN UNITED STATES OF AMERICA

When in the Course of human events, it becomes necessary for one people to dissolve the political bands, which have connected them with another, and to assume among the powers of the earth, the separate and equal station to which the Laws of Nature and of Nature's God entitle them, a decent respect to the opinions of mankind requires that they should declare the causes which impel them to the separation.—We hold these truths to be self-evident, that all men are created equal, that they are endowed by their Creator with certain unalienable Rights, that among these are Life, Liberty and the pursuit of Happiness.—That to secure these rights, Governments are instituted among Men, deriving their just powers from the consent of the governed,—That whenever any Form of Government becomes destructive of these ends, it is the Right of the People to alter or to abolish it, and to institute new Government, laying its foundation on such principles and organizing its powers in such form, as to them shall seem most likely to effect their Safety and Happiness. Prudence, indeed, will dictate that Governments long established should not be changed for light and transient causes; and accordingly all experience hath shewn, that mankind are more disposed to suffer, while evils are sufferable, than to right themselves by abolishing the forms to which they are accustomed. But when a long train of abuses and usurpations, pursuing invariably the same Object evinces a design to reduce them under absolute Despotism, it is their right, it is their duty, to throw off such Government, and to provide new Guards for their future security.—Such has been the patient sufferance of these Colonies; and such is now the necessity which constrains them to alter their former Systems of Government. The history of the present King of Great Britain is a history of repeated injuries and usurpations, all having in direct object the establishment of an absolute Tyranny over these States. To prove this, let Facts be submitted to a candid world.—He has refused his Assent to Laws, the most wholesome and necessary for the public good.—He has forbidden his Governors to pass Laws of immediate and pressing importance, unless suspended in their operation till his Assent should be obtained; and when so suspended, he has utterly neglected to attend to them. . . . He has dissolved Representative Houses repeatedly, for opposing with manly firmness his invasions on the rights of the people. . . . He has made Judges dependent on his Will alone, for the tenure of their offices, and the amount and payment of their salaries.—He has erected a multitude of New Offices, and sent hither swarms of Officers to harass our people, and eat out their substance.—He has kept among us, in times of peace, Standing Armies without the Consent of our legislatures.—He has affected to render the Military independent of and superior to the Civil power.—He has combined with others to subject us to a jurisdiction foreign to our constitution, and unacknowledged by our laws; giving his Assent to their Acts of pretended Legislation.—For quartering large bodies of armed troops among us:—For protecting them, by a mock Trial, from punishment for any Murders which they should commit on the Inhabitants of these States:—For cutting off our Trade with all parts of the world:—For imposing Taxes on us without our Consent:—For depriving us in many cases, of the benefits of Trial by Jury:—For transporting us beyond Seas to be tried for pretended offenses:—For abolishing the free System of English Laws in a neighboring Province, establishing therein an Arbitrary government, and enlarging its Boundaries so as to render it at once an example and fit instrument for introducing the same absolute rule into these Colonies:—For taking away our Charters, abolishing our most valuable Laws, and altering fundamentally the Forms of our Governments:—For suspending our own Legislatures, and declaring themselves invested with power to legislate for us in all cases whatsoever.—He has abdicated Government here, by declaring us out of his Protection and waging War against us.—He has plundered our seas, ravaged our Coasts, burnt our towns, and destroyed the lives of our people.—He is at this time transporting large Armies of foreign Mercenaries to compleat the works of death, desolation and tyranny, already begun with circumstances of Cruelty & perfidy scarcely paralleled in the most barbarous ages, and totally unworthy the Head of a civilized nation.—He has constrained our fellow Citizens taken Captive on the high Seas to bear Arms against their Country, to become the executioners of their friends and Brethren, or to fall themselves by their Hands.—He has excited domestic insurrections amongst us, and has endeavoured to bring on the inhabitants of our frontiers, the merciless Indian Savages, whose known rule of warfare, is an undistinguished destruction of all ages, sexes and conditions. In every stage of these Oppressions We have Petitioned for Redress in the most humble terms: Our repeated Petitions have been answered only by repeated injury. A Prince whose character is thus marked by every act which may define a Tyrant, is unfit to be the ruler of a free people. Nor have We been wanting in attentions to our Brittish brethren. We have warned them from time to time of attempts by their legislature to extend an unwarrantable jurisdiction over us. We have reminded them of the circumstances of our emigration and settlement here. We have appealed to their native justice and magnanimity, and we have conjured them by the ties of our common kindred to disavow these usurpations, which would inevitably interrupt our connections and correspondence. They too have been deaf to the voice of justice and of consanguinity. We must, therefore, acquiesce in the necessity, which denounces our Separation, and hold them, as we hold the rest of mankind, Enemies in War, in Peace Friends.—

We, therefore, the Representatives of the united States of America, in General Congress, Assembled, appealing to the Supreme Judge of the world for the rectitude of our intentions do, in the Name, and by Authority of the good People of these Colonies, solemnly publish and declare, That these United Colonies are, and of Right ought to be Free and Independent States; that they are Absolved from all Allegiance to the British Crown, and that all political connection between them and the State of Great Britain, is and ought to be totally dissolved: and that as Free and Independent States, they have full Power to levy War, conclude Peace, contract Alliances, establish Commerce, and to do all other Acts and Things which Independent States may of right do.—And for the support of this Declaration, with a firm reliance on the protection of divine Providence, we mutually pledge to each other our Lives, our Fortunes and our sacred Honor.

17
Adam Smith, *The Wealth of Nations* (1776). An Attack on Mercantilism

Adam Smith (1723–1790), a Scot, a friend of David Hume, Samuel Johnson, and Voltaire, and for a time a professor of moral philosophy at Glasgow, published in 1776 one of the world's most influential books. *An Inquiry into the Nature and Causes of the Wealth of Nations* was a refutation of the mercantilistic doctrine that wealth consisted of bullion, or gold and silver, and that it was a role of government to foster its accumulation by means of laws restricting imports and encouraging exports. Wealth, he argued, was a country's ability to produce things. Smith, in the spirit of the eighteenth century, was looking for natural laws governing the conduct of human beings. He was in the tradition of Isaac Newton (1642–1727), who explained the workings of the material universe by the laws of gravity. Smith asserted that a nation's economy did not require government regulation; it was better regulated by the natural working of the marketplace. By "an invisible hand," human selfishness and competitiveness were converted into a self-regulating system that optimized benefits and produced a mounting prosperity. All restrictions on the free market, either by government regulation or by individuals, served only as a brake on the growth of capital and, thus, on further production and prosperity.

Although Smith discerned the advantages of laissez-faire and division of labor, he did not foresee the effects of the Industrial

Source: Adam Smith, *An Inquiry into the Nature and Causes of the Wealth of Nations,* edited by Edwin Cannan, New York: Random House, Inc., Modern Library, Inc., 1937, pp. 417–418, 421, 423–425.

Revolution with its huge factories and corporations. He saw only
the bustling competition of countless small shops and manufacto-
ries, which characterized the Britain of his own day. His coining of
the term "the mercantile system" to describe the restrictions he ab-
horred reflected his suspicion of merchants. Elsewhere he wrote,
"People of the same trade seldom meet together but the conversation ends in a conspiracy against the public, or in some diversion
to raise prices." His concern was for the consumer. It is ironic that
his fame came when merchants and manufacturers chose to ignore
his slighting remarks and championed his general idea of a free
market, unhindered by regulations or restrictions. Thus, *The
Wealth of Nations,* appropriated by the defenders of untrammeled
business, was cited to justify opposition to any government regulation.

   I thought it necessary, though at the hazard of being tedious, to examine at
full length this popular notion that wealth consists in money, or in gold and silver. Money in common language, as I have already observed, frequently signi-
fies wealth; and this ambiguity of expression has rendered this popular notion so
familiar to us, that even they, who are convinced of its absurdity, are very apt to
forget their own principles, and in the course of their reasonings to take it for
granted as a certain and undeniable truth. Some of the best English writers upon
commerce set out with observing, that the wealth of a country consists, not in its
gold and silver only, but in its lands, houses, and consumable goods of all different kinds. In the course of their reasonings, however, the lands, houses, and consumable goods seem to slip out of their memory, and the strain of their argument
frequently supposes that all wealth consists in gold and silver, and that to multi-
ply those metals is the great object of national industry and commerce.
   The two principles being established, however, that wealth consisted in gold
and silver, and that those metals could be brought into a country which had no
mines only by the balance of trade, or by exporting to a greater value than it imported; it necessarily became the great object of political economy to diminish
as much as possible the importation of foreign goods for home consumption,
and to increase as much as possible the exportation of the produce of domestic
industry. Its two great engines for enriching the country, therefore, were restraints upon importation, and encouragements to exportation. . . .
   The general industry of the society never can exceed what the capital of the
society can employ. As the number of workmen that can be kept in employment
by any particular person must bear a certain proportion to his capital, so the
number of those that can be continually employed by all the members of a great
society, must bear a certain proportion to the whole capital of that society, and
never can exceed that proportion. No regulation of commerce can increase the

quantity of industry in any society beyond what its capital can maintain. It can only divert a part of it into a direction into which it might not otherwise have gone; and it is by no means certain that this artificial direction is likely to be more advantageous to the society than that into which it would have gone of its own accord.

Every individual is continually exerting himself to find out the most advantageous employment for whatever capital he can command. It is his own advantage, indeed, and not that of the society, which he has in view. But the study of his own advantage naturally, or rather necessarily leads him to prefer that employment which is most advantageous to the society. . . .

As every individual, therefore, endeavours as much as he can both to employ his capital in the support of domestic industry, and so to direct that industry that its produce may be of the greatest value; every individual necessarily labours to render the annual revenue of the society as great as he can. He generally, indeed, neither intends to promote the public interest, nor knows how much he is promoting it. By preferring the support of domestic to that of foreign industry, he intends only his own security; and by directing that industry in such a manner as its produce may be of the greatest value, he intends only his own gain, and he is in this, as in many other cases, led by an invisible hand to promote an end which was no part of his intention. Nor is it always the worse for the society that it was no part of it. By pursuing his own interest he frequently promotes that of the society more effectually than when he really intends to promote it. I have never known much good done by those who affected to trade for the public good. It is an affectation, indeed, not very common among merchants, and very few words need be employed in dissuading them from it.

What is the species of domestic industry which his capital can employ, and of which the produce is likely to be of the greatest value, every individual, it is evident, can, in his local situation, judge much better than any statesman or lawgiver can do for him. The statesman, who should attempt to direct private people in what manner they ought to employ their capitals, would not only load himself with a most unnecessary attention, but assume an authority which could safely be trusted, not only to no single person, but to no council or senate whatever, and which would nowhere be so dangerous as in the hands of a man who had folly and presumption enough to fancy himself fit to exercise it.

To give the monopoly of the home-market to the produce of domestic industry, in any particular art or manufacture, is in some measure to direct private people in what manner they ought to employ their capitals, and must, in almost all cases, be either a useless or a hurtful regulation. If the produce of domestic can be bought there as cheap as that of foreign industry, the regulation is evidently useless. If it cannot, it must generally be hurtful. It is the maxim of every prudent master of a family, never to attempt to make at home what it will cost him more to make than to buy. The taylor does not attempt to make his own shoes, but buys them of the shoemaker. The shoemaker does not attempt to make his own clothes, but employs a taylor. The farmer attempts to make neither the one nor the other, but employs those different artificers. All of them find it for their interest to employ their whole industry in a way in which they have some advantage over their neighbours, and to purchase with a part of its produce, or what is the same thing, with the price of a part of it, whatever else they have occasion for.

What is prudence in the conduct of every private family, can scarce be folly in that of a great kingdom. If a foreign country can supply us with a commodity cheaper than we ourselves can make it, better buy it of them with some part of the produce of our own industry, employed in a way in which we have some advantage. The general industry of the country, being always in proportion to the capital which employs it, will not thereby be diminished, no more than that of the above-mentioned artificers; but only left to find out the way in which it can be employed with the greatest advantage. It is certainly not employed to the greatest advantage, when it is thus directed towards an object which it can buy cheaper than it can make. The value of its annual produce is certainly more or less diminished, when it is thus turned away from producing commodities evidently of more value than the commodity which it is directed to produce. According to the supposition, that commodity could be purchased from foreign countries cheaper than it can be made at home. It could, therefore, have been purchased with a part only of the commodities, or, what is the same thing, with a part only of the price of the commodities, which the industry employed by an equal capital would have produced at home, had it been left to follow its natural course. The industry of the country, therefore, is thus turned away from a more, to a less advantageous employment, and the exchangeable value of its annual produce, instead of being increased, according to the intention of the lawgiver, must necessarily be diminished by every such regulation.

By means of such regulations, indeed, a particular manufacture may sometimes be acquired sooner than it could have been otherwise, and after a certain time may be made at home as cheap or cheaper than in the foreign country. But though the industry of the society may be thus carried with advantage into a particular channel sooner than it could have been otherwise, it will by no means follow that the sum total, either of its industry, or of its revenue, can ever be augmented by any such regulation. The industry of the society can augment only in proportion as its capital augments, and its capital can augment only in proportion to what can be gradually saved out of its revenue. But the immediate effect of every such regulation is to diminish its revenue, and what diminishes its revenue is certainly not very likely to augment its capital faster than it would have augmented of its own accord, had both capital and industry been left to find out their natural employments.

Though for want of such regulations the society should never acquire the proposed manufacture, it would not, upon that account, necessarily be the poorer in any one period of its duration. In every period of its duration its whole capital and industry might still have been employed, though upon different objects, in the manner that was most advantageous at the time. In every period its revenue might have been the greatest which its capital could afford, and both capital and revenue might have been augmented with the greatest possible rapidity.

18

Jeremy Bentham, *A Fragment on Government* (1776), and *An Introduction to the Principles of Morals and Legislation* (1780)

William Blackstone's *Commentaries on the Laws of England* (1765–1769) became justly famous as a description of the evolved perfection of England's common law and constitution. However, in many respects, what he had written was an idealization; he gloried in the fictions that hid the seamy realities. Jeremy Bentham (1748–1832), who as a young law student at Oxford had listened to the lectures that Blackstone later converted into his *Commentaries,* spent his long life protesting the contradictions between the law as it actually was and Blackstone's idealization of it.

Bentham countered Blackstone's justification of the law as tradition with his own utilitarian "measure of right and wrong." Law and governmental action should promote "the greatest happiness of the greatest number." In *A Fragment on Government* (1776), his first published work, he applied this principle of criticism specifically to Blackstone. Four years later, in the opening paragraphs of *An Introduction to the Principles of Morals and Legislation,* he wrote his clearest and most succinct description "Of the Principle of Utility." By the turn of the century he was attracting a school of followers. As "Utilitarians" or "Philosophical Radicals," they influenced reform and legislation across a wide spectrum of nineteenth-century life.

It is not difficult to ridicule or poke holes in the hedonistic basis of utilitarianism. Is all pleasure of equal value? Is poetry no better

Source: The Works of Jeremy Bentham, edited by John Bowring, 11 vols., 1838–1843, New York: Russell & Russell, 1962, I, 227, 230, 1–2. Reprinted by permission of Russell & Russell, Publishers.

than "pushpin"—a petty form of gambling once popular in tav-
erns? Nevertheless, Bentham and his followers, by asserting that
people could best judge their own happiness, expressed a principle that was at the heart of liberalism. Bentham's insistence that
tradition need not be blindly revered but, instead, should be
judged by a principle as straightforward and understandable as
utility provided probably the most effective argument for reform in
the nineteenth century.

A FRAGMENT ON GOVERNMENT

Preface

The age we live in is a busy age; an age in which knowledge is rapidly advancing towards perfection. In the natural world, in particular, every thing teems
with discovery and with improvement. The most distant and recondite regions of
the earth traversed and explored—the all-vivifying and subtle element of the air
so recently analyzed and made known to us,—are striking evidences, were all
others wanting, of this pleasing truth.

Correspondent to *discovery* and *improvement* in the natural world, is *reformation* in the moral. . . . Perhaps among such observations as would be best
calculated to serve as grounds for reformation, are some which, being observations of matters of fact hitherto either incompletely noticed, or not at all, would,
when produced, appear capable of bearing the name of discoveries: with so little
method and precision have the consequences of this fundamental axiom, *It is the
greatest happiness of the greatest number that is the measure of right and
wrong,* been as yet developed.

Be this as it may, if there be room for making, and if there be use in publishing, *discoveries* in the *natural* world, surely there is not much less room for
making, nor much less use in proposing, *reformation* in the *moral.* If it be a matter of importance and of use to us to be made acquainted with *distant* countries,
surely it is not a matter of much less importance, nor of much less use to us, to
be made better and better acquainted with the chief means of living happily in
our *own:* If it be of importance and of use to us to know the principles of the element we breathe, surely it is not of much less importance, nor of much less use,
to comprehend the principles, and endeavour at the improvement of those *laws,*
by which alone we breathe it in security. If to this endeavour we should fancy
any author, especially any author of great name, to *be,* and as far as could in
such case be expected, to *avow himself,* a determined and persevering enemy,
what should we say of him? We should say that the interests of reformation, and
through them the welfare of mankind, were inseparably connected with the
downfall of his works: of a great part, at least, of the esteem and influence which
these works might, under whatever title, have acquired.

Such an enemy it has been my misfortune (and not mine only) to see, or fancy at least I saw, in the Author of the celebrated COMMENTARIES *on the* LAWS *of* ENGLAND: an author whose works have had, beyond comparison, a more extensive circulation, have obtained a greater share of esteem, of applause, and consequently of influence (and that by a title on many grounds so indisputable), than any other writer who on that subject has ever yet appeared.

It is on this account that I conceived, some time since, the design of pointing out some of what appeared to me the capital blemishes of that work, particularly this grand and fundamental one, the antipathy to reformation; or rather, indeed, of laying open and exposing the universal inaccuracy and confusion which seemed to my apprehension to pervade the whole. .

It is wonderful how forward some have been to look upon it as a kind of presumption, and ingratitude, and rebellion, and cruelty, and I know not what besides, not to allege only, nor to own, but to suffer any one so much as to imagine, that an old-established law could in any respect be a fit object of condemnation. Whether it has been a kind of *personification* that has been the cause of this, as if the Law were a living creature, or whether it has been the mechanical veneration for antiquity, or what other delusion of the fancy, I shall not here inquire. For my part, I know not for what good reason it is that the merit of justifying a law when right, should have been thought greater than that of censuring it when wrong. Under a government of laws, what is the motto of a good citizen? *To obey punctually; to censure freely.*

Thus much is certain; that a system that is never to be censured, will never be improved: that if nothing is ever to be found fault with, nothing will ever be mended: and that a resolution to justify every thing at any rate, and to disapprove of nothing, is a resolution which, pursued in future, must stand as an effectual bar to all the *additional* happiness we can ever hope for; pursued hitherto, would have robbed us of that share of happiness which we enjoy already.

Nor is a disposition to find "every thing as it should be," less at variance with itself, than with reason and utility.

AN INTRODUCTION TO THE PRINCIPLES OF MORALS AND LEGISLATION

Chapter I. Of the Principle of Utility

Nature has placed mankind under the governance of two sovereign masters, *pain* and *pleasure*. It is for them alone to point out what we ought to do, as well as to determine what we shall do. On the one hand the standard of right and wrong, on the other the chain of causes and effects, are fastened to their throne. They govern us in all we do, in all we say, in all we think: every effort we can make to throw off our subjection, will serve but to demonstrate and confirm it. In words a man may pretend to abjure their empire: but in reality he will remain subject to it all the while. The *principle of utility* recognizes this subjection, and assumes it for the foundation of that system, the object of which is to rear the fabric of felicity by the hands of reason and of law. . . .

III.

By utility is meant that property in any object, whereby it tends to produce benefit, advantage, pleasure, good, or happiness (all this in the present case comes to the same thing), or (what comes again to the same thing) to prevent the happening of mischief, pain, evil, or unhappiness to the party whose interest is considered: if that party be the community in general, then the happiness of the community: if a particular individual, then the happiness of that individual.

IV.

The interest of the community is one of the most general expressions that can occur in the phraseology of morals: no wonder that the meaning of it is often lost. When it has a meaning, it is this. The community is a fictitious *body,* composed of the individual persons who are considered as constituting as it were its *members.* The interest of the community then is, what?—the sum of the interests of the several members who compose it.

V.

It is in vain to talk of the interest of the community, without understanding what is the interest of the individual. A thing is said to promote the interest, or to be *for* the interest, of an individual, when it tends to add to the sum total of his pleasures: or, what comes to the same thing, to diminish the sum total of his pains.

VI.

An action then may be said to be conformable to the principle of utility, or, for shortness sake, to utility (meaning with respect to the community at large), when the tendency it has to augment the happiness of the community is greater than any it has to diminish it.

19

James Ogden, *A Description of Manchester* (1783). The Industrial Revolution

James Ogden (1718–1802), although he witnessed a revolution, failed to appreciate the fact until late in life. He was born in Manchester, then a prosperous little textile town of perhaps 10,000 people. Like many of Manchester's young men, he was soon a part of the textile industry, which was still under the domestic system and devoid of large factories. Ogden later became a schoolmaster, spending much of his time writing volumes of "turgid" verse, including the never-to-be-remembered *British Lion Rous'd; or Acts of the British Worthies: a Poem in Nine Books* (8 vols., 1762). While Ogden was thus pleasantly engaged, Manchester was transformed by the Industrial Revolution. Canals to nearby coalfields and the port of Liverpool made the town after 1760 a natural center for large-scale industry. The introduction of modern textile machinery inaugurated the factory system. By 1800 Manchester had changed; it was an industrial center with a population of almost 100,000.

Late in life, Ogden developed an interest in the economic changes occurring about him. His *Description of Manchester* (1783) was reprinted several times because of its historical value. In his discussion of the introduction of machinery, at least two things are worth noting. First, it is apparent that some people did not share his enthusiasm for the blessings of modern technology, viewing industrialization with skepticism if not distrust. Second, it is interesting that Ogden attributed much of Manchester's economic success to its lack of a corporate structure. It was fortunate in being "only a market town," without the traditional guild regulations, which obstructed industrial growth and commerce, and without parliamentary representation, whose elections periodically distracted and divided the people. This widespread attitude among the wealthy and educated was a great obstacle to social and political reform in the nineteenth century.

Source: James Ogden, *A Description of Manchester . . . By a Native of the Town,* Manchester, 1783, pp. 87–94.

These were first used by the country people on a confined scale, twelve spindles being thought a great affair at first, and the aukward posture required to spin on them, was discouraging to grown up people, while they saw with a degree of surprize, children, from nine to twelve years of age, manage them with dexterity, which brought plenty into families, that were before overburthened with children, and delivered many a poor endeavouring weaver out of bondage to which they were exposed, by the insolence of spinners, and abatement of their work, for which evils there was no remedy till spinning-jennies were invented. . . .

The plenty of weft produced by this means gave uneasiness to the country people, and the weavers were afraid lest the manufacturers should demand finer weft woven at the former prices, which occasioned some risings, and the jennies were opposed, some being demolished before those who used them could be protected, or convince others of their general utility, till *Dorning Rasbotham,* Esq; a worthy magistrate who lived in that part of the country, towards *Bolton,* where they were used, convinced the weavers, in a sensible printed address, that it was their true interest to encourage jennies, urging the former insolence of spinners, and the happiness of such as had already relieved themselves, and procured employment for their children; and appealed to their own experience of the fly shuttle, against which the like clamour had been raised, and the inventor driven to *France,* where he found encouragement, while his shuttles are yet in such estimation here, as to be used generally even on narrow goods, to the benefit of trade in general, without any bad consequence in the experience of several years, but they are rather of particular benefit to the weavers.

This seasonable address produced a general acquiescence in the use of these engines, to a certain number of spindles, but they were soon multiplied to three or four times the quantity; nor did the invention of ingenious mechanics rest here, for the demand of twist for warps was greater as weft grew plenty, therefore engines were soon constructed for this purpose: one in particular was purchased at a price which was a considerable reward for the contriver's ingenuity, and exposed at the Exchange, where he spun on it, and all that were disposed to see the operation, were admitted gratis.

The improvements kept increasing till the capital engines for twist were perfected; and it is amazing to see what thousands of spindles may be put in motion by a water wheel, and managed mostly by children, without confusion, and with less waste of cotton than the former methods: but the carding and slubbing, preparatory to twisting, required a greater range of invention than the twisting engines, and there were sufficient motives to encourage the attempt; for while carding was performed by common cards, and slubbing by the hand, these operations took half the price of spinning.

The first attempts were in carding engines, which are very curious, and now brought to great perfection, though they are still improving; and an engine has now been contrived, for converting the carded wool to slubbing, by drawing it to about the thickness of candle-wick, preparatory to throwing it into twist. /•••/

We suppose, and even wish that the principle of this last engine may be applied to reduce combed sheeps wool to a slubbing, for the purpose of spinning it upon the more complex machines, which would be a great acquisition to some branches of trade here. It is already spun on the common flax wheel with a fly (which has been adopted by these engines) the length way of the combing, which is capable of being handled and divided at pleasure, and may be prepared as a slubbing for the spinning machines, by any contrivance in the drawing out, which has a respect to the length of staple and cohesion of parts, wherein combed wool differs from carded cotton.

When the larger machines were first set to work by water, they produced such excellent twist for warps, that they soon outrivalled the makers of warps on the larger jennies, some of whom had several at work, and had reaped a good harvest of profit by them; but as the larger machines were encouraged, they suffered abatement in proportion; and one of them concerned, making his complaint to others when they were intoxicated at the alehouse, a resolution was taken to destroy the water machines, and some were demolished before the owners could be protected, or the deluded country people who joined them could reflect, that if more warps were made, there would be a greater demand for weft from their jennies, and a better price for it. . . .

We are now hastening to a conclusion, and shall observe by the way, that perhaps nothing has more contributed to the improvements in trade here, than the free admission of workmen in every branch, whereby the trade has been kept open to strangers of every description, who contribute to its improvement by their ingenuity; for *Manchester* being only a market town, governed by Constables, is not subject to such regulations as are made in corporations, to favour freemen in exclusion of strangers: and, indeed, nothing could be more fatal to its trading interest, if it should be incorporated, and have representatives in Parliament. For such is the general course of popular contests, that in places where the immediate dependence of the inhabitants is not upon trade, the health and morals of the people are ruined upon those occasions. How much more fatal would the effects be in such a town as this, where, to the above evils, there would be added the interruption of trade, and perpetuation of ill-will between masters and workmen, who were independent; while those who had nothing to depend on but labour, would contract habits of idleness and drunkenness, or fly to other places, where they could be free from the tyrannical restrictions and partial usage which generally prevail in corporations.

20
Archeology and the Industrial Revolution

The past thirty years have seen an explosion of interest among economic historians in a new area of study—"industrial archeology." This term, first used in 1955 by Michael Rix, produced a number of questions over its meaning. Its focus is clear; the industrial archeologist, usually an above-ground archeologist, seeks through field studies to use physical remains to assist in understanding Britain's industrial development. Industrial archeologists are also interested in preserving or "recording" their finds, and they have taken a leading role in persuading local governments and such national offices as the Ministry of Works to protect important industrial monuments and open them to the public. The Gladstone Pottery Museum, the New Lanark cotton mills, and the Ironbridge Gorge Museum are good examples of this historic preservation campaign.

The controversy over the definition of "industrial archeology" lies largely in its chronological scope. The Inspectorate of Ancient Monuments at the Ministry of Works concluded in 1962 that an industrial monument was a site "especially" associated with "the period of the Industrial Revolution" and "illustrat[ing] the beginning and development of industrial and technical processes, including means of communication." This definition has been widely accepted, but some scholars, such as Kenneth Hudson, believe it too restrictive, preventing an understanding of the processes of industrialization which began before 1700 and which continue to this day. These critics argue that more appreciation needs to be paid to the later industrial revolution, which produced the "tin lizzy, the crystal set and the biplane." Disagreements have also developed between the amateur industrial archeologists, often interested merely in preserving the past, and the professional archeologists/historians, who emphasize the interpretation or understanding in a historical context of these monuments.

Despite these disputes, expected in any new field of study, the investigation of industrial remains can obviously aid the historian in understanding the processes which transformed not only England's economy and society but her landscape as well. The following illustrations reveal the rich heritage of Britain, the mother of the industrial revolution.

James Hargreaves's spinning jenny of 1770 (Plate A), reflects the interest in preserving and, more frequently, reconstructing machinery of the first industrial revolution. Few machines from the eighteenth century have survived in their original form. The Gladstone Pottery at Stoke-on-Trent (Plate B), preserved as an industrial museum, is a monument to the industry made famous by Josiah

PLATE A
Spinning Jenny (Reproduced by permission of the Trustees of the Science Museum).

Wedgwood at his Etruria works, razed in 1968. Plate C shows the excavations of an Abraham Darby furnace at Coalbrookdale, where iron was first smelted with coke in 1709.

The growing use of iron as well as the progress made in improving transport facilities, an important part of the Industrial Revolution, is illustrated by Ironbridge (Plate D). Designed by Abraham Darby III and completed in 1781, it had a span of 100 feet and bridged the Severn River at Coalbrookdale. The construction of an elaborate canal system, principally in the years 1780 to 1820, was fundamental to Britain's industrial growth. Finally, the change in the life-style of the new industrial workers of the eighteenth and early nineteenth centuries is reflected in Tea Kettle Row (Plate E), workers' cottages in Coalbrookdale dating from the 1740s, and in Robert Owen's New Lanark mills and housing (Plate F). Both New Lanark and the older cotton mills of Samuel Arkwright at Cromford in Derbyshire are open to the public.

PLATE B
Gladstone Pottery (Weidenfeld & Nicolson Archives).

PLATE C
Abraham Darby Furnace (By permission of Ironbridge Gorge Museum Trust).

PLATE D
Ironbridge (By permission of Ironbridge Gorge Museum Trust).

PLATE E
Tea Kettle Row (By permission of Ironbridge Gorge Museum Trust).

PLATE F
New Lanark Mills (Cambridge University Collection: copyright reserved).

21
Thomas Clarkson, Sermon (1787).
The African Slave Trade

Originally destined for a career in the church, Thomas Clarkson (1760–1846) instead devoted his life to the greatest humanitarian movement of the late eighteenth century–the crusade against the African slave trade. Joining such established figures as Granville Sharp and William Wilberforce, he became a prominent member of the Clapham Sect. Within the movement, Clarkson had two primary functions. First, he was its chief investigator, spending considerable time in Bristol and Liverpool collecting data on the slave trade. He was particularly interested in, and appalled by, conditions on the slave vessels during the middle passage, the trip from Africa to the Western Hemisphere (see Plate A). The data he collected were used by Wilberforce in his parliamentary efforts to abolish the British slave trade, ultimately successful in 1807.

Clarkson was also largely responsible for mobilizing public opinion against the slave trade and for gathering petitions for presentation to Parliament. These petitions strengthened the position of reforming MPs like Wilberforce. In 1787, Clarkson preached a sermon in Manchester condemning the evils of the slave trade. In so doing, he followed the example of other social reformers. By preaching, reformers were assured of a building, a ready audience and, in most instances, a favorable response that could be transformed into a parliamentary petition. The excerpts from Clarkson's sermon are taken from his *History of the Abolition of the African Slave-Trade by the British Parliament* (1808), one of the most important sources of information on the actions of the Clapham Sect. Not content with their victory of 1807, Clarkson and his colleagues worked to ensure that the laws against the slave trade were enforced and, later, attacked the institution of slavery itself. In 1833, Clarkson, an old man, saw Parliament declare slavery illegal throughout the British Empire.

Text. "Thou shalt not oppress a stranger, for ye know the heart of a stranger, seeing ye were strangers in the land of Egypt."

Source: Thomas Clarkson, *The History of the Rise, Progress, and Accomplishment of the Abolition of the African Slave-Trade by the British Parliament,* 2 vols., London: Frank Cass, Reprint, 1968, I, 418, 420–425. Reprinted by permission of Valentine, Mitchell, London, 1968.

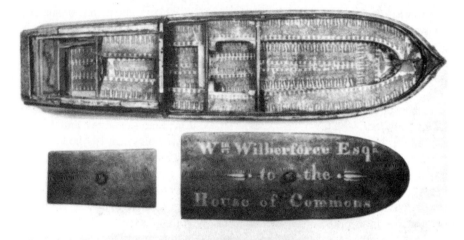

PLATE A
Model of Slave Ship (courtesy of Wilberforce House Museum, Hull).

This being the case, and this law of Moses being afterwards established into a fundamental precept of Christianity, I must apply it to facts of the present day, and I am sorry that I must apply it to—ourselves.

And first, Are there no strangers, whom we oppress? I fear the wretched African will say, that he drinks the cup of sorrow, and that he drinks it at our hands. Torn from his native soil, and from his family and friends, he is immediately forced into a situation, of all others the most degrading, where he and his progeny are considered as cattle, as possessions, and as the possessions of a man to whom he never gave offence.

It is a melancholy fact, but it can be abundantly proved, that great numbers of the unfortunate strangers, who are carried from Africa to our colonies, are fraudulently and forcibly taken from their native soil. To descant but upon a single instance of the kind must be productive of pain to the ear of sensibility and freedom. Consider the sensations of the person, who is thus carried off by the ruffians, who have been lurking to intercept him. Separated from every thing which he esteems in life, without the possibility even of bidding his friends adieu, behold him overwhelmed in tears—wringing his hands in despair—looking backwards upon the spot where all his hopes and wishes lay,—while his family at home are waiting for him with anxiety and suspense—are waiting, perhaps, for sustenance—are agitated between hope and fear—till length of absence confirms the latter, and they are immediately plunged into inconceivable misery and distress.

If this instance, then, is sufficiently melancholy of itself, and is at all an act of

oppression, how complicated will our guilt appear, who are the means of snatch-
ing away thousands annually in the same manner, and who force them and their
families into the same unhappy situation, without either remorse or shame! . . .

If, then, we oppress the stranger, as I have shown, and if, by a knowledge of
his heart, we find that he is a person of the same passions and feelings as ourselves, we are certainly breaking, by means of the prosecution of the Slave-
trade, that fundamental principle of Christianity, which says, that we shall not do
that unto another, which we wish should not be done unto ourselves, and, I fear,
cutting ourselves off from all expectation of the Divine blessing. For how inconsistent is our conduct! We come into the temple of God; we fall prostrate before
him; we pray to him, that he will have mercy upon us. But how shall he have
mercy upon us, who have had no mercy upon others! We pray to him, again, that
he will deliver us from evil. But how shall he deliver us from evil, who are daily
invading the rights of the injured African, and heaping misery on his head! . . .

If, then, we wish to avert the heavy national judgment which is hanging over
our heads (for must we not believe that our crimes towards the innocent
Africans lie recorded against us in heaven) let us endeavour to assert their cause.
Let us nobly withstand the torrent of the evil, however inveterately it may be
fixed among the customs of the times; not, however, using our liberty as a cloak
of maliciousness against those, who perhaps without due consideration, have the
misfortune to be concerned in it, but upon proper motives, and in a proper spirit,
as the servants of God; so that if the sun should be turned into darkness, and the
moon into blood, and the very heaven should fall upon us, we may fall in the
general convulsion without dismay, conscious that we have done our duty in endeavouring to succour the distressed, and that the stain of the blood of Africa is
not upon us.

22

Edmund Burke, *Reflections on the Revolution in France* (1790)

Edmund Burke (1729–1797) wrote his *Reflections on the Revolution in France* to counter the popular support in England for the dramatic events then taking place in France. It was also a statement of the principles he had expressed and acted on consistently in his writing and during his political career. As the personal secretary of the Whig leader, the marquis of Rockingham, and himself a Whig intellectual and a member of Parliament, he had been an outspoken critic of the government of George III (1760–1820), especially for its policy toward the American colonies. Burke led the fight to reduce the influence of the king and his ministers in Parliament, and he spearheaded the movement to impeach and convict Warren Hastings for his treatment of natives during his governor-generalship of India. The apex of his career came in 1790 with the writing of his *Reflections.*

At the heart of Burke's political thinking was a profound distrust of abstract political theory and natural law based on reason. Like William Blackstone, he believed that a sound system of law and government must rest on a foundation of tradition, on institutions and practice that had evolved slowly and had been proved effective by generations of usage. The state "becomes a partnership not only between those who are living, but between those who are living, those who are dead, and those who are to be born." Unlike the Glorious Revolution of England and the American Revolution, which sought to preserve and restore the constitutional usage of the past, the French Revolution was destroying tradition. Relying only on abstract reason, the French would, he accurately predicted, only prove again how difficult or impossible it was to make a revolutionary government legitimate and acceptable.

When Burke wrote his *Reflections* in 1790, most Britons were still applauding the French for copying the English example of 1688. However, the popularity of Burke's book, which went through eleven editions the first year, and the radical and violent turn of events in France produced a rush toward conservatism. The

Source: Edmund Burke, *Reflections on the Revolution in France and Other Essays,* Introduction and Notes by A. J. Grieve, Everyman's Library Edition, London: E. P. Dutton & Co., Inc., 1940, pp. 57–59, 242–243. Used with the permission of E. P. Dutton & Co., Inc., and J M Dent & Sons, Ltd. Publishers, London.

political shift in Parliament, led by Burke himself, and the parallel
reaction in the country as a whole revived the Tory party and gave
it unprecedented dominance for nearly forty years. Burke's ideas
are still the beginning of any intelligent conservative political philosophy.

Government is not made in virtue of natural rights, which may and do exist in
total independence of it; and exist in much greater clearness, and in a much
greater degree of abstract perfection: but their abstract perfection is their practical defect. By having a right to everything they want everything. Government is
a contrivance of human wisdom to provide for human *wants.* Men have a right
that these wants should be provided for by this wisdom. Among these wants is
to be reckoned the want, out of civil society, of a sufficient restraint upon their
passions. Society requires not only that the passions of individuals should be
subjected, but that even in the mass and body, as well as in the individuals, the
inclinations of men should frequently be thwarted, their will controlled, and
their passions brought into subjection. This can only be done *by a power out of
themselves;* and not, in the exercise of its function, subject to that will and to
those passions which it is its office to bridle and subdue. In this sense the restraints on men, as well as their liberties, are to be reckoned among their rights.
But as the liberties and the restrictions vary with times and circumstances, and
admit of infinite modifications, they cannot be settled upon any abstract rule;
and nothing is so foolish as to discuss them upon that principle.

The moment you abate anything from the full rights of men, each to govern
himself, and suffer any artificial, positive limitation upon those rights, from that
moment the whole organization of government becomes a consideration of convenience. This it is which makes the constitution of a state, and the due distribution of its powers, a matter of the most delicate and complicated skill. It requires
a deep knowledge of human nature and human necessities, and of the things
which facilitate or obstruct the various ends, which are to be pursued by the
mechanism of civil institutions. The state is to have recruits to its strength, and
remedies to its distempers. What is the use of discussing a man's abstract right
to food or medicine? The question is upon the method of procuring and administering them. In that deliberation I shall always advise to call in the aid of the
farmer and the physician, rather than the professor of metaphysics. . . .

The science of government being therefore so practical in itself, and intended
for such practical purposes, a matter which requires experience, and even more
experience than any person can gain in his whole life, however sagacious and
observing he may be, it is with infinite caution that any man ought to venture
upon pulling down an edifice, which has answered in any tolerable degree for
ages the common purposes of society, or on building it up again, without having
models and patterns of approved utility before his eyes. . . .

To make a government requires no great prudence. Settle the seat of power; teach obedience: and the work is done. To give freedom is still more easy. It is not necessary to guide; it only requires to let go the rein. But to form a *free government;* that is, to temper together these opposite elements of liberty and restraint in one consistent work, requires much thought, deep reflection, a sagacious, powerful, and combining mind. This I do not find in those who take the lead in the National Assembly. Perhaps they are not so miserably deficient as they appear. I rather believe it. It would put them below the common level of human understanding. But when the leaders choose to make themselves bidders at an auction of popularity, their talents, in the construction of the state, will be of no service. They will become flatterers instead of legislators; the instruments, not the guides, of the people. If any of them should happen to propose a scheme of liberty, soberly limited, and defined with proper qualifications, he will be immediately outbid by his competitors, who will produce something more splendidly popular. Suspicions will be raised of his fidelity to his cause. Moderation will be stigmatized as the virtue of cowards; and compromise as the prudence of traitors; until, in hopes of preserving the credit which may enable him to temper, and moderate, on some occasions, the popular leader is obliged to become active in propagating doctrines, and establishing powers, that will afterwards defeat any sober purpose at which he ultimately might have aimed.

But am I so unreasonable as to see nothing at all that deserves commendation in the indefatigable labours of this Assembly? I do not deny that, among an infinite number of acts of violence and folly, some good may have been done. They who destroy everything certainly will remove some grievance. They who make everything new, have a chance that they may establish something beneficial. To give them credit for what they have done in virtue of the authority they have usurped, or which can excuse them in the crimes by which that authority has been acquired, it must appear, that the same things could not have been accomplished without producing such a revolution. Most assuredly they might; because almost every one of the regulations made by them, which is not very equivocal, was either in the cession of the king, voluntarily made at the meeting of the states, or in the concurrent instructions to the orders. Some usages have been abolished on just grounds; but they were such, that if they had stood as they were to all eternity, they would little detract from the happiness and prosperity of any state. The improvements of the National Assembly are superficial, their errors fundamental.

Whatever they are, I wish my countrymen rather to recommend to our neighbours the examples of the British constitution, than to take models from them for the improvement of our own. In the former they have got an invaluable treasure. They are not, I think, without some causes of apprehension and complaint; but these they do not owe to their constitution, but to their own conduct. I think our happy situation owing to our constitution; but owing to the whole of it, and not to any part singly; owing in a great measure to what we have left standing in our several reviews and reformations, as well as to what we have altered or super-added. Our people will find employment enough for a truly patriotic, free, and independent spirit, in guarding what they possess from violation. I would not exclude alteration neither; but even when I changed, it should be to preserve. I should be led to my remedy by a great grievance. In what I did, I should follow the example of our ancestors. I would make the reparation as nearly as possible in the style of the building.

23
Mary Wollstonecraft, *A Vindication of the Rights of Woman* (1792)

Mary Wollstonecraft (1759–1797) wrote what is perhaps still the most powerful plea for the equality of women. Her *Vindication of the Rights of Woman* (1792) was a product of the English debate on natural rights resulting from the French Revolution. It championed the ideas of the Enlightenment against the conservative reaction. More specifically, it was the sequel to *A Vindication of the Rights of Men,* which she wrote hurriedly in 1790 in reply to Edmund Burke. To Burke's assertion that the idea of natural rights was foolish and dangerous, she countered, "It is necessary emphatically to repeat that there are rights which men inherit at their birth, as rational creatures . . . not from their forefathers but from God." In her second book, she simply extended to women in particular what she had formerly said of mankind in general. Only when women were taught and treated "as part of the human species" and not "as a kind of subordinate being" would they acquire the virtue of which they were capable and which was essential to make them the equals of men. Indeed, it was this same denial of human dignity that made men unequal.

Mary Wollstonecraft was as much an emancipated woman as the eighteenth century and her own inclinations would allow. After helping operate a private school and then working as a governess, from which position she was dismissed because the chil-

Source: Mary Wollstonecraft, *A Vindication of the Rights of Woman with Strictures on Political and Moral Subjects*, edited by Charles W. Hagelman, Jr., pp. 31–33, 49–50, 52–53, 55, 283–284, 286–287. Norton Library Edition. Copyright © 1967 by W. W. Norton & Company, Inc., New York, N. Y.

dren loved her more than they did their mother, she became a writer. At first she wrote exclusively on women's and children's topics, but later she was accepted as capable of dealing even with contemporary intellectual topics. The success of her *Rights of Woman* made her prominent in the literary circles of London and then of Paris, where she went in 1792 to view the Revolution. Her affair with the American Gilbert Imlay gave Mary a daughter and led her, in her despair, at its termination to jump off the Putney bridge. In 1797, she married William Godwin, the English radical and freethinker, who had written denouncing the institution of marriage. This happy and successful union of two high-spirited and independent individuals ended when Mary died giving birth to their daughter, who became Mary Shelley, the author of the romantic novel *Frankenstein*.

A Vindication of the Rights of Woman went through two English editions in 1792 as well as one Irish and two American editions in that and the following year. It has gone through numerous other editions since.

The conduct and manners of women, in fact, evidently prove that their minds are not in a healthy state; for, like the flowers which are planted in too rich a soil, strength and usefulness are sacrificed to beauty; and the flaunting leaves, after having pleased a fastidious eye, fade, disregarded on the stalk, long before the season when they ought to have arrived at maturity. One cause of this barren blooming I attribute to a false system of education, gathered from the books written on this subject by men who, considering females rather as women than human creatures, have been more anxious to make them alluring mistresses than affectionate wives and rational mothers; and the understanding of the sex has been so bubbled by this specious homage, that the civilized women of the present century, with a few exceptions, are only anxious to inspire love, when they ought to cherish a nobler ambition, and by their abilities and virtues exact respect. . . .

In the true style of Mahometanism, they are treated as a kind of subordinate beings, and not as a part of the human species, when improveable reason is allowed to be the dignified distinction which raises men above the brute creation, and puts a natural sceptre in a feeble hand. . . .

In the government of the physical world it is observable that the female in point of strength is, in general, inferior to the male. This is the law of nature; and it does not appear to be suspended or abrogated in favour of woman. A degree of physical superiority cannot, therefore, be denied—and it is a noble prerogative! But not content with this natural pre-eminence, men endeavour to sink us still lower, merely to render us alluring objects for a moment; and women, intoxicated by the adoration which men, under the influence of their senses, pay them, do not seek to obtain a durable interest in their hearts, or to become the friends of the fellow creatures who find amusement in their society.

I am aware of an obvious inference:—from every quarter have I heard exclamations against masculine women; but where are they to be found? If by this appellation men mean to inveigh against their ardour in hunting, shooting, and gaming, I shall most cordially join in the cry; but if it be against the imitation of manly virtues, or, more properly speaking, the attainment of those talents and virtues, the exercise of which ennobles the human character, and which raise females in the scale of animal being, when they are comprehensively termed mankind;—all those who view them with a philosophic eye must, I should think, wish with me, that they may every day grow more and more masculine. . . .

To account for, and excuse the tyranny of man, many ingenious arguments have been brought forward to prove, that the two sexes, in the acquirement of virtue, ought to aim at attaining a very different character; or, to speak explicitly, women are not allowed to have sufficient strength of mind to acquire what really deserves the name of virtue. Yet it should seem, allowing them to have souls, that there is but one way appointed by Providence to lead *mankind* to either virtue or happiness.

If then women are not a swarm of ephemeron triflers, why should they be kept in ignorance under the specious name of innocence? Men complain, and with reason, of the follies and caprices of our sex, when they do not keenly satirize our headstrong passions and grovelling vices. Behold, I should answer, the natural effect of ignorance! The mind will ever be unstable that has only prejudices to rest on, and the current will run with destructive fury when there are no barriers to break its force. Women are told from their infancy, and taught by the example of their mothers, that a little knowledge of human weakness, justly termed cunning, softness of temper, *outward* obedience, and a scrupulous attention to a puerile kind of propriety, will obtain for them the protection of man; and should they be beautiful, everything else is needless, for, at least, twenty years of their lives. . . .

Consequently, the most perfect education, in my opinion, is such an exercise of the understanding as is best calculated to strengthen the body and form the heart. Or, in other words, to enable the individual to attain such habits of virtue as will render it independent. In fact, it is a farce to call any being virtuous whose virtues do not result from the exercise of its own reason. This was Rousseau's opinion respecting men: I extend it to women, and confidently assert that they have been drawn out of their sphere by false refinement, and not by an endeavour to acquire masculine qualities. Still the regal homage which they receive is so intoxicating, that till the manners of the times are changed, and formed on more reasonable principles, it may be impossible to convince them that the illegitimate power, which they obtain, by degrading themselves, is a curse, and that they must return to nature and equality, if they wish to secure the placid satisfaction that unsophisticated affections impart. But for this epoch we must wait—wait, perhaps, till kings and nobles, enlightened by reason, and, preferring the real dignity of man to childish state, throw off their gaudy hereditary trappings: and if then women do not resign the arbitrary power of beauty—they will prove that they have *less* mind than man. . . .

As a proof that education gives this appearance of weakness to females, we may instance the example of military men, who are, like them, sent into the world before their minds have been stored with knowledge or fortified by principles. The consequences are similar; soldiers acquire a little superficial knowledge, snatched from the muddy current of conversation, and, from continually mixing with society, they gain, what is termed a knowledge of the world; and this acquaintance with manners and customs has frequently been confounded with a knowledge of the human heart. But can the crude fruit of casual observation, never brought to the test of judgment, formed by comparing speculation and experience, deserve such a distinction? Soldiers, as well as women, practice the minor virtues with punctilious politeness. Where is then the sexual difference, when the education has been the same? All the difference that I can discern, arises from the superior advantage of liberty, which enables the former to see more of life. . . .

Moralists have unanimously agreed, that unless virtue be nursed by liberty, it will never attain due strength—and what they say of man I extend to mankind, insisting that in all cases morals must be fixed on immutable principles; and that the being cannot be termed rational or virtuous who obeys any authority but that of reason.

To render women truly useful members of society, I argue that they should be led, by having their understandings cultivated on a large scale, to acquire a rational affection for their country, founded on knowledge, because it is obvious that we are little interested about what we do not understand. And to render this general knowledge of due importance, I have endeavoured to show that private duties are never properly fulfilled unless the understanding enlarges the heart; and that public virtue is only an aggregate of private. . . .

Asserting the rights which women in common with men ought to contend for, I have not attempted to extenuate their faults; but to prove them to be the natural consequence of their education and station in society. If so, it is reasonable to suppose that they will change their character, and correct their vices and follies, when they are allowed to be free in a physical, moral, and civil sense.

Let women share the rights and she will emulate the virtues of man; for she must grow more perfect when emancipated, or justify the authority that chains such a weak being to her duty. If the latter, it will be expedient to open a fresh trade with Russia for whips: a present which a father should always make to his son-in-law on his wedding day, that a husband may keep his whole family in order by the same means; and without any violation of justice reign, wielding this sceptre, sole master of his house, because he is the only being in it who has reason:—the divine, indefeasible earthly sovereignty breathed into man by the Master of the universe. Allowing this position, women have not any inherent rights to claim; and by the same rule their duties vanish, for rights and duties are inseparable.

24
Robert Burns (1759–1796), Poems and Songs

Robert Burns (1759–1796), best known today for his "Auld Lang Syne," is Scotland's greatest poet and perhaps Britain's foremost songwriter. Born in Ayrshire in the western Lowlands into a poor, devout farm family, he discovered his ability to rhyme, he said, when he was fifteen and in love. Though acclaimed as the untaught, genius plowman poet, he was, in fact, well educated. Through reading, he mastered the poetic tradition of Scotland and was familiar with English literature and contemporary British writing.

Though he lived a life of poverty and hard work, he enjoyed the company of his drinking companions and especially the fairer sex. He wrote love poems, satires of the Presbyterian Church, and poetic commentaries on acquaintances and situations found in ordinary life. A failure at farming and rejected by the family of the woman bearing his child (twins as it turned out), he resolved to go to the West Indies but before leaving to publish a volume of his verses. This Kilmarnock edition of 1786, named for the town where it was printed, took Scotland by storm and made Burns a celebrity. An Edinburgh edition earned some money with which he traveled in the Highlands. Not finding place or fortune, Burns returned to Ayrshire, married Jean Armour, who had earlier rejected him, and failed once more at farming. He eventually found some degree of financial security as an exciseman. He spent his last few years collecting the folk songs of Scotland for two Edinburgh publishers, a patriotic task for which he refused to be

Source: The Poems and Songs of Robert Burns, edited by James Kinsley, Oxford: At the Clarendon Press, 1968, I, 127–128; II, 707–708, 734–735. By permission of Oxford University Press.

compensated. No other people has had such a genius devoted to saving and improving its musical folk heritage.

In "To a Mouse," published in the Kilmarnock edition, Burns celebrated an ordinary subject, using the Scots dialect of ordinary people and revealing his ideas of humanity's place in the larger scheme of things. "Robert Bruce's March to Bannockburn," written in 1793, was both a remembrance of Scotland's tradition of independence, best recalled in Bruce's victory in 1314, and an imitation of the patriotic fervor found in "La Marseillaise" of revolutionary France. "A red, red Rose" is one of the best examples of Burns's ability to create immortal songs from the lyric fragments and old tunes that were still alive in Scotland's folk memory.

Burns is not considered one of the Romantic poets, like William Blake (1757–1827) or William Wordsworth (1770–1850). But his love of nature, his regard for human feelings and emotion, and his appreciation of both individualism and national sentiment make him a transitional figure in Scottish and British literature, helping prepare the way for Sir Walter Scott (1771–1832), whose Waverley novels were an embodiment of the Romantic movement.

To a Mouse, On turning her up in her Nest, with the Plough, November, 1785.

Wee, sleeket, cowran, tim'rous *beastie*,
O, what a panic's in thy breastie!
Thou need na start awa sae hasty,
      Wi' bickering brattle!
I wad be laith to rin an' chase thee,
      Wi' murd'ring *pattle*!

I'm truly sorry Man's dominion
Has broken Nature's social union,
An' justifies that ill opinion,
      Which makes thee startle,
At me, thy poor, earth-born companion,
      An' *fellow-mortal*!

I doubt na, whyles, but thou may *thieve;*
What then? poor beastie, thou maun live!
A *daimen-icker* in a *thrave*
      'S a sma' request:
I'll get a blessin wi' the lave,
      An' never miss't!

Thy wee-bit *housie,* too, in ruin!
It's silly wa's the win's are strewin!
An' naething, now, to big a new ane,
   O' foggage green!
An' bleak *December's winds* ensuin,
   Baith snell an' keen!

Thou saw the fields laid bare an' wast,
An' weary *Winter* comin fast,
An' cozie here, beneath the blast,
   Thou thought to dwell,
Till crash! the cruel *coulter* past
   Out thro' thy cell.

That wee-bit heap o' leaves an' stibble,
Has cost thee monie a weary nibble!
Now thou's turn'd out, for a' thy trouble,
   But house or hald,
To thole the Winter's *sleety dribble,*
   An' *cranreuch* cauld!

But Mousie, thou art no thy-lane,
In proving *foresight* may be vain:
The best laid schemes o' *Mice* an' *Men,*
   Gang aft agley,
An' lea'e us nought but grief an' pain,
   For promis'd joy!

Still, thou art blest, compar'd wi' *me!*
The *present* only toucheth thee:
But Och! I *backward* cast my e'e,
   On prospects drear!
An' *forward,* tho' I canna *see,*
   I *guess* an' *fear!*

Robert Bruce's March to Bannockburn—

Scots, wha hae wi' WALLACE bled,
Scots, wham BRUCE has aften led,
Welcome to your gory bed,—
  Or to victorie.—

Now's the day, and now's the hour;
See the front o' battle lour;
See approach proud EDWARD's power,
  Chains and Slaverie.—

Wha will be a traitor-knave?
Wha can fill a coward's grave?
Wha sae base as be a Slave?
   —Let him turn and flie:—

Wha for SCOTLAND's king and law,
Freedom's sword will strongly draw,
FREE-MAN stand, or FREE-MAN fa',
   Let him follow me.—

By Oppression's woes and pains!
By your Sons in servile chains!
We will drain our dearest veins,
   But they *shall* be free!

Lay the proud Usurpers low!
Tyrants fall in every foe!
LIBERTY's in every blow!
   Let us Do—OR DIE!!!

A red, red Rose

O MY Luve's like a red, red rose,
   That's newly sprung in June;
O my Luve's like the melodie
   That's sweetly play'd in tune.—

As fair art thou, my bonie lass,
   So deep in luve am I;
And I will love thee still, my Dear,
   Till a' the seas gang dry.—

Till a' the seas gang dry, my Dear,
   And the rocks melt wi' the sun:
I will love thee still, my Dear,
   While the sands o' life shall run.—

And fare thee weel, my only Luve!
   And fare thee weel, a while!
And I will come again, my Luve,
   Tho' it were ten thousand mile!—

25

Thomas Robert Malthus, *An Essay on the Principle of Population* (1798)

There was a deep seam of optimism running through the eighteenth-century Enlightenment. By using their ability to reason, people were capable of discovering the natural laws that governed not only the material universe but also economic and political behavior. Such knowledge would enable them to transcend the shortcomings of the present and produce in the future a utopian happy state. One of England's most radical and optimistic advocates of "progress" was William Godwin (1756–1836), the husband of Mary Wollstonecraft and the author of the weighty *Enquiry concerning Political Justice* (1793), which at a cost of three guineas was thought by the government to be sufficiently restricted not to merit censure.

Thomas Robert Malthus (1766–1834), a Church of England clergyman and later, at the East India Company college at Haileybury, Britain's first professor of economics, was provoked by his father's enthusiasm for Godwin to publish his own counterarguments. Appearing as a pamphlet in 1798, Malthus's *Essay on the Principle of Population as it Affects the Future Improvement of Society* crushed the optimists and has remained an anxiety to thinking people ever since. The passage below gives the gist of Malthus's argument, that population will necessarily increase more rapidly than the food supply and will be kept in check by it. There will always be suffering and starving people. Politicians and others opposed to reform cited Malthus as proof that improvements in the condition of the poor were counterproductive. Any improvement brought by reform could only be temporary, for it would be swamped by the increased population it encouraged. It is not surprising that Thomas Carlyle (1795–1881) on reading Malthus should have dubbed economics, perhaps unfairly, "the dismal science."

Malthus's doubts regarding his conclusion can be detected in the lengthened edition of 1803. He removed some of the mathematical certainty that he had used to support his earlier conclusions and asserted that voluntary "moral restraint" might ease the

Source: Thomas Robert Malthus, *Population: The First Essay*, Ann Arbor: University of Michigan Press, 1959, pp. 1, 4–6, 120–121. By permission of the University of Michigan Press.

pressure of population on the food supply. The expansion of arable land, especially in newly discovered and exploited continents, and better farming and manufacturing techniques bolstered and heartened the champions of progress. However, the growing world population, never far behind the expanding food supply, may yet demonstrate the awful applicability of Malthus's predictions.

It has been said that the great question is now at issue, whether man shall henceforth start forwards with accelerated velocity towards illimitable, and hitherto unconceived improvement, or be condemned to a perpetual oscillation between happiness and misery, and after every effort remain still at an immeasurable distance from the wished-for goal. . . .

In entering upon the argument I must premise that I put out of the question, at present, all mere conjectures, that is, all suppositions, the probable realization of which cannot be inferred upon any just philosophical grounds. . . .

I think I may fairly make two postulata.

First, That food is necessary to the existence of man.

Secondly, That the passion between the sexes is necessary and will remain nearly in its present state.

These two laws, ever since we have had any knowledge of mankind, appear to have been fixed laws of our nature, and, as we have not hitherto seen any alteration in them, we have no right to conclude that they will ever cease to be what they now are, without an immediate act of power in that Being who first arranged the system of the universe, and for the advantage of his creatures, still executes, according to fixed laws, all its various operations.

I do not know that any writer has supposed that on this earth man will ultimately be able to live without food. . . . Towards the extinction of the passion between the sexes, no progress whatever has hitherto been made. It appears to exist in as much force at present as it did two thousand or four thousand years ago. . . .

Assuming then, my postulata as granted, I say, that the power of population is indefinitely greater than the power in the earth to produce subsistence for man.

Population, when unchecked, increases in a geometrical ratio. Subsistence increases only in an arithmetical ratio. A slight acquaintance with numbers will shew the immensity of the first power in comparison of the second.

By that law of our nature which makes food necessary to the life of man, the effects of these two unequal powers must be kept equal.

This implies a strong and constantly operating check on population from the difficulty of subsistence. This difficulty must fall some where and must necessarily be severely felt by a large portion of mankind.

Through the animal and vegetable kingdoms, nature has scattered the seeds of life abroad with the most profuse and liberal hand. She has been comparatively sparing in the room and the nourishment necessary to rear them. The germs of existence contained in this spot of earth, with ample food, and ample room to expand in, would fill millions of worlds in the course of a few thousand years. Necessity, that imperious all pervading law of nature, restrains them within the prescribed bounds. The race of plants, and the race of animals shrink under this great restrictive law. And the race of man cannot, by any efforts of reason, escape from it. Among plants and animals its effects are waste of seed, sickness, and premature death. Among mankind, misery and vice. The former, misery, is an absolutely necessary consequence of it. Vice is a highly probable consequence, and we therefore see it abundantly prevail, but it ought not, perhaps, to be called an absolutely necessary consequence. The ordeal of virtue is to resist all temptation to evil.

This natural inequality of the two powers of population and of production in the earth and that great law of our nature which must constantly keep their effects equal form the great difficulty that to me appears insurmountable in the way to the perfectability of society. All other arguments are of slight and subordinate consideration in comparison of this. I see no way by which man can escape from the weight of this law which pervades all animated nature. No fancied equality, no agrarian regulations in their utmost extent, could remove the pressure of it even for a single century. And it appears, therefore, to be decisive against the possible existence of a society, all the members of which should live in ease, happiness, and comparative leisure; and feel no anxiety about providing the means of subsistence for themselves and families.

Consequently, if the premises are just, the argument is conclusive against the perfectibility of the mass of mankind. . . .

It is, undoubtedly a most disheartening reflection that the great obstacle in the way to any extraordinary improvement in society is of a nature that we can never hope to overcome. The perpetual tendency in the race of man to increase beyond the means of subsistence is one of the general laws of animated nature which we can have no reason to expect will change. Yet discouraging as the contemplation of this difficulty must be to those whose exertions are laudably directed to the improvement of the human species, it is evident that no possible good can arise from any endeavours to slur it over or keep it in the back ground. On the contrary the most baleful mischiefs may be expected from the unmanly conduct of not daring to face truth because it is unpleasing.

26
An Act for the Preservation of the Health and Morals of Apprentices (1802)

The Industrial Revolution had by the 1790s transformed the economy of many parts of England. This was particularly true of the industrial frontier, the new factory towns in the Midlands and the north of England. Slum housing, street crime, and child labor were only the most obvious new hardships facing the people. For a number of reasons, however, the government was slow in attempting to alleviate the situation. Some problems, such as child labor, were simply not recognized as social evils, particularly by a government preoccupied with the war with France. Even more important, the laissez-faire principles of Adam Smith had become a dogma to many politicians, who were convinced that any tampering with the "natural laws" of economics would result in greater injury to the people and the nation. In view of these obstacles, it is a testimony to the ability of Sir Robert Peel the Elder (1750–1830), a wealthy cotton magnate, that he was able to persuade Parliament to accept the reform legislation below.

Peel's Act for the Preservation of the Health and Morals of Apprentices has been variously interpreted by historians. Because it improved, if only slightly, working conditions and provided for "visitors" to ensure that its provisions were enforced, some have viewed it as a "factory act," establishing the government's right to regulate industry and providing a precedent for the factory acts of 1819, 1829, and 1833. There are, however, difficulties with this interpretation. As the following selection shows, the act dealt primarily with apprentice children, orphans sent to the factories by local officials anxious to cut welfare costs. Because these children were not free agents who had agreed to work in the factories, Peel argued that his legislation was not an attack on laissez-faire. The 1802 act was an attempt to protect wards of the state, a poor law and not a factory act. Some historians agree, arguing that the Factory Act of 1819, which dealt with "free" children, those coerced by their parents rather than government officers, was more innovative and important. Still other historians emphasize the act's educational provisions and see it as the first national education

Source: The Statutes At Large, XLIII, 632–635 (42 George III. c. 73).

act. The fact that this controversial legislation has remained subject to several interpretations is probably the best indication of its importance.

AN ACT FOR THE PRESERVATION OF THE HEALTH AND MORALS OF APPRENTICES AND OTHERS, EMPLOYED IN COTTON AND OTHER MILLS, AND COTTON AND OTHER FACTORIES.

Whereas *it hath of late become a practice in cotton and woollen mills, and . . . factories, to employ a great number of male and female apprentices, and other persons, in the same building; in consequence of which certain regulations are become necessary to preserve the health and morals of such apprentices and other persons;* be it therefore enacted . . . That . . . all such mills and factories within *Great Britain* and *Ireland,* wherein three or more apprentices, or twenty or more other persons, shall at any time be employed, shall be subject to the several rules and regulations contained in this act. . . .

II. And be it enacted, That . . . the rooms and apartments in or belonging to any such mill or factory shall, twice at least in every year, be well and sufficiently washed with quick lime and water over every part of the walls and ceiling thereof; and that due care and attention shall be paid . . . to provide a sufficient number of windows and openings in such rooms . . . to insure a proper supply of fresh air. . . .

III. And be it further enacted, That every such master or mistress shall constantly supply every apprentice, during the term of his or her apprenticeship, with two whole and complete suits of cloathing, with suitable linen, stockings, hats, and shoes; one new complete suit being delivered to such apprentice once at least in every year.

IV. And be it further enacted, That no apprentice . . . shall be employed or compelled to work for more than twelve hours in any one day, (reckoning from six of the clock in the morning to nine of the clock at night), exclusive of the time that may be occupied by such apprentice in eating the necessary meals: provided always, that . . . no apprentice shall be emloyed . . . between the hours of nine . . . at night and six . . . in the morning.

VI. And be it further enacted, That every such apprentice shall be instructed, in some part of every working day, for the first four years at least of his or her apprenticeship . . . in the usual hours of work, in reading, writing, and arithmetick, or either of them, according to the age and abilities of such apprentice, by some discreet and proper person, to be provided and paid by the master or mistress of such apprentice, in some room or place in such mill or factory to be set apart for that purpose. . . .

IX. And be it further enacted, That the justices of the peace . . . yearly . . . appoint two persons, not interested in, or in any way connected with, any such mills or factories . . . one of whom shall be a justice of peace . . . and the other shall be a clergyman of the established church of *England* or *Scotland* and the said visitors, or either of them, shall have full power and authority . . . to enter into and inspect any such mill or factory, at any time of the day, or during the hours of employment, as they shall think fit; and such visitors shall report from time to time in writing, to the quarter sessions of the peace, the state and condition of such mills and factories, and of the apprentices therein, and whether the same are or are not conducted and regulated according to the directions of this act, and the laws of the realm.

27
The Times (1805). The Battle of Trafalgar

The eighteenth century witnessed the birth and death of numerous newspapers, a major source of evidence for historians. Most of these newspapers were short-lived, being established for a specific purpose and for a limited group of readers. For example, the most important early newspaper was probably *The Craftsman* (1726–1736), used by Viscount Bolingbroke and William Pulteney to attack Sir Robert Walpole. One of these topical, partisan papers survived to become a national institution.

The *Times* was founded by John Walter (1738–1812), a bankrupt coal merchant who became interested in printing. In 1784 Walter launched *The Daily Universal Register* to cater to the business community and to promote his other printing enterprises. Soon the title was changed to *The Times,* reflecting his decision to broaden the appeal of his paper. Although *The Times* in the 1790s was a faithful supporter of Pitt's government, in the early nineteenth century it adopted a new, more critical approach to news coverage. By then *The Times* was a well-established paper with a daily circulation of more than 5000. Later, under its great editor Thomas Barnes (1831–1841), it became known popularly as "The Thunderer." To promote its independence from the government, *The Times* pioneered in the use of its own correspondents and acquired in the process a reputation for fresh, accurate news.

Despite the use of its own correspondents, *The Times* in its

Source: The Times, November 7, 1805, p. 1. Reproduction from *The Times* by permission.

early years still relied on governmental sources for much of its foreign news. The dispatch from Admiral Collingwood describing
Horatio Nelson's naval victory and death off Cape Trafalgar on
October 21, 1805, is typical of these official news releases. In this
particular case, the government could afford to be honest with the
public. The dispatch described the defeat of the combined navies
of Spain and France. British naval supremacy was confirmed, and
the English were given a new national hero.

ADMIRALTY-OFFICE, NOV. 6

Dispatches, of which the following are Copies, were received at the Admiralty
this day, at one o'clock A.M. from Vice-Admiral Collingwood, Commander in
Chief of his Majesty's ships and vessels off Cadiz:–

Euryalus, off Cape Trafalgar, Oct. 22, 1805

SIR,

The ever-to-be-lamented death of Vice-Admiral Lord Viscount Nelson, who,
in the late conflict with the enemy, fell in the hour of victory, leaves to me the
duty of informing my Lords Commissioners of the Admiralty, that on the 19th
instant, it was communicated to the Commander in Chief, from the ships watching the motions of the enemy in Cadiz, that the Combined Fleet had put to sea;
as they sailed with light winds westerly, his Lordship concluded their destination
was the Mediterranean, and immediately made all sail for the Streights' entrance, with the British Squadron, consisting of twenty-seven ships, three of
them sixty-fours, where his Lordship was informed, by Captain Blackwood
(whose vigilance in watching, and giving notice of the enemy's movements, has
been highly meritorious), that they had not yet passed the Streights.

On Monday the 21st instant, at day-light, when Cape Trafalgar bore E. by S.
about seven leagues, the enemy was discovered six or seven miles to the
Eastward, the wind about West, and very light; the Commander in Chief immediately made the signal for the fleet to bear up in two columns, as they are
formed in order of sailing; a mode of attack his Lordship had previously directed,
to avoid the inconvenience and delay in forming a line of battle in the usual manner. The enemy's line consisted of thirty-three ships (of which eighteen were
French, and fifteen Spanish), commanded in Chief by Admiral Villeneuve: the
Spaniards, under the direction of Gravina, wore, with their heads to the North-
ward, and formed their line of battle with great closeness and correctness. . . .

The Commander in Chief, in the *Victory,* led the weather column, and the
Royal Sovereign, which bore my flag, the lee.

The action began at twelve o'clock, by the leading ships of the columns
breaking through the enemy's line, the Commander in Chief about the tenth ship
from the van, the Second in Command about the twelfth from the rear, leaving

the van of the enemy unoccupied; the succeeding ships breaking through, in all parts, astern of their leaders, and engaging the enemy at the muzzles of their guns; the conflict was severe; the enemy's ships were fought with a gallantry highly honourable to their Officers; but the attack on them was irresistible, and it pleased the Almighty Disposer of all events to grant his Majesty's arms a complete and glorious victory. . . .

After such a Victory, it may appear unnecessary to enter into encomiums on the particular parts taken by the several Commanders; the conclusion says more on the subject than I have language to express; the spirit which animated all was the same: when all exert themselves zealously in their country's service, all deserve that their high merits should stand recorded; and never was high merit more conspicuous than in the battle I have described. . . .

A circumstance occurred during the action, which so strongly marks the invincible spirit of British seamen, when engaging the enemies of their country, that I cannot resist the pleasure I have in making it known to their Lordships; the *Temeraire* was boarded by accident, or design, by a French ship on one side, and a Spaniard on the other; the contest was vigorous, but, in the end, the Combined Ensigns were torn from the poop, and the British hoisted in their places.

Such a battle could not be fought without sustaining a great loss of men. I have not only to lament, in common with the British Navy, and the British Nation, in the Fall of the Commander in Chief, the loss of a Hero, whose name will be immortal, and his memory ever dear to his country; but my heart is rent with the most poignant grief for the death of a friend, to whom, by many years intimacy, and a perfect knowledge of the virtues of his mind, which inspired ideas superior to the common race of men, I was bound by the strongest ties of affection; a grief to which even the glorious occasion in which he fell, does not bring the consolation which, perhaps, it ought: his Lordship received a musket ball in his left breast, about the middle of the action, and sent an Officer to me immediately with his last farewell; and soon after expired. . . .

Having thus detailed the proceedings of the fleet on this occasion, I beg to congratulate their Lordships on a victory which, I hope, will add a ray to the glory of his Majesty's crown, and be attended with public benefit to our country, I am, etc.

(Signed)
C. COLLINGWOOD

28
A Declaration by the Framework Knitters (1812). The Luddites

By a standard dictionary definition a Luddite is "one of a band of workmen who tried to prevent the use of labor-saving machinery by breaking it." The term today connotes an irrational opponent of progress, someone wanting to protect a job that no longer exists, a "featherbedder." This understanding is not entirely fair to the first Luddites, the framework knitters.

The framework knitters did not suddenly begin breaking machinery in 1811; they had a long and very English tradition of such activity. In fact, the historical basis of Luddism derives from an unbalanced artisan, Ned Lud, who destroyed some knitting frames as early as 1779. Later he was transformed into a mythical General Lud or King Lud, who protected his subjects. Machine breaking was seldom the indiscriminate action of workers thrown out of work by new inventions. After all, the framework knitters used machines themselves.

As late as 1800 the framework knitters were a prosperous and well-organized artisan class, possessing a charter from Charles II regulating their hosiery industry. The male leg adorned in fancy hose was still admired as an object of beauty, and thus business was good. However, changes in clothing styles in the early nineteenth century were eroding the economic position of the framework knitters. Also, other knitters suffering from the general trade depression during the Napoleonic Wars began to use larger pantaloon frames to produce material for "cut up" goods, stockings with sewn seams rather than stockings produced from a single, continuous thread. Beginning in 1811, the framework knitters first complained that these inferior and cheaper goods were giving the trade a bad name and then began breaking the frames of their rivals. Their 1812 declaration did not object to new machinery but to the unfair business practices of men using old machinery. Although over 1000 frames were broken, the destruction was selective and, for that reason, initially supported by many employers. Only later, when other depressed classes adopted these techniques, did Luddism become a violent attack on machinery in gen-

Source: English Historical Documents, Vol. XI, 1783–1832, edited by A. Aspinall and E. Anthony Smith, 1959, Oxford University Press, Inc., p. 531. Reprinted by permission of Methuen London.

eral. When the government stepped in and suppressed the movement, Ned Lud became, like Robin Hood, a hero to the oppressed in England's popular folk mythology.

BY THE FRAMEWORK KNITTERS

A Declaration

Whereas by the charter granted by our late sovereign Lord Charles II by the Grace of God King of Great Britain France and Ireland, the framework knitters are empowered to break and destroy all frames and engines that fabricate articles in a fraudulent and deceitful manner and to destroy all framework knitters' goods whatsoever that are so made and whereas a number of deceitful unprincipled and intriguing persons did attain an Act to be passed in the 28th year of our present sovereign Lord George III whereby it was enacted that persons entering by force into any house shop or place to break or destroy frames should be adjudged guilty of felony and as we are fully convinced that such Act was obtained in the most fraudulent interested and electioneering manner and that the honourable the Parliament of Great Britain was deceived as to the motives and intentions of the persons who obtained such Act we therefore the framework knitters do hereby declare the aforesaid Act to be null and void to all intents and purposes whatsoever as by the passing of this Act villainous and imposing persons are enabled to make fraudulent and deceitful manufactures to the discredit and utter ruin of our trade. And whereas we declare that the aforementioned Charter is as much in force as though no such Act had been passed. . . . And we do hereby declare to all hosiers lace manufacturers and proprietors of frames that we will break and destroy all manner of frames whatsoever that make the following spurious articles and all frames whatsoever that do not pay the regular prices heretofore agreed to [by] the masters and workmen—All print net frames making single press and frames not working by the rack and rent and not paying the price regulated in 1810: warp frames working single yarn or two coarse hole—not working by the rack, not paying the rent and prices regulated in 1809—whereas all plain silk frames not making work according to the gage—frames not marking the work according to quality, whereas all frames of whatsoever description the workmen of whom are not paid in the current coin of the realm will invariably be destroyed. . . .

Given under my hand this first day of January 1812.
God protect the Trade.

Ned Lud's Office
Sherwood Forest

29

The Roman Catholic Emancipation Act (1829)

English prejudice against Roman Catholics had by the late eighteenth century begun to soften. By 1793, Catholics enjoyed freedom of worship, but old laws limiting their political activity still remained on the books. The Corporation Act of 1661 prohibited non-Anglicans from being members of municipal governments. The Test Act of 1673 similarly restricted admission to offices of the royal government and required officeholders to take an oath offensive to Roman Catholics. The Test Act of 1678 forbade Catholics to sit in either house of Parliament. Protestant dissenters suffered less from this legislation, and in 1828 the applicability of these acts to them was completely removed.

As Irish crisis produced the Catholic Emancipation Act of 1829. Although the Roman Catholic majority in Ireland obtained the right to vote in parliamentary elections in 1793 and retained it by the Act of Union of 1800, they were still denied public office. This disappointment, added to their dislike for the political union with Britain and their poor economic condition, led many Irish Catholics to rowdiness and disorder, which by the late 1820s absorbed much of the attention of the British army. Daniel O'Connell (1775–1847), a Catholic barrister, and his Catholic Association, founded in 1823, worked to elect members of Parliament favorable to Catholic emancipation and repeal of the union. In 1828, he contested a by-election, even though his Roman Catholicism disqualified him from sitting in Parliament. His winning foretold the possibility of scores of Catholic victors at the next general election. If these were overturned by a Protestant Parliament, Irish outrage was a certainty. The Tories, led by the duke of Wellington, therefore, passed the act that appears in part below. Although Roman Catholics received political rights denied them for more than two and one-half centuries, they were still distrusted by the Protestant establishment. This is shown by the oath required of Catholic members of Parliament, by the strictures against Jesuits, and by the act passed a short time later raising the property qualifications of Irish voters. This act can also be considered as the be-

Source: Statutes At Large, LXV, pt. ii, 49–53, 57 (10 George IV. c. 7).

100

ginning of nineteenth-century reform. It demonstrated the pragmatism of the Tories, who passed legislation they did not believe in, because the situation demanded it. But, by striking the first blow against the constitution the Tories denied themselves the sanctity they later claimed as its chief defenders.

AN ACT FOR THE RELIEF OF HIS MAJESTY'S ROMAN CATHOLIC SUBJECTS (13TH APRIL 1829)

Whereas by various Acts of Parliament certain Restraints and Disabilities are imposed on the Roman Catholic Subjects of His Majesty, to which other Subjects of His Majesty are not liable: And Whereas it is expedient that such Restraints and Disabilities shall be from henceforth discontinued: And Whereas by various Acts certain Oaths and certain Declarations, commonly called the Declaration against Transubstantiation, and the Declaration against Transubstantiation and the Invocation of Saints and the Sacrifice of the Mass, as practised in the Church of *Rome,* are or may be required to be taken, made, and subscribed by the Subjects of His Majesty, as Qualifications for sitting and voting in Parliament, and for the Enjoyment of certain Offices, Franchises, and Civil Rights: Be it enacted by the King's most Excellent Majesty, by and with the Advice and Consent of the Lords Spiritual and Temporal, and Commons, in this present Parliament assembled, and by the Authority of the same, That from and after the Commencement of this Act all such Parts of the said Acts as require the said Declarations, or either of them, to be made or subscribed by any of His Majesty's Subjects, as a Qualification for sitting and voting in Parliament, or for the Exercise or Enjoyment of any Office, Franchise, or Civil Right, be and the same are (save as hereinafter provided and excepted) hereby repealed.

II. And be it enacted, That from and after the Commencement of this Act it shall be lawful for any Person professing the Roman Catholic Religion, being a Peer, or who shall after the Commencement of this Act be returned as a Member of the House of Commons, to sit and vote in either House of Parliament respectively, being in all other respects duly qualified to sit and vote therein, upon taking and subscribing the following Oath, instead of the Oaths of Allegiance, Supremacy, and Abjuration:

I *A. B.* do sincerely promise and swear, That I will be faithful and bear true Allegiance to His Majesty King *George* the Fourth, and will defend him to the utmost of my Power against all Conspiracies and Attempts whatever, which shall be made against his Person, Crown, or Dignity; and I will do my utmost Endeavour to disclose and make known to His Majesty, His Heirs and Successors, all Treasons and traitorous Conspiracies which may be formed against Him or Them: And I do faithfully promise to maintain, support, and defend, to the utmost of my Power, the Succession of the Crown, which Succession, by an Act, intituled *An Act for the further Limitation of the Crown, and better securing the Rights and Liberties of the Subject,* is and stands limited to the Princess *Sophia,* Electress of *Hanover,* and the Heirs of her Body, being Protestants; hereby utterly renouncing and abjuring any Obedience or Allegiance unto any other Person claiming or pretending a Right to the Crown of this Realm: And I do further declare, That it is not an Article of my Faith, and that I do renounce, reject, and abjure the Opinion, that Princes excommunicated or deprived by the Pope, or any other Authority of the See of *Rome,* may be deposed or murdered by their Subjects, or by any Person whatsoever: And I do declare, That I do not believe that the Pope of *Rome,* or any other Foreign Prince, Prelate, Person, State, or Potentate, hath or ought to have any Temporal or Civil Jurisdiction, Power, Superiority, or Pre-eminence, directly or indirectly, within this Realm. I do swear, That I will defend to the utmost of my Power the Settlement of Property within this Realm, as established by the Laws: And I do hereby disclaim, disavow, and solemnly abjure any Intention to subvert the present Church Establishment, as settled by Law within this Realm: And I do solemnly swear, That I never will exercise any Privilege to which I am or may become entitled, to disturb or weaken the Protestant Religion or Protestant Government in the United Kingdom: And I do solemnly, in the presence of God, profess, testify, and declare, That I do make this Declaration, and every Part thereof, in the plain and ordinary Sense of the Words of this Oath, without any Evasion, Equivocation, or mental Reservation whatsoever.

So help me GOD

V. And be it further enacted, That it shall be lawful for Persons professing the Roman Catholic Religion to vote at Elections of Members to serve in Parliament for *England* and for *Ireland,* and also to vote at the Elections of Representative Peers of *Scotland* and of *Ireland,* and to be elected such Representative Peers, being in all other respects duly qualified, upon taking and subscribing the Oath hereinbefore appointed and set forth. . . .

X. And be it enacted, That it shall be lawful for any of His Majesty's Subjects professing the Roman Catholic Religion to hold, exercise, and enjoy all Civil and Military Offices and Places of Trust or Profit under His Majesty, His Heirs or Successors, and to exercise any other Franchise or Civil Right, except as hereinafter excepted. . . .

XIV. And be it enacted, That it shall be lawful for any of His Majesty's Subjects professing the Roman Catholic Religion to be a Member of any Lay Body Corporate, and to hold any Civil Office or Place of Trust or Profit therein, and to do any Corporate Act, or vote in any Corporate Election or other Proceeding, upon taking and subscribing the Oath hereby appointed and set forth. . . .

XXIX. And be it further enacted, That if any Jesuit, or Member of any such Religious Order, Community, or Society as aforesaid, shall, after the Commencement of this Act, come into this Realm, he shall be deemed and taken to be guilty of a Misdemeanor, and being thereof lawfully convicted, shall be sentenced and ordered to be banished from the United Kingdom for the Term of his natural Life.

30
Lord John Russell, Speech in Commons (1831). The Great Reform Bill

In 1831, when Lord John Russell (1792–1878) delivered this speech, the House of Commons was a venerable institution, having served Britain well for centuries. Some of its features, however, had little relevance to current conditions, especially the dramatic changes produced by the Industrial Revolution. The county franchise had not been altered since it became the 40-shilling freeholder in 1430, and in the boroughs there was a hodgepodge of different qualifications. No new boroughs had been created since 1677 and only one had been suppressed. Thus there were dilapidated boroughs like Old Sarum, which had no residents at all. William Pitt the Elder (1708–1778), who once represented Old Sarum, in his speech on the Stamp Act referred to such phenomena as "the rotten part of the Constitution."

Although popular agitation for reform had existed as early as John Wilkes's Middlesex elections in 1768 and 1769, no ministry seriously proposed parliamentary reform until 1831, when Lord Grey (1765–1845) and the Whigs produced the bill proposed by Russell. When the bill, which was surprisingly radical, was defeated, Grey obtained a dissolution of Parliament. The Whig cry, "the bill, the whole bill, and nothing but the bill," won the ensuing election, but a second bill was defeated by the Lords. The following year, a third bill was accepted, but only after William IV (1830–1837) had pledged to create, if necessary, enough new peers to force its passage.

The final bill, much like the one Russell had introduced in 1831, did not make Britain a parliamentary democracy, nor did it

Source: Hansard's Parliamentary Debates: Third Series, II, (1831), 1061, 1063–1064, 1066, 1068–1073, 1085, 1088–1089.

intend to do so. It abolished only the worst of the rotten boroughs, distributing most of the seats among the counties and the new industrial towns. It extended the franchise and made it uniform in the counties and in the boroughs, doubling the number of eligible voters to nearly a million out of a total population of more than 16 million. Thus, the middle classes of the towns joined the landlords as the practical rulers of Britain. Although the Reform Act did not enfranchise the working class and, in fact, disfranchised some, it did momentarily quiet the popular unrest that many feared would lead to revolution on the European model of 1830. Though this bill was intended to be the final reform of Parliament, it was in reality only the first of a series (1867, 1884, 1918, 1928) which during the next century extended the suffrage to virtually all adult subjects.

Although the legal ban on publishing parliamentary debates ended in 1771, systematic recording and publishing did not begin until 1803 under the direction of William Cobbett (1762–1835). His printer, T. C. Hansard, assumed the primary responsibility for the project. The debates, still being printed today, are referred to simply as *Hansard.*

Lord *John Russell* then rose and spoke to the following effect:

The measure I have now to bring forward, is a measure, not of mine, but of the Government, in whose name I appear—the deliberate measure of a whole Cabinet, unanimous upon this subject, and resolved to place their measure before this House, in redemption of their pledge to their Sovereign, the Parliament, and to their country. . . .

Allow me to imagine, for a moment, a stranger from some distant country, who should arrive in England to examine our institutions. All the information he had collected would have told him that this country was singular for the degree which it had attained in wealth, in science, and in civilization. He would have learned, that in no country have the arts of life been carried further, no where the inventions of mechanical skill been rendered more conducive to the comfort and prosperity of mankind. He would have made himself acquainted with its fame in history, and above all, he would have been told, that the proudest boast of this celebrated country was its political freedom. If, in addition to this he had heard that once in six years this country, so wise, so renowned, so free, chose its Representatives to sit in the great Council, where all the ministerial affairs were discussed and determined; he would not be a little curious to see the process by which so important and solemn an operation was effected. What then would be his surprise, if he were taken by his guide, whom he had asked to conduct him to one of the places of election, to a green mound and told, that this green mound sent two Members to Parliament—or, to be taken to a stone wall, with three niches in it, and told that these three niches sent two Members to Parliament. . . . But his surprise would increase to astonishment if he were carried into the North of England, where he would see large flourishing towns, full of trade and activity, containing vast magazines of wealth and manufactures, and were told that these places had no Representatives in the Assembly which was said to represent the people. Suppose him, after all, for I will not disguise any part of the case, suppose him to ask for a specimen of popular election, and to be carried, for that purpose, to Liverpool; his surprise would be turned into disgust at the gross venality and corruption which he would find to pervade the electors. After seeing all this, would he not wonder that a nation which had made such progress in every kind of knowledge, and which valued itself for its freedom, should permit so absurd and defective a system of representation any longer to prevail? . . . The chief grievances of which the people complain are these;—First, the nomination of Members by individuals? Second, the Elections by close Corporations; third, the Expense of Elections. . . .

We propose that every borough which . . . had less than 2,000 inhabitants, shall altogether lose the right of sending Members to Parliament. The effect will be, utterly to disfranchise sixty boroughs. . . . We find that there are forty-seven boroughs, of only 4,000 inhabitants, and these we shall deprive of the right of sending more than one Member to Parliament . . . making in the whole 168 vacancies. . . . As I have already said, we do not mean to allow that the remaining boroughs should be in the hands of select Corporations—that is to say, in the possession of a small number of persons, to the exclusion of the great body of the inhabitants, who have property and interest in the place represented. . . . We therefore propose that the right of voting shall be given to householders paying rates for, or occupying a house of, the yearly value of 10*l*. and upwards. . . . I shall now proceed to the manner in which we propose to extend the franchise in counties. The Bill I wish to introduce will give all copyholders to the value of 10*l*. a year . . . and all leaseholders for not less than twenty-one years, . . . a right to vote for the return of Knights of the Shire. . . . The right will depend upon a lease for twenty-one years, where the annual rent is not less than fifty pounds. It will be recollected that, when speaking of the numbers disfranchised, I said, that 168 vacancies would be created. . . . We propose . . . to fill up a certain number of the vacancies, but not the whole of them. We intend that seven large towns shall send two Members each, and that twenty other towns shall send one Member each. . . . A great portion of the Metropolis and its neighbourhood, amounting in population to 800,000 or 900,000, is not represented, and we propose to give eight members to the unrepresented. . . .

Next we propose an addition to the Members for the larger counties . . . two additional Members to each of twenty-seven counties, where the inhabitants exceed 150,000. Everybody will expect that Yorkshire, divided into three Ridings—the East, West, and North—should have two Members for each

Riding. . . . Besides this, it is proposed that the Isle of Wight shall return one Member. . . .

The names of electors are to be enrolled, by which means we hope that the disputes regarding qualification will be in a great measure avoided. We propose that all electors in counties, cities, towns, or boroughs, shall be registered, and for this purpose, machinery will be put in motion. . . .

I arrive at last at the objections which may be made to the plan we propose. I shall be told, in the first place, that we overturn the institutions of our ancestors. I maintain, that in departing from the letter, we preserve the spirit of those institutions. Our opponents say, our ancestors gave Old Sarum Representatives, therefore we should give Old Sarum Representatives.—We say, our ancestors gave Old Sarum Representatives, because it *was* a large town; therefore we give Representatives to Manchester, which *is* a large town. . . . I . . . think I am justified in saying, that we are to be believed when we come forward and state, that we consider some effectual measure of Reform to be necessary. I say, that we have a right to be believed when we assert that it is not for any sinister end of our own we bring forward the present measure, but because we are interested in the future welfare of this country, which welfare we conceive to be best consulted by the adoption of a timely and an effective Reform—because we think, that, by such a course alone we shall be enabled to give permanency to that Constitution which has been so long the admiration of nations, on account of its popular spirit, but which cannot exist much longer, unless strengthened by an additional infusion of popular spirit, commensurate with the progress of knowledge and the increased intelligence of the age. To establish the Constitution on a firm basis, you must show that you are determined not to be the representatives of a small class, or of a particular interest; but to form a body, who, representing the people, springing from the people, and sympathising with the people, can fairly call on the people to support the future burthens of the country, and to struggle with the future difficulties which it may have to encounter; confident that those who call upon them are ready to join them heart and hand: and are only looking, like themselves, to the glory and welfare of England. I conclude, Sir, by moving for leave to bring in a bill for amending the state of the Representation in England and Wales.

31
Ebenezer Elliott, *Corn Law Rhymes* (1831). The Free Trade Movement

The Corn Law of 1815 was the most consistently controversial statute in early nineteenth-century England. This act, prohibiting the importation of foreign corn, or grain, into England unless domestic wheat was selling for at least 80s. a quarter (eight bushels), was an attempt by the landed interests to maintain agricultural prices at the artificially high levels of the Napoleonic Wars era. Other economic and social groups in England, however, regarded the Corn Law as class legislation. Blaming the landlords for the high price of bread, the lower classes rioted in many towns. Although the rioting eventually ceased, the resentment remained and festered into the 1830s. The middle classes argued that the protection of domestic grain necessarily resulted in higher wages and made English manufactured goods less competitive in world markets. They complained that industry was subsidizing the inefficiency of the landlords. Despite modifications in the 1820s, the Corn Law remained controversial. The Anti-Corn Law League, founded in 1838 and led by Richard Cobden and John Bright, helped to persuade Prime Minister Peel in 1846 to repeal the corn duties. The victory of Cobden and Bright symbolized the economic triumph of free trade and the political ascendancy of the middle class. The loss of the Corn Law, "the ark of the Tory Covenant," marked a major defeat for those who had previously regarded themselves as the rightful rulers of England.

Ebenezer Elliott (1781–1849) was one of the most vocal critics of the Corn Law. The son of an English Jacobin, "Devil Elliott," Ebenezer divided his time between poetry and business. He failed in both. Although some of his early poetry rose to the level of mediocrity, all of it was ignored. His iron business went bankrupt in the 1820s. Personally frustrated, Elliott began writing his famous "corn-law rhymes," directed against what he believed to be the source of his and England's economic woes. These rhymes, published in several editions and widely read, made him something of a popular hero. In the following selections, the intensity of his feelings is apparent. To the historian seeking to understand the passions aroused by the Corn Law, Elliott's rhymes are worth more

Source: Ebenezer Elliott, *Corn Law Rhymes*, 3rd ed., London: B. Steill, 1831, pp. 29–30, 31, 45, 60, 65.

than all the cerebral speeches entombed between the covers of *Hansard.*

What Is Bad Government?

WHAT is bad government, thou slave,
  Whom robbers represent?
What is bad government, thou knave,
  Who lov'st bad government?
It is the deadly *will,* that takes
  What labour ought to keep;
It is the deadly *power,* that makes
  Bread dear, and labour cheap.

The Four Dears

DEAR sugar, dear tea, and dear corn
  Conspired with dear representation,
To laugh worth and honour to scorn,
  And beggar the whole British nation.

Let us bribe the dear sharks, said dear tea;
  Bribe, bribe, said dear representation;
Then buy with their own the dear humbugg'd, and be
  The bulwarks of tory dictation.
Dear sugar and tea, said dear corn,
  Be true to dear representation;
And then the dear crown will be worn,
  But to dignify dearest taxation.

Dear sugar, dear corn, and dear tea,
  Stick to me, said dear representation;
Let us still pull together, and we
  Shall still rob the dear British nation.

Caged Rats

YE coop us up, and tax our bread,
  And wonder why we pine:
But ye are fat, and round, and red,
  And fill'd with tax-bought wine.

Thus, twelve rats starve while three rats thrive,
　　(Like you on mine and me,)
When fifteen rats are caged alive,
　　With food for nine and three.

Haste! havoc's torch begins to glow,
　　The ending is begun;
Make haste; destruction thinks ye slow;
　　Make haste to be undone!
Why are ye call'd 'my lord,' and 'squire,'
　　While fed by mine and me,
And wringing food, and clothes, and fire
　　From bread-tax'd misery?

Make haste, slow rogues! *prohibit* trade,
　　Prohibit honest gain;
Turn all the good that God hath made
　　To fear, and hate, and pain;
Till beggars all, assassins all,
　　All cannibals we be,
And death shall have no funeral
　　From shipless sea to sea.

The Jacobin's Prayer

AVENGE the plunder'd poor, oh Lord!
But not with fire, but not with sword,
Not as at Peterloo they died,
Beneath the hoofs of coward pride.
Avenge our rags, our chains, our sighs,
The famine in our children's eyes!
But not with sword—no, not with fire
Chastise Thou Britain's locustry!
Lord, let them feel thy heavier ire;
Whip them, oh Lord! with poverty!
Then, cold in soul as coffin'd dust,
Their hearts as tearless, dead, and dry,
Let them in outraged mercy trust,
And *find* that mercy they deny!

Yon cotton-prince, at Peterloo,
Found easy work, and glory, too,
Corn laws, quoth he, make labour cheap,
And famine from our trenches keep;

He sees but wealth in want and woe;
Men starve, he owns, and justly so;
But if they marry and get brats,
Must *he* provide their shirts and hats?
Lord, fill his ledger with bad debts!
Let him be learn'd in gazettes!

32
Sadler Committee, Testimony (1832). Child Labor in England

Despite Peel's apprentice act of 1802 and the factory acts of 1819 and 1829, child labor remained a controversial social issue. This and similar problems in the 1820s and 1830s produced demands that the government intervene and correct the worst abuses of laissez-faire capitalism. Logically, many of the early reformers were Tories, who represented not only the landed classes but an older, paternalistic concern for the welfare of England's poor. Richard Oastler and Michael Sadler in the early 1830s and Benjamin Disraeli's Young England movement later reflected this sense of social responsibility.

Michael Sadler (1780–1835), a Tory MP associated with several reform movements in the 1820s, led the attack on the abuses of child labor. To publicize the problem, he persuaded Parliament to appoint a select committee to hear testimony on the working conditions of children and, if necessary, to propose remedial legislation. The committee achieved Sadler's objective, becoming, as one historian has described it, "the chief source of horror stories" about child labor. The resulting Factories Regulations Act (1833) prohibited the employment in textile mills of children under the age of nine and limited the workday of children under the age of thirteen and of youths under eighteen to 9 and 12 hours, respectively. More important, the act provided for full-time factory inspectors to ensure that its provisions were enforced. It represented a major attack on the economic principles of laissez-faire.

Source: "Report of the Select Committee on the Factories Bill," *Industrial Revolution: Children's Employment,* II, 157–159, 163–164, in the Irish University Press 1000-volume series of *British Parliamentary Papers,* Shannon, 1968–1972.

The testimony before the Sadler Committee was published as a "parliamentary paper." These papers, beginning in about 1801 and totaling almost 7000 volumes for the nineteenth century, are for the study of modern Britain the most important printed government records. These "Blue Books," so-called because of their blue paper covers, consist of several different types of documents. Many, like the one below, are reports of select committees of Parliament. Others are reports of Royal Commissions, composed of both members of Parliament and outside specialists. There were also collections of official correspondence, frequently dealing with foreign or colonial policy, and statistical reports from government agencies. All were arranged chronologically according to parliamentary session, with no attempt at any topical organization.

No complete set of original parliamentary papers exists, although nearly complete sets are found in such obvious places as the British Library. Most copies failed to survive the year of their publication, their folio size making them a ready source of wrapping paper. Today, thanks to the marvels of photography, most major libraries possess microprint editions.

Veneris, 1° die Junii, 1832

MICHAEL THOMAS SADLER, ESQUIRE, IN THE CHAIR.

Joseph Hebergam, Called in and Examined

4143. Where do you reside?—At North Great Huddersfield, in Yorkshire.

4144. What age are you?—I was 17 on the 21st of April.

4145. Are your father and mother living?—No; I have been without a father six years on the 8th of August.

4146. Your mother survives?—Yes.

4147. Have you worked in factories?—Yes.

4148. At what age did you commence?—Seven years of age.

4149. At whose mill?—George Addison's, Bradley Mill, near Huddersfield.

4150. What was the employment?—Worsted-spinning.

4151. What were your hours of labour at that mill?—From 5 in the morning till 8 at night.

4152. What intervals had you for refreshment and rest?—Thirty minutes at noon.

4153. Had you no time for breakfast or refreshment in the afternoon?—No, not one minute; we had to eat our meals as we could; standing or otherwise.

4154. You had fourteen and a half hours of actual labour at 7 years of age?—Yes.

4155. What wages had you at that time?—Two shillings and sixpence a week.

4164. What means were taken to keep you at your work so long?—There were three overlookers; there was a head overlooker, and then there was one man kept to grease the machines, and then there was one kept on purpose to strap.

4165. Was the main business of one of the overlookers that of strapping the children up to this excessive labour?—Yes, the same as strapping an old restive horse that has fallen down and will not get up.

4166. Was that the constant practice?—Yes, day by day.

4167. Were there straps regularly provided for that purpose?—Yes, he is continually walking up and down with it in his hand.

4176. Where is your brother John working now?—He died three years ago.

4177. What age was he when he died?—Sixteen years and eight months.

4178. To what was his death attributed by your mother and the medical attendants?—It was attributed to this, that he died from working such long hours, and that it had been brought on by the factory. They have to stop the flies with their knees, because they go so swift they cannot stop them with their hands; he got a bruise on the shin by a spindleboard, and it went on to the degree that it burst; the surgeon cured that, then he was better; then he went to work again; but when he had worked about two months more his spine became affected, and he died.

4181. What effect had this labour upon your own health?—It had a great deal; I have had to drop it several times in the year.

4182. How long was it before the labour took effect on your health?—Half a year.

4183. And did it at length begin to affect your limbs?—When I had worked about half a year, a weakness fell into my knees and ankles; it continued, and it has got worse and worse.

4187. How far did you live from the mill?—A good mile.

4188. Was it very painful for you to move?—Yes, in the morning I could scarcely walk, and my brother and sister used out of kindness to take me under each arm, and run with me to the mill, and my legs dragged on the ground in consequence of the pain; I could not walk.

4189. Were you sometimes too late?—Yes; and if we were five minutes too late, the overlooker would take a strap, and beat us till we were black and blue.

4190. The overlooker nevertheless knew the occasion of your being a little too late?—Yes.

4191. Did you state to him the reason?—Yes, he never minded that; and he used to watch us out of the windows.

4192. Did the pain and weakness in your legs increase?—Yes.

4193. Just show the Committee the situation in which your limbs are now?—

[The Witness accordingly stood up, and showed his limbs.]

4194. Were you originally a straight and healthy boy?—Yes, I was straight and healthful as any one when I was 7 years and a quarter old.

4306. How long have you been in the Leeds Infirmary?—A week last Saturday night; if I had been this week at Leeds I should have been a fortnight next Saturday.

4307. Have any cases of accidents in mills or factories been brought into the Infirmary since you were there?—Yes, last Tuesday but one there was a boy brought in about 5 or 6 o'clock in the evening from a mill; he had got catched with the shaft, and he had both his thighs broke, and from his knee to his hip the flesh was ripped up the same as if it had been cut by a knife, his head was bruised, his eyes were nearly torn out, and his arms broken. His sister, who ran to pull him off, got both her arms broke and her head bruised, and she is bruised all over her body. The boy died last Thursday night but one, about 8 o'clock; I do not know whether the girl is dead, but she was not expected to live.

4310. Something has been said about the fear of giving evidence regarding this factory question; do you know whether any threats have ever been used on that account?—Yes; Dr. Walker ordered me to wear irons from the ankle to the thigh; my mother was not able to get them, and he said he would write a note, and she might go to some gentlemen in the town, and give them that note, and see if they would not give her something towards them; and so she did, and I have got the bare irons made; and I was coming into the yard where I live; and there was a man who worked at the same place that I did, asked me to let him look at them; I told him I could not get money to line them with, and he said, "I will tell you where there is a gentleman who will give you the money;" he told me of Mr. Oastler, and he said, "I will go and see if he is at home, that you may not lose your trouble." Mrs. Oastler was at home, and said I was to be there at 8 o'clock in the morning, because he wanted to go off on a journey; I got there about half-past 8. Mr. Wood of Bradford gave me a sovereign, and Mr. Oastler gave me 3*s.* 6*d.*, and so I had them made. He asked me questions what my lameness came on with, and I told him, and he happened to mention it at the County Meeting at York; my master saw it in the newspaper; I think it was in Mr. Baines's newspaper, of Leeds; he is an enemy to the Ten Hours' Bill, and he happened to see it in the paper, and he sent the foreman on to our house where I lived; he had not patience to read it, and he said to my mother, "I suppose it is owing to our place that your Joseph got the use of his limbs taken away?" and my mother said he was informed wrong, that he had it before he went to that factory; but he said, "If he has said anything about our factory, we shall certainly turn him off, and both his brothers." I have two little brothers working at the same place.

4311. Did the foreman say this to you?—To my mother and me; he said he did not know exactly how it was, but he would go back and see the paper himself, and if he found out that we said anything about the factory system, that we should be turned off.

4312. Have you been turned off?—I have not, but my master will not speak to me or look at me: I do not know whether he will let me start again or not.

4335. You stated that you found it your duty to go to those mills, in order to maintain your mother, who is a widow, and very poor?—Yes.

33
Thomas Babington Macaulay, Minute on Indian Education (1835)

In acquiring a world empire, Britain created a number of administrative problems, one of the most constant being whether to "Anglicize," i.e., civilize, native populations. This issue, first raised in French Canada after 1763, remained controversial in the African colonies well into the twentieth century.

The consolidation of British control in India in the early nineteenth century led to a major debate between the "Orientalists" and the "Anglicists." The former defended the vitality and sophistication of Indian culture. The latter in the 1820s conducted a vigorous campaign against what they viewed as barbarism and superstition, attacking in particular the *suttee,* a Hindu religious practice of burning alive a man's widow on his funeral pyre. The decision of the East India Company in 1833 to admit Indians into its civil service precipitated a new round in this old debate. Although both sides agreed that the education of Indians should be promoted, they differed on its proposed form. The Orientalists favored Arabic and Sanskrit learning. The Anglicists urged the introduction of western scholarship taught in English.

The most prominent westernizer was Thomas Babington Macaulay (1800–1859), a member of the Supreme Council of India. Already a distinguished essayist, and later renowned for his *History of England from the Accession of James the Second,* Macaulay never doubted the superiority of English civilization. The history of England since 1688 was, he wrote, "eminently the history of physical, of moral, and of intellectual improvement." It

Source: Speeches by Lord Macaulay with his Minute on Indian Education, edited by G. M. Young, London: Oxford University Press, 1935, pp. 348–350, 352–353, 357–359.

was Britain's duty therefore to uplift the Indians by blessing them with western learning, an argument made most dogmatically in his Minute on Indian Education (1835). Macaulay was not a racist. Indians were not inferior as people; they simply had an inferior culture. As Greece had civilized Rome and Rome had civilized Britain, now Britain, a link in the chain of progress, must transfer that benefit to India.

Macaulay and others recognized that education might contribute to the end of British political rule in India. Nevertheless, Britain would create a more enduring empire:

> The sceptre may pass from us. Victory may be inconstant to our arms. But there are triumphs which are followed by no reverse. There is an empire exempt from all natural cause of decay. Those triumphs are the pacific triumphs of reason over barbarism; that empire is the imperishable empire of our arts and our morals, our literature and our laws.

Regardless of the merits of the case, the government of India's adoption of Macaulay's recommendations was of great importance. Although alienating many Indians and perhaps contributing to the Indian Mutiny of 1857, the westernization and modernization of India was begun.

We have a fund to be employed as Government shall direct for the intellectual improvement of the people of this country. The simple question is, what is the most useful way of employing it?

All parties seem to be agreed on one point, that the dialects commonly spoken among the natives of this part of India, contain neither literary nor scientific information, and are, moreover, so poor and rude that, until they are enriched from some other quarter, it will not be easy to translate any valuable work into them. It seems to be admitted on all sides, that the intellectual improvement of those classes of the people who have the means of pursuing higher studies can at present be effected only by means of some language not vernacular amongst them.

What then shall that language be? One-half of the Committee maintain that it should be the English. The other half strongly recommended the Arabic and Sanscrit. The whole question seems to me to be, which language is the best worth knowing?

I have no knowledge of either Sanscrit or Arabic.—But I have done what I could to form a correct estimate of their value. I have read translations of the most celebrated Arabic and Sanscrit works. I have conversed both here and at home with men distinguished by their proficiency in the Eastern tongues. I am quite ready to take the Oriental learning at the valuation of the Orientalists themselves. I have never found one among them who could deny that a single shelf of a good European library was worth the whole native literature of India and Arabia. The intrinsic superiority of the Western literature is, indeed, fully admitted by those members of the Committee who support the Oriental plan of education.

It will hardly be disputed, I suppose, that the department of literature in which the eastern writers stand highest is poetry. And I certainly never met with any Orientalist who ventured to maintain that the Arabic and Sanscrit poetry could be compared to that of the great European nations. But when we pass from works of imagination to works in which facts are recorded, and general principles investigated, the superiority of the Europeans becomes absolutely immeasurable. It is, I believe, no exaggeration to say, that all the historical information which has been collected from all the books written in the Sanscrit language is less valuable than what may be found in the most paltry abridgments used at preparatory schools in England. In every branch of physical or moral philosophy, the relative position of the two nations is nearly the same.

How, then, stands the case? We have to educate a people who cannot at present be educated by means of their mother-tongue. We must teach them some foreign language. The claims of our own language it is hardly necessary to recapitulate. It stands preeminent even among the languages of the west. It abounds with works of imagination not inferior to the noblest which Greece has bequeathed to us; with models of every species of eloquence; with historical compositions, which, considered merely as narratives, have seldom been surpassed, and which, considered as vehicles of ethical and political instruction, have never been equalled; with just and lively representations of human life and human nature; with the most profound speculations on metaphysics, morals, government, jurisprudence, and trade; with full and correct information respecting every experimental science which tends to preserve the health, to increase the comfort, or to expand the intellect of man. Whoever knows that language has ready access to all the vast intellectual wealth, which all the wisest nations of the earth have created and hoarded in the course of ninety generations. It may safely be said, that the literature now extant in that language is of far greater value than all the literature which three hundred years ago was extant in all languages of the world together. Nor is this all. In India, English is the language spoken by the ruling class. It is spoken by the higher class of natives at the seats of Government. It is likely to become the language of commerce throughout the seas of the East. . . .

And what are the arguments against that course which seems to be alike recommended by theory and by experience? It is said that we ought to secure the co-operation of the native public, and that we can do this only by teaching Sanscrit and Arabic. . . .

It is said that the Sanscrit and Arabic are the languages in which the sacred books of a hundred millions of people are written, and that they are, on that account, entitled to peculiar encouragement. Assuredly it is the duty of the British

Government in India to be not only tolerant, but neutral on all religious questions. But to encourage the study of a literature admitted to be of small intrinsic value, only because that literature inculcates the most serious errors on the most important subjects, is a course hardly reconcileable with reason, with morality, or even with that very neutrality which ought, as we all agree, to be sacredly preserved. It is confessed that a language is barren of useful knowledge. We are to teach it because it is fruitful of monstrous superstitions. We are to teach false History, false Astronomy, false Medicine, because we find them in company with a false religion. We abstain, and I trust shall always abstain, from giving any public encouragement to those who are engaged in the work of converting natives to Christianity. And while we act thus, can we reasonably and decently bribe men out of the revenues of the state to waste their youth in learning how they are to purify themselves after touching an ass, or what text of the Vedas they are to repeat to expiate the crime of killing a goat?

It is taken for granted by the advocates of Oriental learning, that no native of this country can possibly attain more than a mere smattering of English. . . . They assume it as undeniable, that the question is between a profound knowledge of Hindoo and Arabian literature and science on the one side, and a superficial knowledge of the rudiments of English on the other. This is not merely an assumption, but an assumption contrary to all reason and experience. We know that foreigners of all nations do learn our language sufficiently to have access to all the most abstruse knowledge which it contains, sufficiently to relish even the more delicate graces of our most idiomatic writers. There are in this very town natives who are quite competent to discuss political or scientific questions with fluency and precision in the English language. I have heard the very question on which I am now writing discussed by native gentlemen with a liberality and an intelligence which would do credit to any member of the Committee of Public Instruction. Indeed it is unusual to find, even in the literary circles of the continent, any foreigner who can express himself in English with so much facility and correctness as we find in many Hindoos. Nobody, I suppose, will contend that English is so difficult to a Hindoo as Greek to an Englishman. Yet an intelligent English youth, in a much smaller number of years than our unfortunate pupils pass at the Sanscrit college, becomes able to read, to enjoy, and even to imitate, not unhappily, the compositions of the best Greek Authors. Less than half the time which enables an English youth to read Herodotus and Sophocles, ought to enable a Hindoo to read Hume and Milton.

To sum up what I have said, I think it clear that we are not fettered by the Act of Parliament of 1813; that we are not fettered by any pledge expressed or implied; that we are free to employ our funds as we choose; that we ought to employ them in teaching what is best worth knowing; that English is better worth knowing than Sanscrit or Arabic; that the natives are desirous to be taught English, and are not desirous to be taught Sanscrit or Arabic; that neither as the languages of law, nor as the languages of religion, have the Sanscrit and Arabic any peculiar claim to our engagement; that it is possible to make natives of this country thoroughly good English scholars, and that to this end our efforts ought to be directed.

In one point I fully agree with the gentlemen to whose general views I am opposed. I feel with them, that it is impossible for us, with our limited means, to attempt to educate the body of the people. We must at present do our best to form a class who may be interpreters between us and the millions whom we govern; a class of persons, Indian in blood and colour, but English in taste, in opinions, in morals, and in intellect. To that class we may leave it to refine the vernacular dialects of the country, to enrich those dialects with terms of science borrowed from the Western nomenclature, and to render them by degrees fit vehicles for conveying knowledge to the great mass of the population.

34
The National Petition (1839).
The Chartist Program

In the late 1830s and 1840s, Britain witnessed a revival of lower-class political agitation. The "Hungry Forties" brought widespread unemployment, reduced wages, and poverty that in some cases became actual starvation. The suffering lower classes felt betrayed. The Reform Act of 1832, which had enfranchised the "moneymongers and shopocrats," appeared simply to have transferred power from an exploitive landed class to an oppressive middle class. This widely held view was confirmed by the Poor Act of 1834, which refused governmental assistance to the needy unless they entered a workhouse, and by the Factory Act of 1833, which regulated the hours of work only of the young. These economic and political frustrations produced Chartism.

The Chartist movement, led initially by William Lovett (1800–1877), was on the surface a movement for political reform. The petition of 1839 indicates, however, that the real objective was social and economic reform; political change was simply a means to an end. It is also interesting for its deferential tone, indicating an initial willingness of the Chartists to work within the sys-

Source: William Lovett, *The Life and Struggles of William Lovett,* London: Trübner & Co., 1876, pp. 469–473.

tem. Its rejection in the House of Commons by a vote of 235 to 46, however, undermined the moderates' position and contributed to the rise of "physical force" Chartists such as Feargus O'Connor, an Irish demagogue who radicalized but also weakened the movement in the 1840s. It should be noted that this petition mentions only five of the six political demands usually associated with Chartism, that for equal electoral districts being omitted.

The rejection of this petition foreshadowed the failure of Chartism. The middle class became more interested in the Anti-Corn Law League. The moderate worker turned increasingly to trade unionism. Only the radicals remained; and the failure of their monster petitions in 1842 and 1848 and the prosperity of the 1850s ended even this last phase. Chartism, though it failed to achieve its immediate objective, awakened people to the economic and political problems facing Britain. It developed in working people a class consciousness, and it forced politicians to realize that the political reform of 1832 might not in fact be final.

NATIONAL PETITION

Unto the Honourable the Commons of the United Kingdom of Great Britain and Ireland in Parliament assembled, the Petition of the undersigned, their suffering countrymen,

HUMBLY SHEWETH,

That we, your petitioners, dwell in a land whose merchants are noted for enterprise, whose manufacturers are very skilful, and whose workmen are proverbial for their industry.

The land itself is goodly, the soil rich, and the temperature wholesome; it is abundantly furnished with the materials of commerce and trade; it has numerous and convenient harbours; in facility of internal communication it exceeds all others.

For three-and-twenty years we have enjoyed a profound peace.

Yet, with all these elements of national prosperity, and with every disposition and capacity to take advantage of them, we find ourselves overwhelmed with public and private suffering.

We are bowed down under a load of taxes; which, notwithstanding, fall greatly short of the wants of our rulers; our traders are trembling on the verge of bankruptcy; our workmen are starving; capital brings no profit, and labour no remuneration; the home of the artificer is desolate, and the warehouse of the pawnbroker is full; the workhouse is crowded, and the manufactory is deserted.

We have looked on every side, we have searched diligently in order to find out the causes of a distress so sore and so long continued.

We can discover none in nature, or in Providence.

Heaven has dealt graciously by the people; but the foolishness of our rulers has made the goodness of God of none effect.

The energies of a mighty kingdom have been wasted in building up the power of selfish and ignorant men, and its resources squandered for their aggrandisement.

The good of a party has been advanced to the sacrifice of the good of the nation; the few have governed for the interest of the few, while the interest of the many has been neglected, or insolently and tyrannously trampled upon.

It was the fond expectation of the people that a remedy for the greater part, if not for the whole, of their grievances, would be found in the Reform Act of 1832.

They were taught to regard that Act as a wise means to a worthy end; as the machinery of an improved legislation, when the will of the masses would be at length potential.

They have been bitterly and basely deceived.

The fruit which looked so fair to the eye has turned to dust and ashes when gathered.

The Reform Act has effected a transfer of power from one domineering faction to another, and left the people as helpless as before.

Our slavery has been exchanged for an apprenticeship to liberty, which has aggravated the painful feeling of our social degradation, by adding to it the sickening of still deferred hope.

We come before your Honourable House to tell you, with all humility, that this state of things must not be permitted to continue; that it cannot long continue without very seriously endangering the stability of the throne and the peace of the kingdom. . . .

We tell your Honourable House that the capital of the master must no longer be deprived of its due reward; that the laws which make food dear, and those which by making money scarce, makes labour cheap, must be abolished; that taxation must be made to fall on property, not on industry; that the good of the many, as it is the only legitimate end, so must it be the sole study of the Government.

As a preliminary essential to these and other requisite changes; as means by which alone the interests of the people can be effectually vindicated and secured, we demand that those interests be confided to the keeping of the people.

When the state calls for defenders, when it calls for money, no consideration of poverty or ignorance can be pleaded in refusal or delay of the call.

Required as we are, universally, to support and obey the laws, nature and reason entitle us to demand, that in the making of the laws, the universal voice shall be implicitly listened to.

We perform the duties of freemen; we must have the privileges of freemen.

WE DEMAND UNIVERSAL SUFFRAGE. . . .

WE DEMAND THE BALLOT. . . .

WE DEMAND ANNUAL PARLIAMENTS. . . .

We demand that in the future election of members of your Honourable House, the approbation of the constituency shall be the sole qualification; and that to every representative so chosen, shall be assigned, out of the public taxes, a fair and adequate remuneration for the time which he is called upon to devote to the public service. . . .

The management of this mighty kingdom has hitherto been a subject for contending factions to try their selfish experiments upon.

We have felt the consequences in our sorrowful experience—short glimmerings of uncertain enjoyment swallowed up by long and dark seasons of suffering.

If the self-government of the people should not remove their distresses, it will at least remove their repinings.

Universal suffrage will, and it alone can, bring true and lasting peace to the nation; we firmly believe that it will also bring prosperity.

May it therefore please your honourable House to take this our petition into your most serious consideration; and to use your utmost endeavours, by all constitutional means, to have a law passed, granting to every male of lawful age, sane mind, and unconvicted of crime, the right of voting for members of Parliament; and directing all future elections of members of Parliament to be in the way of secret ballot; and ordaining that the duration of Parliaments so chosen shall in no case exceed one year; and abolishing all property qualifications in the members; and providing for their due remuneration while in attendance on their Parliamentary duties.

AND YOUR PETITIONERS, &C.

35

Lord Durham, *Report on the Affairs of British North America* (1839). Self-Government in the Colonies

Even after the loss of thirteen colonies, Britain retained settlements in North America. Besides those on the Atlantic coast—Nova Scotia, Newfoundland, Prince Edward Island, and New Brunswick—there was Quebec, initially French, but after the American Revolution enlarged by the influx of Loyalists. In 1791, Quebec was divided into two parts, Upper Canada, today called Ontario, populated by Loyalists and recent British immigrants, and French Lower Canada, today called Quebec. Rebellions erupted in 1837 in both colonies protesting the authority of the British governors and the power of the local oligarchies. Although the revolts were easily suppressed, the British government recognized the danger and sent an important official to study the political problems facing the Canadas.

The man sent was John George Lambton, the earl of Durham (1792–1840), often called "Radical Jack" for his Benthamite leanings and for his outspoken liberalism. The son-in-law of Prime Minister Lord Grey, he had played an important role in the drafting of the Great Reform Bill. He also subscribed to the "Systematic Colonization" of Edward Gibbon Wakefield, who called for a more rational alienation of Crown lands and greater self-government in the colonies. In Canada, Durham had the opportunity to practice both his liberalism and his advanced ideas on colonial government.

For five months in 1838, Durham ruled Canada as High Commissioner and Governor-in-Chief. Resigning in a huff, he returned to England to write his report, which advocated two things. First, the two Canadas should be united. The French, by being thrown in with the rapidly growing English population, would thereby become Anglicized and thus more easily controlled. The political union was accomplished in 1840, but the French have never accepted the idea of losing their unique identity. Second, as the selection below shows, Durham advocated that Canada be

Source: Arthur Berriedale Keith, ed., *Selected Speeches and Documents on British Colonial Policy, 1763–1917*, London: Oxford University Press, 1948, pp. 129–131, 134–135, 138–142. Reprinted by permission of Oxford University Press.

given responsible government. In internal affairs the governor must accept the advice of members responsible to the legislative assembly, just as in Britain the monarch was supposedly controlled by a cabinet responsible to the House of Commons. Although this recommendation was not endorsed by the British government, it was introduced in 1849 by Governor Lord Elgin. Canada played her traditional role of colonial bellwether; almost immediately the principle was extended to the other white settlement colonies, not only in North America but in Australasia and southern Africa as well.

Since the Revolution of 1688, the stability of the English constitution has been secured by that wise principle of our Government which has vested the direction of the national policy, and the distribution of patronage, in the leaders of the Parliamentary majority. However partial the monarch might be to particular ministers, or however he might have personally committed himself to their policy, he has invariably been constrained to abandon both, as soon as the opinion of the people has been irrevocably pronounced against them through the medium of the House of Commons. The practice of carrying on a representative government on a different principle, seems to be the rock on which the continental imitations of the British Constitution have invariably split; and the French Revolution of 1830 was the necessary result of an attempt to uphold a ministry with which no Parliament could be got to act in concert. It is difficult to understand how any English statesman could have imagined that representative and irresponsible government could be successfully combined. There seems, indeed, to be an idea, that the character of representative institutions ought to be thus modified in colonies; that it is an incident of colonial dependence that the officers of government should be nominated by the Crown, without any reference to the wishes of the community, whose interests are entrusted to their keeping. It has never been very clearly explained what are the imperial interests, which require this complete nullification of representative government. But if there be such a necessity, it is quite clear that a representative government in a colony must be a mockery, and a source of confusion. For those who support this system have never yet been able to devise, or to exhibit in the practical working of colonial government, any means for making so complete an abrogation of political influence palatable to the representative body. It is not difficult to apply the case to our own country. Let it be imagined that at a general election the opposition were to return 500 out of 658 members of the House of Commons, and that the whole policy of the ministry should be condemned, and every Bill introduced by it, rejected by this immense majority. Let it be supposed that the Crown should consider it a point of honour and duty to retain a ministry so condemned and so thwarted; that repeated dissolutions should in no way increase, but should even diminish, the ministerial minority, and that the only result which could be obtained by such a development of the force of the opposition were not the slightest change in the policy of the ministry, not the removal of a single minister, but simply the election of a Speaker of the politics of the majority; and, I think, it will not be difficult to imagine the fate of such a system of government. Yet such was the system, such literally was the course of events in Lower Canada, and such in character, though not quite in degree, was the spectacle exhibited in Upper Canada, and, at one time or another, in every one of the North American Colonies. . . .

The preceding pages have sufficiently pointed out the nature of those evils, to the extensive operation of which, I attribute the various practical grievances, and the present unsatisfactory condition of the North American Colonies. It is not by weakening, but strengthening the influence of the people on its Government; by confining within much narrower bounds than those hitherto allotted to it, and not by extending the interference of the imperial authorities in the details of colonial affairs, that I believe that harmony is to be restored, where dissension has so long prevailed; and a regularity and vigour hitherto unknown, introduced into the administration of these Provinces. It needs no change in the principles of government, no invention of a new constitutional theory, to supply the remedy which would, in my opinion, completely remove the existing political disorders. It needs but to follow out consistently the principles of the British constitution, and introduce into the Government of these great Colonies those wise provisions, by which alone the working of the representative system can in any country be rendered harmonious and efficient. We are not now to consider the policy of establishing representative government in the North American Colonies. That has been irrevocably done; and the experiment of depriving the people of their present constitutional power, is not to be thought of. To conduct their Government harmoniously, in accordance with its established principles, is now the business of its rulers; and I know not how it is possible to secure that harmony in any other way, than by administering the Government on those principles which have been found perfectly efficacious in Great Britain. . . .

Perfectly aware of the value of our colonial possessions, and strongly impressed with the necessity of maintaining our connexion with them, I know not in what respect it can be desirable that we should interfere with their internal legislation in matters which do not affect their relations with the mother country. The matters, which so concern us, are very few. The constitution of the form of government,—the regulation of foreign relations, and of trade with the mother country, the other British Colonies, and foreign nations,—and the disposal of the public lands, are the only points on which the mother country requires a control. This control is now sufficiently secured by the authority of the Imperial Legislature; by the protection which the Colony derives from us against foreign enemies; by the beneficial terms which our laws secure to its trade; and by its share of the reciprocal benefits which would be conferred by a wise system of colonization. A perfect subordination, on the part of the Colony, on these points, is secured by the advantages which it finds in the continuance of its connexion with the Empire. It certainly is not strengthened, but greatly weakened, by a vexatious interference on the part of the Home Government, with the enactment of laws for regulating the internal concerns of the Colony, or in the selection of the persons entrusted with their execution. The colonists may not always know what laws are best for them, or which of their countrymen are the fittest for conducting their affairs; but, at least, they have a greater interest in coming to a right judgement on these points, and will take greater pains to do so, than those whose welfare is very remotely and slightly affected by the good or bad legislation of these portions of the Empire. If the colonists make bad laws, and select improper persons to conduct their affairs, they will generally be the only, always the greatest, sufferers; and, like the people of other countries, they must bear the ills which they bring on themselves, until they choose to apply the remedy. . . .

My own observation convinces me, that the predominant feeling of all the English population of the North American Colonies is that of devoted attachment to the mother country. . . . The attachment constantly exhibited by the people of these Provinces towards the British Crown and Empire has all the characteristics of a strong national feeling. They value the institutions of their country, not merely from a sense of the practical advantages which they confer, but from sentiments of national pride; and they uphold them the more, because they are accustomed to view them as marks of nationality, which distinguish them from their Republican neighbours. I do not mean to affirm that this is a feeling which no impolicy on the part of the mother country will be unable to impair; but I do most confidently regard it as one which may, if rightly appreciated, be made the link of an enduring and advantageous connexion. The British people of the North American Colonies are a people on whom we may safely rely, and to whom we must not grudge power. For it is not to the individuals who have been loudest in demanding the change, that I propose to concede the responsibility of the Colonial administration, but to the people themselves.

36

Lord Palmerston, Speech in Commons (1850). The Don Pacifico Affair

Britain reached the apex of her world power in the fifty years following the Congress of Vienna, a power based on industrial leadership, naval and imperial supremacy, and the relative political stability and self-confidence of her people. The man best symbolizing this preeminence was Henry John Temple, third Viscount Palmerston (1784–1865). Palmerston, a man of great political ability, was the Tory secretary-at-war from 1809 to 1828, the Whig foreign secretary throughout the 1830s and from 1846 to 1851, and finally prime minister from 1855 to 1858 and again from 1859 to 1865. Unlike some patrician statesmen, he was loved by the public. Cartoonists often portrayed "Pam" with a straw in his mouth, symbolic of his devil-may-care attitude, which led him in 1840 at the age of 56 to attempt, unsuccessfully, to seduce one of the Queen's ladies-in-waiting.

Palmerston's foreign policy reflected his life-style; it was arrogant, unpredictable, and often controversial. Specifically, his use of gunboat diplomacy to protect Englishmen in foreign countries was the subject of much debate. To foreign governments, Pam was the image of the "Ugly Englishman" of the nineteenth century, a meddlesome, overbearing bully. To his critics at home, including Victoria, he was too strong-willed and independent, giving deference neither to the cabinet nor to the queen. His admirers, however, saw him as John Bull, ever ready to defend a British subject in his just quarrel with a foreign government. Palmerston denied being a bully, arguing that even small nations were responsible for their actions: "The weaker a government is, the more inexcusable becomes its insolence or injustice."

Palmerston's greatest speech, reproduced below, was on the Don Pacifico affair, which threatened his entire approach to diplomacy. Palmerston's aggressive attempts to collect from the Greek government damages for Don Pacifico, a Portuguese Jew born at Gibraltar, whose house in Athens had been burned by a mob in 1847, created grave diplomatic problems. When in 1850 France

Source: Hansard's Parliamentary Debates, Third Series, CXII (1850), 380–381, 383, 394–397, 443–444.

withdrew her ambassador from London in protest, the House of Lords voted censure on Palmerston for his handling of the dispute. Lord John Russell, hoping to salvage British prestige as well as his foreign secretary, arranged for a vote of confidence in the House of Commons, thus giving Palmerston a chance to defend himself. He rose to speak at 9:45 in the evening of June 25, 1850, and concluded his moving, impromptu oration four and one-half hours later at 2:20 in the morning to prolonged cheers. Palmerston not only saved his career, but added luster to a reputation that was fast becoming a legend.

When I say that this is an important question, I say it in the fullest expression of the term. It is a matter which concerns not merely the tenure of office by one individual, or even by a Government; it is a question that involves principles of national policy, and the deepest interests as well as the honour and dignity of England. . . .

Now, the resolution of the House of Lords involves the future as well as the past. It lays down for the future a principle of national policy, which I consider totally incompatible with the interests, with the rights, with the honour, and with the dignity of the country; and at variance with the practice, not only of this, but of all other civilised countries in the world. . . . The country is told that British subjects in foreign lands are entitled—for that is the meaning of the resolution—to nothing but the protection of the laws and the tribunals of the land in which they happen to reside. The country is told that British subjects abroad must not look to their own country for protection, but must trust to that indifferent justice which they may happen to receive at the hands of the Government and tribunals of the country in which they may be. . . .

I say, then, that our doctrine is, that, in the first instance, redress should be sought from the law courts of the country; but that in cases where redress cannot be so had—and those cases are many—to confine a British subject to that remedy only, would be to deprive him of the protection which he is entitled to receive.

Then the question arises, how does this rule apply to the demands we have made upon Greece? . . .

Then we come to the claim of M. Pacifico—a claim which has been the subject of much unworthy comment. . . . I don't care what M. Pacifico's character is. I do not, and cannot admit, that because a man may have acted amiss on some other occasion, and in some other matter, he is to be wronged with impunity by others. . . .

The rights of a man depend on the merits of the particular case; and it is an abuse of argument to say, that you are not to give redress to a man, because in some former transaction he may have done something which is questionable.

Punish him if you will—punish him if he is guilty, but don't pursue him as a Pariah through life.

What happened in this case? In the middle of the town of Athens, in a house . . . —a house as good as the generality of those which existed in Athens before the Sovereign ascended the throne—M. Pacifico, living in this house, within forty yards of the great street, within a few minutes' walk of a guardhouse, where soldiers were stationed, was attacked by a mob. Fearing injury, when the mob began to assemble, he sent an intimation to the British Minister, who immediately informed the authorities. Application was made to the Greek Government for protection. No protection was afforded. The mob, in which were soldiers and gens-d'armes, who, even if officers were not with them, ought, from a sense of duty, to have interfered and to have prevented plunder—that mob, headed by the sons of the Minister of War, not children of eight or ten years old, but older—that mob, for nearly two hours, employed themselves in gutting the house of an unoffending man, carrying away or destroying every single thing the house contained, and left it a perfect wreck. . . .

The Greek Government having neglected to give the protection they were bound to extend, and having abstained from taking means to afford redress, this was a case in which we were justified in calling on the Greek Government for compensation for the losses, whatever they might be, which M. Pacifico had suffered. I think that claim was founded in justice. The amount we did not pretend to fix. If the Greek Government had admitted the principle of the claim, and had objected to the account sent in by M. Pacifico—if they had said, "This is too much, and we think a less sum sufficient," that would have been a question open to discussion. . . . But the Greek Government denied altogether the principle of the claim. . . .

M. Pacifico having, from year to year, been treated either with answers wholly unsatisfactory, or with a positive refusal, or with pertinacious silence, it came at last to this, either that his demand was to be abandoned altogether, or that, in pursuance of the notice we had given the Greek Government a year or two before, we were to proceed to use our own means of enforcing the claim. . . .

Well, then, was there anything so uncourteous in sending, to back our demands, a force which should make it manifest to all the world that resistance was out of the question? Why, it seems to me, on the contrary, that it was more consistent with the honour and dignity of the Government on whom we made those demands, that there should be placed before their eyes a force, which it would be vain to resist, and before which it would be no indignity to yield. . . .

While we have seen . . . the political earthquake rocking Europe from side to side—while we have seen thrones shaken, shattered, levelled; institutions overthrown and destroyed—while in almost every country of Europe the conflict of civil war has deluged the land with blood, from the Atlantic to the Black Sea, from the Baltic to the Mediterranean; this country has presented a spectacle honourable to the people of England, and worthy of the admiration of mankind.

We have shown that liberty is compatible with order; that individual freedom is reconcilable with obedience to the law. We have shown the example of a nation, in which every class of society accepts with cheerfulness the lot which Providence has assigned to it; while at the same time every individual of each class is constantly striving to raise himself in the social scale—not by injustice and wrong, not by violence and illegality—but by persevering good conduct, and by the steady and energetic exertion of the moral and intellectual faculties with which his Creator has endowed him. To govern such a people as this, is indeed an object worthy of the ambition of the noblest man who lives in the land; and therefore I find no fault with those who may think any opportunity a fair one, for endeavouring to place themselves in so distinguished and honourable a position. But I contend that we have not in our foreign policy done anything to forfeit the confidence of the country. We may not, perhaps, in this matter or in that, have acted precisely up to the opinions of one person or of another—and hard indeed it is, as we all know by our individual and private experience, to find any number of men agreeing entirely in any matter, on which they may not be equally possessed of the details of the facts, and circumstances, and reasons, and conditions which led to action. But, making allowance for those differences of opinion which may fairly and honourably arise among those who concur in general views, I maintain that the principles which can be traced through all our foreign transactions, as the guiding rule and directing spirit of our proceedings, are such as deserve approbation. I therefore fearlessly challenge the verdict which this House, as representing a political, a commercial, a constitutional country, is to give on the question now brought before it; whether the principles on which the foreign policy of Her Majesty's Government has been conducted, and the sense of duty which has led us to think ourselves bound to afford protection to our fellow subjects abroad, are proper and fitting guides for those who are charged with the Government of England; and whether, as the Roman, in days of old, held himself free from indignity, when he could say *Civis Romanus sum*; so also a British subject, in whatever land he may be, shall feel confident that the watchful eye and the strong arm of England, will protect him against injustice and wrong.

37
The Victoria and Albert Museum (1852)

The word "museum," derived from the Greek *mouseion,* the "seat of the Muses," originally referred to a place of contemplation, much like a modern university. Museums remain places of study, and the collections housed in increasingly grand buildings are documents reflecting important historical trends. Britain played a leading role in the development of modern museums, one of the oldest being the Ashmolean in Oxford (1683). In 1753, Parliament founded the British Museum "not only for the inspection and entertainment of the learned and the curious, but for the general use and benefit of the public." In the nineteenth century, not only "national" but municipal and topical museums proliferated. Frequently they were designed not to amuse the populace but to promote economic growth and scientific and technical progress. This environment produced the Victoria and Albert Museum, arguably the most "British" of all collections.

Founded in 1852 as the Museum of Manufactures, the Victoria and Albert stressed decorative design and aimed at helping British artisans understand "the arts and crafts of past ages." The original collection, housed in Marlborough House, had been displayed at the Crystal Palace Exhibition in Hyde Park in 1851. The library, today containing more than 700,000 items on the applied arts, dates from 1837, when it was founded by the Board of Trade as a part of the Government School of Design. Growing rapidly in the late nineteenth century, the museum was in 1899 renamed by Queen Victoria in memory of her husband. The modern building housing the collection (Plate A) was opened in South Kensington in 1909 by Edward VII. The V&A remains in the same location, although five branch museums have been added.

Although the Victoria and Albert contains artifacts from throughout the world, it increasingly emphasized the development of British decorative arts. The prize of the Furniture and Interior Design Department is undoubtedly the Great Bed of Ware (Plate B), which is mentioned in Shakespeare's play *Twelfth Night* and dates from about 1590. The Ceramics and Glass Department boasts a fine collection of early Wedgwood jasperware, including a copy of the Portland Vase (Plate C), the original of which is in the British Museum. Other departments are of even greater interest to the student of material culture who seeks a greater understanding of the past through a study of everyday possessions. These "social archeologists" are drawn to the Dress Collection, which traces costume design from the Stuart era to the present (Plate D), to such games as "Snakes and Ladders" (Plate E), which reflected society's expectations for children, and to the dollhouse (Plate F), complete with the knickknacks so associated with the Victorian and Edwardian middle classes who made the V&A their museum.

PLATE A
The Victoria and Albert Museum (With permission of Victoria and Albert Museum).

PLATE B
The Great Bed of Ware (With permission of Victoria and Albert Museum).

PLATE C
Wedgwood copy of the Portland Vase (With permission of Victoria and Albert Museum).

PLATE D
The Costume Court (With permission of Victoria and Albert Museum).

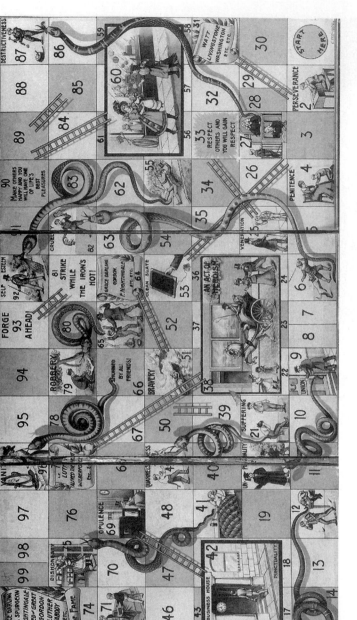

PLATE E
Snakes and Ladders (With permission of Victoria and Albert Museum).

PLATE F
Victorian Doll House (With permission of Victoria and Albert Museum).

38

William Howard Russell, Dispatches to *The Times* (1854). The Charge of the Light Brigade

Britain's involvement in the Crimean War (1854–1856), to check Russian expansion against the Turks and potentially against India, proved an embarrassment. Many viewed it as unnecessary, the product of a series of unforgivable diplomatic blunders. Furthermore, the war revealed serious defects in the British war machine, especially in supply and medical facilities. Britain suffered 21,000 noncombat deaths. The army was also poorly led, resulting in such glorious disasters as the charge of the Light Brigade described below. The commander-in-chief, Lord Raglan, had lost an arm at Waterloo (1815), and he had seen no combat since. The best that could be said for Lord Cardigan and Lord Lucan, who commanded the cavalry, was that they were gentlemen, both having purchased their commissions and never having been in battle. Cardigan, perhaps the most despised officer in the army, avoided the hardships of war by sleeping on his private yacht on the Black Sea.

The Crimean War was the first campaign fully covered by newspaper reporters, the most famous being William Howard Russell (1820–1907) of *The Times.* Russell's lively reports to *The Times* stirred in the English an admiration for the courage of the suffering British troops, the men of the Light Brigade and "the thin red line," as he described the infantry at Balaclava. His revelations of gross inefficiency in the army also produced outrage and contributed to the fall of the weak Aberdeen government in 1855 and, later, to the reform of the civil service and the army. Russell subsequently covered the Indian Mutiny (1857), the American Civil War (1861–1865), Bismarck's wars (1866–1871), and the British invasion of Egypt (1882). His career, reflecting a more literate populace eager for news and vicarious excitement, was a model for such later war correspondents as H. M. Stanley, made famous by his expedition to Africa to find David Livingstone, and Winston Churchill.

Source: W. H. Russell, *The War: From the Landing at Gallipoli to the Death of Lord Raglan,* London: George Routledge & Co., 1855, pp. 230–232.

And now occurred the melancholy catastrophe which fills us all with sorrow. It appears that the Quartermaster-General, Brigadier Airey, thinking that the Light Cavalry had not gone far enough in front when the enemy's horse had fled, gave an order in writing to Captain Nolan, 15th Hussars, to take to Lord Lucan, directing his Lordship "to advance" his cavalry nearer to the enemy. A braver soldier than Captain Nolan the army did not possess. . . .

Properly led, the British Hussar and Dragoon could in his mind break square, take batteries, ride over columns of infantry, and pierce any other cavalry in the world as if they were made of straw. He thought they had not had the opportunity of doing all that was in their power, and that they had missed even such chances as they had offered to them,— that, in fact, they were in some measure disgraced. A matchless horseman and a first-rate swordsman, he held in contempt, I am afraid, even grape and canister. He rode off with his orders to Lord Lucan. . . .

When Lord Lucan received the order from Captain Nolan, and had read it, he asked, we are told, "Where are we to advance to?" Captain Nolan pointed with his finger to the line of the Russians, and said, "There are the enemy, and there are the guns, sir, before them; it is your duty to take them," or words to that effect, according to the statements made since his death. Lord Lucan, with reluctance, gave the order to Lord Cardigan to advance upon the guns, conceiving that his orders compelled him to do so. The noble Earl, though he did not shrink, also saw the fearful odds against him. . . . It is a maxim of war, that "cavalry never act without a support," that "infantry should be close at hand when cavalry carry guns, as the effect is only instantaneous," and that it is necessary to have on the flank of a line of cavalry some squadrons in column, the attack on the flank being most dangerous. The only support our light cavalry had was the reserve of heavy cavalry at a great distance behind them, the infantry and guns being far in the rear. There were no squadrons in column at all, and there was a plain to charge over, before the enemy's guns were reached, of a mile and a half in length.

At ten minutes past eleven, our Light Cavalry brigade advanced. The whole brigade scarcely made one effective regiment, according to the numbers of continental armies; and yet it was more than we could spare. As they rushed towards the front, the Russians opened on them from the guns in the redoubt on the right, with volleys of musketry and rifles. They swept proudly past, glittering in the morning sun in all the pride and splendour of war. We could scarcely believe the evidence of our senses! Surely that handful of men are not going to charge an army in position? Alas! it was but too true—their desperate valour knew no bounds, and far indeed was it removed from its so-called better part—discretion. They advanced in two lines, quickening their pace as they closed towards the enemy. A more fearful spectacle was never witnessed than by those who, without the power to aid, beheld their heroic countrymen rushing to the arms of death. At the distance of 1200 yards the whole line of the enemy belched forth, from thirty iron mouths, a flood of smoke and flame, through which hissed the deadly balls. Their flight was marked by instant gaps in our ranks, by dead men and horses, by steeds flying wounded or riderless across the plain. The first line is broken, it is joined by the second, they never halt or check their speed an instant; with diminished ranks, thinned by those thirty guns, which the Russians had laid with the most deadly accuracy, with a halo of flashing steel above their heads, and with a cheer which was many a noble fellow's death-cry, they flew into the smoke of the batteries, but ere they were lost from view the plain was strewn with their bodies and with the carcasses of horses. They were exposed to an oblique fire from the batteries on the hills on both sides, as well as to a direct fire of musketry. Through the clouds of smoke we could see their sabres flashing as they rode up to the guns and dashed between them, cutting down the gunners as they stood. We saw them riding through the guns, as I have said; to our delight we saw them returning, after breaking through a column of Russian infantry, and scattering them like chaff, when the flank of fire of the battery on the hill swept them down, scattered and broken as they were. Wounded men and dismounted troopers flying towards us told the sad tale—demi-gods could not have done what we had failed to do. At the very moment when they were about to retreat, an enormous mass of Lancers was hurled on their flank. Colonel Shewell, of the 8th Hussars, saw the danger, and rode his few men straight at them, cutting his way through with fearful loss. The other regiments turned and engaged in a desperate encounter. With courage too great almost for credence, they were breaking their way through the columns which enveloped them, when there took place an act of atrocity without parallel in the modern warfare of civilized nations. The Russian gunners, when the storm of cavalry passed, returned to their guns. They saw their own cavalry mingled with the troopers who had just ridden over them, and, to the eternal disgrace of the Russian name, the miscreants poured a murderous volley of grape and canister on the mass of struggling men and horses, mingling friend and foe in one common ruin. It was as much as our Heavy Cavalry brigade could do to cover the retreat of the miserable remnants of that band of heroes as they returned to the place they had so lately quitted in all the pride of life. At thirty-five minutes past eleven not a British soldier, except the dead and dying, was left in front of these bloody Muscovite guns.

39

Anthony Trollope, *The Three Clerks* (1858). The Unreformed Civil Service

Anthony Trollope (1815–1882) had two careers. He was a civil servant, a prominent postal official, and also a popular novelist. His novels, the most famous describing life in the imaginary provincial town of Barchester, dealt primarily with the middle class. He emphasized character development and atmosphere rather than action or plot and, partially for that reason, his novels were seen by many later critics as "Victorian," and hence respectable to the point of dullness. When Trollope died in 1882, *The Times* observed that, "It would be rash to prophesy that his work will long be read; most of it lacks some of the qualifications which that stern official who draws up the passports for the Land of Matters Unforgot insists upon." In the short run it was an accurate prediction. The poignancy of Charles Dickens's descriptions of the urban poor and the urbanity of William Makepeace Thackeray's portrayals of the aristocracy never lost their appeal, but Trollope had to await the twentieth century's rediscovery of the charm and complexity of Victorian England.

By studying the popular literature of any period, the historian can learn much about the attitudes and interests of the general public. In the case of Trollope, Dickens, and Thackeray, who often satirized or directly attacked the conditions they observed, the historian can gain insight into the problems facing Victorian England. In the selection from *The Three Clerks* (1858), Trollope ridicules in a gentle but effective manner the patronage system of recruitment for the civil service. A decade later, William Ewart Gladstone was to correct this problem by introducing open competition.

The London world, visitors as well as residents, are well acquainted also with Somerset House; and it is moreover tolerably well known that Somerset House is a nest of public offices, which are held to be of less fashionable repute than those situated in the neighbourhood of Downing Street, but are not so decidedly plebeian as the Custom House, Excise, and Post Office.

Source: Anthony Trollope, *The Three Clerks,* introduction by W. Teignmouth Shore, London: Oxford University Press, 1907, pp. 10, 12–15. Reprinted by permission of Oxford University Press.

But there is one branch of the Civil Service located in Somerset House, which has little else to redeem it from the lowest depths of official vulgarity than the ambiguous respectability of its material position. This is the office of the Commissioners of Internal Navigation. The duties to be performed have reference to the preservation of canal banks, the tolls to be levied at locks, and disputes with the Admiralty as to points connected with tidal rivers. The rooms are dull and dark, and saturated with the fog which rises from the river, and their only ornament is here and there some dusty model of an improved barge. . . .

Charles Tudor, the third of the three clerks alluded to in our title-page, is the son of a clergyman, who has a moderate living on the Welsh border, in Shropshire. Had he known to what sort of work he was sending his son, he might probably have hesitated before he accepted for him a situation in the Internal Navigation Office. He was, however, too happy in getting it to make inquiries as to its nature. We none of us like to look a gift-horse in the mouth. Old Mr. Tudor knew that a clerkship in the Civil Service meant, or should mean, a respectable maintenance for life, and having many young Tudors to maintain himself, he was only too glad to find one of them provided for.

Charley Tudor was some few years younger than his cousin Alaric when he came up to town, and Alaric had at that time some three or four years' experience of London life. The examination at the Internal Navigation was certainly not to be so much dreaded as that at the Weights and Measures; but still there was an examination; and Charley, who had not been the most diligent of schoolboys, approached it with great dread after a preparatory evening passed with the assistance of his cousin and Mr. Norman.

Exactly at ten in the morning he walked into the lobby of his future workshop, and found no one yet there but two aged seedy messengers. He was shown into a waiting-room, and there he remained for a couple of hours, during which every clerk in the establishment came to have a look at him. At last he was ushered into the Secretary's room.

"Ah!" said the Secretary, "your name is Tudor, isn't it?" Charley confessed to the fact. . . .

"And you wish to serve the Queen?" said the Secretary.

Charley, not quite knowing whether this was a joke or not, said that he did. . . .

"The Internal Navigation requires great steadiness, good natural abilities, considerable education, and—and—and no end of application. Come, Mr. Tudor, let us see what you can do." And so saying, Mr. Oldeschole, the Secretary, motioned him to sit down at an office table opposite to himself.

Charley did as he was bid, and took from the hands of his future master an old, much-worn quill pen, with which the great man had been signing minutes.

"Now," said the great man, "just copy the few first sentences of that leading article—either one will do," and he pushed over to him a huge newspaper.

To tell the truth, Charley did not know what a leading article was, and so he sat abashed, staring at the paper.

"Why don't you write?" asked the Secretary.

"Where shall I begin, sir!" stammered poor Charley, looking piteously into the examiner's face.

"God bless my soul! there; either of those leading articles," and leaning over the table, the Secretary pointed to a particular spot.

Hereupon Charley began his task in a large, ugly, round hand, neither that of a man nor of a boy, and set himself to copy the contents of the paper. "The name of Pacifico stinks in the nostril of the British public. It is well known to all the world how sincerely we admire the versitility of Lord Palmerston's genius; how cordially we simpathize with his patriotic energies. But the admiration which even a Palmerston inspires must have a bound, and our simpathy may be called on too far. When we find ourselves asked to pay——." By this time Charles had half covered the half-sheet of foolscap which had been put before him, and here at the word "pay" he unfortunately suffered a large blot of ink to fall on the paper.

"That won't do, Mr. Tudor, that won't do—come, let us look," and stretching over again, the Secretary took up the copy.

"Oh dear! oh dear! this is very bad; versatility with an 'i!'—sympathy with an 'i!' sympathize with an 'i!' Why, Mr. Tudor, you must be very fond of 'i's' down in Shropshire."

Charley looked sheepish, but of course said nothing.

"And I never saw a viler hand in my life. Oh dear, oh dear, I must send you back to Sir Gilbert. Look here, Snape, this will never do—never do for the Internal Navigation, will it?"

Snape, the attendant senior clerk said, as indeed he could not help saying, that the writing was very bad.

"I never saw worse in my life," said the Secretary. "And now, Mr. Tudor, what do you know of arithmetic?"

Charley said that he thought he knew arithmetic pretty well;—"at least some of it," he modestly added.

"Some of it!" said the Secretary, slightly laughing. "Well, I'll tell you what—this won't do at all;" and he took the unfortunate manuscript between his thumb and forefinger. "You had better go home and endeavour to write something a little better than this. Mind, if it is not very much better it won't do. And look here; take care that you do it yourself. If you bring me the writing of any one else, I shall be sure to detect you. I have not any more time now; as to arithmetic, we'll examine you in 'some of it' to-morrow.". . .

He worked thus for an hour before dinner, and then for three hours in the evening, and produced a very legible copy of half a chapter of the "Decline and Fall."

"I didn't think they examined at all at the Navigation," said Norman.

"Well, I believe it's quite a new thing," said Alaric Tudor. "The schoolmaster must be abroad with a vengeance, if he got as far as that."

And then they carefully examined Charley's work, crossed his t's, dotted his i's, saw that his spelling was right, and went to bed.

Again, punctually at ten o'clock, Charley presented himself at the Internal Navigation; and again saw the two seedy old messengers warming themselves at the lobby fire. On this occasion he was kept three hours in the waiting-room, and some of the younger clerks ventured to come and speak to him. At length Mr. Snape appeared, and desired the acolyte to follow him. Charley, supposing that he was again going to the awful Secretary, did so with palpitating heart. But he was led in another direction into a large room, carrying his manuscript neatly rolled in his hand. Here Mr. Snape introduced him to five other occupants of the chamber; he, Mr. Snape himself, having a separate desk there, being, in official parlance, the head of the room. Charley was told to take a seat at a desk, and did so, still thinking that the dread hour of his examination was soon to come. His examination, however, was begun and over. No one ever asked for his calligraphic manuscript, and as to his arithmetic, it may be presumed that his assurance that he knew "some of it," was deemed to be adequate evidence of sufficient capacity. And in this manner, Charley Tudor became one of the Infernal Navvies.

40
Samuel Smiles, *Self Help* (1859)

Samuel Smiles (1812–1904) is best remembered today as the author of *Self Help,* one of the most influential and popular books of the Victorian period. *Self Help,* together with *Character* (1871), *Thrift* (1875), *Duty* (1880), and *Life and Labour* (1887), made Smiles the apostle of individual effort as the key to personal and national progress, a position similar to that of Horatio Alger in the United States.

Smiles's popularity resulted from a number of factors. His message of self-reliance was congenial to the laissez-faire atmosphere of the mid-nineteenth century. His forceful, pithy style attracted many readers. Finally, his examples of success, courage, and perseverance—such as the story of the conduct of the men aboard the sinking *Birkenhead*—were often drawn from English history and thus appealed to the national pride of his audience.

Smiles has never lacked critics. As early as the 1880s socialists condemned him as an apologist for middle-class values and an obstacle to meaningful reform. Fairness demands, however, a recognition of Smiles's interest in and sympathy with the lower classes. As a young man he edited a radical newspaper and supported some of the ideas of Chartism. Although by the time he wrote *Self Help* he had grown doubtful of the ability of government to legislate solutions to social problems, he was never willing to equate personal success with wealth. Wealth could easily be a bar to good character—the true index of success, well within the reach of every man.

Self Help with Illustrations of Conduct and Perseverance was originally published in 1859. It has since been reprinted numerous times and translated into several languages.

"Heaven helps those who help themselves" is a well-tried maxim, embodying in a small compass the results of vast human experience. The spirit of self-help is the root of all genuine growth in the individual; and, exhibited in the lives of many, it constitutes the true source of national vigour and strength. Help from

Source: Samuel Smiles, *Self Help with Illustrations of Conduct and Perseverance,* introduction by Asa Briggs, London: John Murray, 1958, pp. 35–36, 38, 57, 298–299, 360, 377–379. Reprinted by the permission of John Murray (Publishers) Ltd.

without is often enfeebling in its effects, but help from within invariably invigo-rates. Whatever is done *for* men or classes, to a certain extent takes away the stimulus and necessity of doing for themselves; and where men are subjected to over-guidance and over-government, the inevitable tendency is to render them comparatively helpless. . . .

The Government of a nation itself is usually found to be but the reflex of the individuals composing it. The Government that is ahead of the people will in-evitably be dragged down to their level, as the Government that is behind them will in the long run be dragged up. In the order of nature, the collective character of a nation will as surely find its befitting results in its law and government, as water finds its own level. The noble people will be nobly ruled, and the ignorant and corrupt ignobly. Indeed, all experience serves to prove that the worth and strength of a State depend far less upon the form of its institutions than upon the character of its men. For the nation is only an aggregate of individual conditions, and civilization itself is but a question of the personal improvement of the men, women, and children of whom society is composed.

National progress is the sum of individual industry, energy, and uprightness, as national decay is of individual idleness, selfishness and vice. What we are ac-customed to decry as great social evils, will, for the most part, be found to be but the outgrowth of man's own perverted life; and though we may endeavour to cut them down and extirpate them by means of Law, they will only spring up again with fresh luxuriance in some other form, unless the condition of personal life and character are radically improved. If this view be correct, then it follows that the highest patriotism and philanthropy consist, not so much in altering laws and modifying institutions, as in helping and stimulating men to elevate and improve themselves by their own free and independent individual action. . . .

The spirit of self-help, as exhibited in the energetic action of individuals, has in all times been a marked feature in the English character, and furnishes the true measure of our power as a nation. . . .

In fine, human character is moulded by a thousand subtle influences; by ex-ample and precept; by life and literature; by friends and neighbours; by the world we live in as well as by the spirits of our forefathers, whose legacy of good words and deeds we inherit. But great, unquestionably, though these influ-ences are acknowledged to be, it is nevertheless equally clear that men must nec-essarily be the active agents of their own well-being and well-doing; and that, however much the wise and the good may owe to others, they themselves must in the very nature of things be their own best helpers. . . .

Worldly success, measured by the accumulation of money, is no doubt a very dazzling thing; and all men are naturally more or less the admirers of worldly success. But though men of preserving, sharp, dexterous, and unscrupulous habits, ever on the watch to push opportunities, may and do "get on" in the world, yet it is quite possible that they may not possess the slightest elevation of character, nor a particle of real goodness. He who recognizes no higher logic than that of the shilling, may become a very rich man, and yet remain all the while an exceedingly poor creature. For riches are no proof whatever of moral worth; and their glitter often serves only to draw attention to the worthlessness of their possessor, as the light of the glow-worm reveals the grub. . . .

Riches are oftener an impediment than a stimulus to action; and in many cases they are quite as much a misfortune as a blessing. The youth who inherits wealth is apt to have life made too easy for him, and he soon grows sated with it, because he has nothing left to desire. Having no special object to struggle for, he finds time hang heavy on his hands; he remains morally and spiritually asleep; and his position in society is often no higher than that of a polypus over which the tide floats. . , ,

Character is human nature in its best form. It is moral order embodied in the individual. Men of character are not only the conscience of society, but in every well-governed State they are its best motive power; for it is moral qualities in the main which rule the world. . . .

Notwithstanding the wail which we occasionally hear for the chivalry that is gone, our own age has witnessed deeds of bravery and gentleness—of heroic self-denial and manly tenderness—which are unsurpassed in history. The events of the last few years have shown that our countrymen are as yet an undegenerate race. . . .

The wreck of the *Birkenhead* off the coast of Africa on February 27th, 1852, affords another memorable illustration of the chivalrous spirit of common men acting in this nineteenth century, of which any age might be proud. The vessel was steaming along the African coast with 472 men and 166 women and children on board. The men belonged to several regiments then serving at the Cape, and consisted principally of recruits who had been only a short time in the service. At two o'clock in the morning, while all were asleep below, the ship struck with violence upon a hidden rock, which penetrated her bottom; and it was at once felt that she must go down. The roll of the drums called the soldiers to arms on the upper deck, and the men mustered as if on parade. The word was passed to *save the women and children;* and the helpless creatures were brought from below, mostly undressed, and handed silently into the boats. When they had all left the ship's side, the commander of the vessel thoughtlessly called out, "All those that can swim, jump overboard and make for the boats." But Captain Wright, of the 91st Highlanders, said, "No! if you do that, *the boats with the women must be swamped";* and the brave men stood motionless. There was no boat remaining, and no hope of safety; but not a heart quailed; no one flinched from his duty in that trying moment. "There was not a murmur nor a cry amongst them," said Captain Wright, a survivor, "until the vessel made her final plunge." Down went the ship, and down went the heroic band, firing a *feu de joie* as they sank beneath the waves. Glory and honour to the gentle and the brave. The examples of such men can never die, but, like their memories, are immortal.

41

Charles Darwin, *On the Origin of Species* (1859). The Theory of Evolution

Charles Darwin (1809–1882), intending first to be a physician and then a clergyman, found his vocation when he was invited to become the naturalist aboard the explorer ship, H.M.S. *Beagle*. From 1830 to 1836, he collected and compared specimens found along the coast of South America and on the adjacent islands, particularly the Galápagos Islands. The variations in his specimens argued increasingly for some form of biological evolution. The mechanism by which evolution operated remained, however, a mystery. It was not until 1838 that his reading of Malthus's *Essay on Population* gave him the idea of the "struggle for existence." "It at once struck me," he wrote, "that under these circumstances favourable variations would tend to be preserved and unfavourable ones to be destroyed. The result would be the formation of a new species. Here then I had at last got a theory by which to work." In 1859, after twenty years of observation and study and after learning that another naturalist, Alfred Russell Walace, had arrived at an identical conclusion, Darwin published *On the Origin of Species by Means of Natural Selection or the Preservation of Favoured Races in the Struggle for Life.*

His concluding paragraphs summarize his theory that "natural selection" is a result of the "struggle for life," his confidence that things "will tend to progress toward perfection," and his belief that his theory "accords better with what we know of the laws impressed on matter by the Creator." Just as Sir Isaac Newton (1642–1727) had taken the mystery out of the mechanical operation of the universe by formulating the universal laws of gravity, so Darwin explained how the world, in its present complexity, had evolved by natural means from simple beginnings.

Darwin's book was instantly famous and controversial, the first edition selling out the first day. T. H. Huxley (1825–1895), for his ardent support nicknamed "Darwin's Bulldog," on reading the *Origin of Species* said of himself, "How extremely stupid not to

Source: Charles Darwin, *On the Origin of Species: A Facsimile of the First Edition*, introduction by Ernst Mayr, New York: Atheneum, 1967, pp. 488–490. Reprinted by permission of Harvard University Press.

have thought of that." Despite stubborn pockets of resistance, chiefly on religious grounds, some of which still exist, Darwin's theory of evolution by natural selection was an idea whose time had come. Not only did it gain acceptance in scientific circles but, because of its agreement with the ideas of laissez-faire and progress, it accorded well with popular beliefs in many fields. Rugged individualism and competition between individuals and between nations seemed, by reference to the idea of the "survival of the fittest," to be inevitable and necessary. With questionable justice to Darwin, these were dramatized by the term "Social Darwinism." Darwin's *Origin of Species* has been one of the most influential books of the nineteenth and twentieth centuries.

Authors of the highest eminence seem to be fully satisfied with the view that each species has been independently created. To my mind it accords better with what we know of the laws impressed on matter by the Creator, that the production and extinction of the past and present inhabitants of the world should have been due to secondary causes, like those determining the birth and death of the individual. When I view all beings not as special creations, but as the lineal descendants of some few beings which lived long before the first bed of the Silurian system was deposited, they seem to me to become ennobled. Judging from the past, we may safely infer that not one living species will transmit its unaltered likeness to a distant futurity. And of the species now living very few will transmit progeny of any kind to a far distant futurity; for the manner in which all organic beings are grouped, shows that the greater number of species of each genus, and all the species of many genera, have left no descendants, but have become utterly extinct. We can so far take a prophetic glance into futurity as to foretell that it will be the common and widely-spread species, belonging to the larger and dominant groups, which will ultimately prevail and procreate new and dominant species. As all the living forms of life are the lineal descendants of those which lived long before the Silurian epoch, we may feel certain that the ordinary succession by generation has never once been broken, and that no cataclysm has desolated the whole world. Hence we may look with some confidence to a secure future of equally inappreciable length. And as natural selection works solely by and for the good of each being, all corporeal and mental endowments will tend to progress towards perfection.

It is interesting to contemplate an entangled bank, clothed with many plants of many kinds, with birds singing on the bushes, with various insects flitting about, and with worms crawling through the damp earth, and to reflect that these elaborately constructed forms, so different from each other, and dependent on each other in so complex a manner, have all been produced by laws acting around us. These laws, taken in the largest sense, being Growth with

Reproduction; Inheritance which is almost implied by reproduction; Variability from the indirect and direct action of the external conditions of life, and from use and disuse; a Ratio of Increase so high as to lead to a Struggle for Life, and as a consequence to Natural Selection, entailing Divergence of Character and the Extinction of less-improved forms. Thus, from the war of nature, from famine and death, the most exalted object which we are capable of conceiving, namely, the production of the higher animals, directly follows. There is grandeur in this view of life, with its several powers, having been originally breathed into a few forms or into one; and that, whilst this planet has gone cycling on according to the fixed law of gravity, from so simple a beginning endless forms most beautiful and most wonderful have been, and are being, evolved.

42
John Henry Cardinal Newman, *Apologia Pro Vita Sua* (1864). The Oxford Movement

The Oxford Movement began in 1833 as a reaction to the liberal and Evangelical tendencies of England and the Anglican church. In a series of *Tracts for the Times* (1834–1841), such men as John Henry Newman (1801–1890) and E. B. Pusey (1800–1882) emphasized the historical position of the church as a divine institution, not just a congregation of individual believers. They urged a return to an older tradition of beliefs and ceremonies. Low-church Evangelicals, who saw these ideas as perilously close to Roman Catholicism, had their worst fears realized in 1841, when Newman, the most attractive and talented of the Oxford group, argued in *Tract XC* that the Thirty-Nine Articles of the Church of England were compatible with Roman Catholicism. His misunderstood objective was to reassure those who were leaning toward Rome that they might safely remain Anglican. In the storm of public controversy that ensued, the *Tracts* were discontinued, and Newman left Oxford under a cloud of suspicion. In 1845, he officially joined, and became a priest in, the Roman Catholic church.

Source: John Henry Cardinal Newman, *Apologia Pro Vita Sua: Being a History of His Religious Opinions,* edited by Martin J. Svaglic, pp. 39–40, 54–55, 57, 113, 115, 181, 213. ©1967 Oxford University Press. By permission of the Clarendon Press.

In 1864, after two decades of personal frustration and practical exile, Newman was provoked to reply to an offhand remark impugning the honesty of the Roman church and of himself personally. *Apologia Pro Vita Sua: Being a History of His Religious Opinions* recounts his attempt to understand his own faith and shows how he was led to break with the Anglican church and join that of Rome. The book was immediately recognized as a literary masterpiece and a spiritual autobiography of the first magnitude. It brought a better and more sympathetic understanding not only of Newman but of Catholics in general. Catholics were finally readmitted to Oxford in 1871, and six years later Newman was appointed a fellow of Trinity College. After an absence of more than three decades he was restored to his beloved university.

The Oxford Movement became, despite Newman's defection, a permanent tendency to restore to the Anglican church the richness of its Catholic heritage. Newman's humanism, so alien to the narrow and beleaguered Catholicism of Pope Pius IX (1846–1878), was more acceptable to Leo XIII (1878–1903), who made Newman a cardinal in 1879, and Newman has been vindicated in the twentieth century by the papacy of John XXIII (1958–1963) and the Second Vatican Council (1962–1965). Newman now appears as the outstanding English churchman of the nineteenth century, noteworthy for his individual attractiveness and for his impact on both of the Christian communions to which he gave his allegiance.

Great events were happening at home and abroad, which brought out into form and passionate expression the various beliefs which had so gradually been winning their way into my mind. Shortly before, there had been a Revolution in France; the Bourbons had been dismissed: and I held that it was unchristian for nations to cast off their governors, and, much more, sovereigns who had the divine right of inheritance. Again, the great Reform Agitation was going on around me as I wrote. The Whigs had come into power; Lord Grey had told the Bishops to set their house in order, and some of the Prelates had been insulted and threatened in the streets of London. The vital question was, how were we to keep the Church from being liberalized? . . . I felt affection for my own Church, but not tenderness; I felt dismay at her prospects, anger and scorn at her do-nothing perplexity. I thought that if Liberalism once got a footing within her, it was sure of the victory in the event. I saw that Reformation principles were powerless to rescue her. As to leaving her, the thought never crossed my imagination; still I ever kept before me that there was something greater than the Established Church, and that that was the Church Catholic and Apostolic, set up from the beginning, of which she was but the local presence and the organ. She was nothing, unless she was this. She must be dealt with strongly, or she would be lost. There was need of a second reformation. . . .

I have spoken of my firm confidence in my position; and now let me state more definitely what the position was which I took up, and the propositions about which I was so confident. These were three:—

1. First was the principle of dogma: my battle was with liberalism; by liberalism I mean the anti-dogmatic principle and its developments. This was the first point on which I was certain. . . . Under this first head I have the satisfaction of feeling that I have nothing to retract, and nothing to repent of. The main principle of the movement is as dear to me now, as it ever was. I have changed in many things: in this I have not. From the age of fifteen, dogma has been the fundamental principle of my religion: I know no other religion; I cannot enter into the idea of any other sort of religion; religion, as a mere sentiment, is to me a dream and a mockery. As well can there be filial love without the fact of a father, as devotion without the fact of a Supreme Being. What I held in 1816, I held in 1833, and I hold in 1864. Please God, I shall hold it to the end. . . .

2. Secondly, I was confident in the truth of a certain definite religious teaching, based upon this foundation of dogma; viz. that there was a visible Church, with sacraments and rites which are the channels of invisible grace. I thought that this was the doctrine of Scripture, of the early Church, and of the Anglican Church. Here again, I have not changed in opinion; I am as certain now on this point as I was in 1833, and have never ceased to be certain. . . .

3. But now, as to the third point on which I stood in 1833, and which I have utterly renounced and trampled upon since,—my then view of the Church of Rome;—I will speak about it as exactly as I can. When I was young, as I have said already, and after I was grown up, I thought the Pope to be Antichrist. . . . From my boyhood and in 1824 I considered, after Protestant authorities, that St. Gregory I. about A.D. 600 was the first Pope that was Antichrist, though, in spite of this, he was also a great and holy man; but in 1832–3 I thought the Church of Rome was bound up with the cause of Antichrist by the Council of Trent. When it was that in my deliberate judgment I gave up the notion altogether in any shape, that some special reproach was attached to her name, I cannot tell; but I had a shrinking from renouncing it, even when my reason so ordered me, from a sort of conscience or prejudice, I think up to 1843. . . .

I had no longer a distinctive plea for Anglicanism. . . . I had, most painfully, to fall back upon my three original points of belief, which I have spoken so much of in a former passage,—the principle of dogma, the sacramental system, and anti-Romanism. Of these three, the first two were better secured in Rome than in the Anglican Church. The Apostolic Succession, the two prominent sacraments, and the primitive Creeds, belonged, indeed, to the latter; but there had been and was far less strictness on matters of dogma and ritual in the Anglican system than in the Roman: in consequence, my main argument for the

Anglican claims lay in the positive and special charges, which I could bring against Rome. I had no positive Anglican theory. . . .

I underwent a great change of opinion. I saw that, from the nature of the case, the true Vicar of Christ must ever to the world seem like Antichrist, and be stigmatized as such, because a resemblance must ever exist between an original and a forgery; and thus the fact of such a calumny was almost one of the notes of the Church. . . .

I have nothing more to say on the subject of the change in my religious opinions. On the one hand I came gradually to see that the Anglican Church was formally in the wrong, on the other that the Church of Rome was formally in the right; then, that no valid reasons could be assigned for continuing in the Anglican, and again that no valid objections could be taken to joining the Roman. . . .

I took leave of my first College, Trinity, which was so dear to me, and which held on its foundation so many who had been kind to me both when I was a boy, and all through my Oxford life. Trinity had never been unkind to me. There used to be much snap-dragon growing on the walls opposite my freshman's rooms there, and I had for years taken it as the emblem of my own perpetual residence even unto death in my University.

On the morning of the 23rd I left the Observatory. I have never seen Oxford since, excepting its spires, as they are seen from the railway.

43

Harriet Martineau, "Middle-Class Education in England: Girls," *The Cornhill Magazine* (1864)

Harriet Martineau (1802–1876) was one of the few women to be included in the *Dictionary of National Biography* (1885–1901), a 22-volume tribute to famous Britons that remains an essential reference work. Such was Martineau's fame that she could not be ignored. Experiencing the personal frustrations typical of women born into the middle class, she ultimately rejected marriage, a restricting institution too often denying a woman the "larger opportunities of usefulness." Nevertheless, she used the title "Mrs." rather than "Miss" because of the greater respect it accorded. Finding fulfillment in writing, first to earn a living and then to advance her feminist ideas, she supported a variety of women's movements. These included reform of the divorce laws, women's suffrage, the protection of married women's property rights, and the elimination of the Contagious Disease Acts, which placed the blame for venereal disease on prostitutes.

Martineau was naturally drawn to the topic of middle-class female education, understanding clearly what modern writers define as "status incongruence." Girls were expected to marry, and their education was traditionally structured to that end. What, however, was to become of a woman who failed in the business of life. Because of her class, she could not easily seek work outside the home without losing status. Therefore, many middle-class women became governesses, and the first women's colleges—Queen's College, Cheltenham Ladies College, and Bedford College— founded between 1848 and 1853, trained ladies for this honorable profession. Such an education would not, however, provide employment for all middle-class women. What was the solution? In the selection below, Martineau argued for a reform of women's education.

The Cornhill Magazine was a natural outlet for her ideas. The Victorian periodical, usually a monthly, was a staple of the era. The genre included *The Edinburgh Review* (1802), *The Quarterly Review* (1824), *The Fortnightly Review* (1865), and *The Contem-*

Source: Harriet Martineau, "Middle-Class Education in England: Girls," *The Cornhill Magazine*, 10 (November 1864): 519, 551, 553–554, 560–561, 566–567.

porary Review (1866). Although varying in their interests and political emphases, all discussed serious issues. Leading novelists, economists, philanthropists, educators, and social reformers, both male and female, graced their pages. *The Cornhill Magazine,* which opened in 1860 with the serialization of Trollope's *Framley Parsonage* and Thackeray's *Lovel the Widower,* attained a circulation of over 100,000. It survived 115 years.

   If the education of middle-class Boys is a vague and cloudy subject to treat in writing, what is that of Girls? At first sight, the subject seems to be too chaotic to be examined on any principle or in any method at all; and perhaps the best purpose to be answered by any examination at all is that of exposing the confusion itself. In the Boys' case there is something like firm ground to stand on in the universal agreement that boys should be somehow educated, and in the old custom of making Latin and Greek the chief studies; but in the case of the Girls, there is no tradition, no common conviction, no established method, no imperative custom,—nothing beyond a supposition that girls must somehow learn to read and write, and to practise whatever accomplishment may be the fashion at the time. . . .
   The custom of giving girls a classical education three centuries ago, ought to have settled for ever the pretended doubt whether the female intellect is adequate to the profitable study of the classics; and, as the practice was by no means confined to the aristocracy, the results should have left no room to question the benefit of such studies. But the religious struggle of the seventeenth century disturbed the natural course of women's training, as it disturbed everything else; and a manifest decline of female intelligence and manners followed the abatement of Puritanism, and the enlargement of social liberty or licence. Our grandmothers did, however,learn something well. Their parents had not fallen into the modern temptation of being ashamed of their station in life, and anxious that their children should attain a higher. The daughters were prepared to be what their mothers had been before them; and the children therefore learned early and thoroughly what their mothers could teach them. . . .
   Their acquirements, such as they were, were obtained at home for the most part; and further, at the writing-school, the sewing-school, or the general day-school. Then followed the period of middle-class girls' boarding-schools. There was a great expansion and multiplication of these during the war which followed the French Revolution. . . . As the parents made war and monopoly profits, an evil emulation entered into too many of them to rise in gentility; and one of the first methods they took was to make sportsmen of their sons, and fine ladies of their daughters. Hence, . . . the mushroom "Ladies' Seminaries" which became a byword long ago,—a representative term for false pretension, vulgarity, and cant. The complaints of dismayed parents that their girls at eighteen could do no

one thing well, and pretended only to read a little French with difficulty, play badly on the piano, and ornament screens, are still fresh in our ears. . . .

There has certainly been some improvement since that time,—half a century ago; and the most striking part of the improvement has been within the last half, and especially the last quarter of those fifty years. This is an encouragement to look into the present state of things,—chaotic as it appears from the highest point of view. What, then, is the state of Girls' education now? . . .

Within half a century the girlhood of the upper middle class has gone through an experience of permanent historical importance. At the beginning of that time, it was assumed in ordinary practice, as in law and politics, that every woman is maintained by her father or her husband, or other male relative. . . . After the suspense and crash of 1825–6, there seemed to be nothing between them and despair. Their fathers or husbands ruined, their brothers thrown destitute on the world, what was to become of the hundreds of thousands of women who had always been told, and had always believed, that they would be taken care of as long as they lived? . . . The greater number, perhaps, could do nothing but accept charity in the form of dependence, with its carking cares and intolerable humiliations; but there was such a rush into governessing as was never seen before. . . . We need not explore the painful subject. It is enough to refer to what each of us can remember of what we knew or have heard of the astonishing ignorance of women who professed to teach; of the bad health, bad manners, bad tempers, and even the bad morals of reduced ladies, driven to obtain a maintenance in any way they could. . . .

It could not but be agreed, in the next place, that girls foredoomed to self-support (such was the view then) should be more or less qualified for some branch of industry. Teaching was as yet the only occupation, besides needlework, which seemed practicable; and the efforts of so many to qualify themselves, ever so little, for a life of teaching constituted a demand for some improvement in female education. At the time at which we are living, it is an indisputable fact that above two millions of the women of England are self-supporting workers: it is an admitted truth that while the customs of English society remain what they are, there must be tens of thousands of middle-class women dependent on their own industry: and it can hardly be doubtful, even to the most reluctant eyes, that the workers ought to be properly trained to the business of their lives. . . .

Let it be understood at once that in claiming for middle-class girls a substantial and liberal development and training of the mind, and, for those who desire it, a special preparation for the educational or other profession in life, nobody contemplates the use of any method which is not in accordance with national custom and English feelings. We should not like to see little girls in our streets parading in laurel crowns, and carrying gilt books,—their prizes of the year,—in their hands. The presence of mamma, or a servant, or elder sister would not give respectability to such a display in our eyes. We should not like to see our boarding-schools thrown open on examination days, for the public, or an invited crowd, to enter and see the pupils exhibit their attainments. The presence of a bishop or some other highly priestly personage, as in France, would not, in our view, neutralize the mischief. . . .

The two colleges in London, *Queen's College* in Harley Street, with its Preparatory School, and the *Ladies' College* in Bedford Square, were striking signs of the times in their institution, and are becoming more and more so in their success. They were sure to bring out all the weaknesses and vices of the popular mind in regard to female education, and to raise up a host of enemies, and treacherous or mischievous friends; and their gradual triumph over such opposition and embarrassment is a sufficient assurance that the cause is safe. If a full disclosure could be made of the experience of the conductors in regard to the applications and criticisms of parents and guardians, one wonders what proportion of the middle class would be astonished, and how many more would be astonished at their astonishment. One wonders whether these colleges have brought into notice all the fathers who grumble over paying five-pound notes for their daughters' education, while cheerfully spending hundreds a year for their boys, at Eton or Harrow. One wonders where the perplexity is when the father first tells his girls that he can give them no fortune whatever, because their brothers cost him so much, and then declares in their hearing that he can't see what women want, beyond what they might easily pick up at home. One wonders whether he ever considers what is to become of them if he dies untimely, leaving them without a maintenance, and without education wherewith to gain one. One wonders how much dread of the father operates on the mother when she slily and yet audaciously manoeuvres to get two girls into a course for the fees of one; or contrives to introduce the governess "just to sit by during the lessons," so that she may learn without pay, and save sending the younger girls at all. Things like these on the one hand, and, on the other, the honest eagerness of the young pupils themselves, and of grown women who enter as pupils, afford guidance and stimulus to all who witness them. So does the generous zeal of the professors. Those who desire a high order of instruction for girls, whether women and girls, or parents and friends, or patriots and philosophers, should persist in the demand; and the right answer will come. Not all the ignorance, the jealousy, the meanness, the prudery, or the profligate selfishness which is to be found from end to end of the middle class, can now reverse the destiny of the English girl, or retard that ennobling of the sex which is a natural consequence of its becoming wiser and more independent, while more accomplished, gracious, and companionable. The briars and brambles are cleared away from the women's avenue to the temple of knowledge. Now they have only to knock, and it will be opened to them.

44
Walter Bagehot, *The English Constitution* (1867).
England on the Eve of Democracy

Walter Bagehot (1826–1877) was a prosperous member of the middle class, a banker and businessman, and probably the foremost journalist of his day. In 1855, he became a joint editor of the *National Review* and, in 1860, the editor of *The Economist,* a position he held until his death. His most famous works include *Lombard Street* (1873), a pioneering study of central banking, and *The English Constitution* (1867), which first appeared as a series of articles in *Fortnightly Review* in 1865 and 1866.

Bagehot's book is the classic description of the nineteenth-century English constitution. Like Bentham, Bagehot detected the disparity between the reality of things and the fictions that people believed, but unlike the Utilitarians he saw the value of both. The "dignified parts of government" gave it "its motive power." Primary among these were the monarchy, the House of Lords, and the old belief in a separation of powers between the executive and the legislature. The "efficient parts" enabled the government to "employ that power." Most important was the cabinet, the "connecting link" that joined the dignified and efficient parts together and gave the British government its remarkable strength. What Bagehot describes below is the system of responsible government that had evolved during the eighteenth century and had been amplified by the Great Reform Bill in 1832. Essential to the working of the constitution was the deferential character of the mass of the people, their willingness to allow their betters to rule on their behalf.

It is noteworthy that Bagehot wrote on the eve of the second reform bill, the Representation of the People Act of 1867, by which Benjamin Disraeli joyfully "dished the Whigs." With help from the radicals, Disraeli gave the British working classes a share of the electorate and took the first step, a "leap in the dark," toward Britain's becoming a democracy. Bagehot, a middle-class liberal, not a democrat, wrote in his book's second edition in 1872 a long introduction explaining the dangers of political leaders bidding

Source: Walter Bagehot, *The English Constitution,* Garden City, N. Y.: Dolphin Books, Doubleday & Company, Inc., n.d., pp. 63–64, 68–73.

against each other for popular support. He was certainly correct in seeing the passing of the British constitution as he knew it. With the rise of highly structured and disciplined political parties, made necessary by a democratic electorate, and with the prime minister wielding more power, the House of Commons and the cabinet have moved some distance in joining the monarch and the House of Lords as dignified, rather than efficient, parts of the government.

No one can approach to an understanding of the English institutions, or of others which, being the growth of many centuries, exercise a wide sway over mixed populations, unless he divide them into two classes. In such constitutions there are two parts (not indeed separable with microscopic accuracy, for the genius of great affairs abhors nicety of division): first, those which excite and preserve the reverence of the population—the *dignified* parts, if I may so call them; and next, the *efficient* parts—those by which it, in fact, works and rules. There are two great objects which every constitution must attain to be successful, which every old and celebrated one must have wonderfully achieved: every constitution must first *gain* authority, and then *use* authority; it must first win the loyalty and confidence of mankind, and then employ that homage in the work of government. . . .

The dignified parts of government are those which bring it force—which attract its motive power. The efficient parts only employ that power. . . .

The brief description of the characteristic merit of the English Constitution is, that its dignified parts are very complicated and somewhat imposing, very old and rather venerable; while its efficient part, at least when in great and critical action, is decidedly simple and rather modern. We have made, or rather stumbled on, a constitution which—though full of every species of incidental defect, though of the worst *workmanship* in all out-of-the-way matters of any constitution in the world—yet has two capital merits: it contains a simple efficient part which, on occasion, and when wanted, *can* work more simply and easily, and better, than any instrument of government that has yet been tried; and it contains likewise historical, complex, august, theatrical parts, which it has inherited from a long past—which *take* the multitude—which guide by an insensible but an omnipotent influence the associations of its subjects. Its essence is strong with the strength of modern simplicity; its exterior is august with the Gothic grandeur of a more imposing age. Its simple essence may, *mutatis mutandis,* be transplanted to many very various countries, but its august outside—what most men think it is—is narrowly confined to nations with an analogous history and similar political materials.

The efficient secret of the English Constitution may be described as the close union, the nearly complete fusion, of the executive and legislative powers. No doubt by the traditional theory, as it exists in all the books, the goodness of our constitution consists in the entire separation of the legislative and executive authorities, but in truth its merit consists in their singular approximation. The connecting link is *the cabinet.* By that new word we mean a committee of the legislative body selected to be the executive body. The legislature has many committees, but this is the greatest. It chooses for this, its main committee, the men in whom it has most confidence. It does not, it is true, choose them directly; but it is nearly omnipotent in choosing them indirectly. A century ago the Crown had a real choice of ministers, though it had no longer a choice in policy. During the long reign of Sir R. Walpole he was obliged not only to manage parliament, but to manage the palace. He was obliged to take care that some court intrigue did not expel him from his place. The nation then selected the English policy, but the Crown chose the English ministers. They were not only in name, as now, but in fact, the Queen's servants. Remnants, important remnants, of this great prerogative still remain. The discriminating favour of William IV made Lord Melbourne head of the Whig party when he was only one of several rivals. At the death of Lord Palmerston it is very likely that the Queen may have the opportunity of freely choosing between two, if not three statesmen. But, as a rule, the nominal prime minister is chosen by the legislature, and the real prime minister for most purposes—the leader of the House of Commons—almost without exception is so. There is nearly always some one man plainly selected by the voice of the predominant party in the predominant house of the legislature to head that party, and consequently to rule the nation. We have in England an elective first magistrate as truly as the Americans have an elective first magistrate. The Queen is only at the head of the dignified part of the constitution. The prime minister is at the head of the efficient part. The Crown is, according to the saying, the "fountain of honour"; but the Treasury is the spring of business. Nevertheless our first magistrate differs from the American. He is not elected directly by the people; he is elected by the representatives of the people. He is an example of "double election." The legislature chosen, in name, to make laws, in fact finds its principal business in making and in keeping an executive. . . .

The cabinet, in a word, is a board of control chosen by the legislature, out of persons whom it trusts and knows, to rule the nation. The particular mode in which the English ministers are selected; the fiction that they are, in any political sense, the Queen's servants; the rule which limits the choice of the cabinet to the members of the legislature—are accidents unessential to its definition—historical incidents separable from its nature. Its characteristic is that it should be chosen by the legislature out of persons agreeable to and trusted by the legislature. Naturally these are principally its own members—but they need not be exclusively so. A cabinet which included persons not members of the legislative assembly might still perform all useful duties. Indeed the Peers, who constitute a large element in modern cabinets are members, nowadays, only of a subordinate assembly. The House of Lords still exercises several useful functions; but the ruling influence—the deciding faculty—has passed to what, using the language of old times, we still call the lower house—to an assembly which, though inferior as a dignified institution, is superior as an efficient institution. A principal advantage of the House of Lords in the present age indeed consists in its thus acting as a *reservoir* of cabinet ministers. Unless the composition of the House of Commons were improved, or unless the rules requiring cabinet ministers to be members of the legislature were relaxed, it would undoubtedly be difficult to find without the Lords, a sufficient supply of chief ministers. But the detail of the composition of a cabinet, and the precise method of its choice, are not to the purpose now. The first and cardinal consideration is the definition of a cabinet. We must not bewilder ourselves with the inseparable accidents until we know the necessary essence. A cabinet is a combining committee—a *hyphen* which joins, a *buckle* which fastens, the legislative part of the state to the executive part of the state. In its origin it belongs to the one, in its functions it belongs to the other. . . .

But a cabinet, though it is a committee of the legislative assembly, is a committee with a power which no assembly would—unless for historical accidents, and after happy experience—have been persuaded to entrust to any committee. It is a committee which can dissolve the assembly which appointed it; it is a committee with a suspensive veto—a committee with a power of appeal. Though appointed by one parliament, it can appeal if it chooses to the next. Theoretically, indeed, the power to dissolve parliament is entrusted to the sovereign only; and there are vestiges of doubt whether in *all* cases a sovereign is bound to dissolve parliament when the cabinet asks him to do so. But neglecting such small and dubious exceptions, the cabinet which was chosen by one House of Commons has an appeal to the next House of Commons. The chief committee of the legislature has the power of dissolving the predominant part of that legislature—that which at a crisis is the supreme legislature. The English system, therefore, is not an absorption of the executive power by the legislative power; it is a fusion of the two. Either the cabinet legislates and acts, or else it can dissolve. It is a creature, but it has the power of destroying its creators. It is an executive which can annihilate the legislature, as well as an executive which is the nominee of the legislature. It *was* made, but it *can* unmake; it was derivative in its origin, but it is destructive in its action.

45

Queen Victoria, Letters to Gladstone (1870–1886).
The Nineteenth-Century Monarchy

Two dominant figures of the late nineteenth century were Victoria (1819–1901), Queen of England from 1837 to 1901, and William Ewart Gladstone (1809–1898), four times Liberal prime minister: 1868–1874, 1880–1885, 1886, 1892–1894. Although their official positions brought them into personal contact for half a century, their association was seldom cordial. Following the death of Prince Albert in 1861, Victoria was a lonely woman needing the affection and understanding that the aloof, unbending Gladstone could not provide. Instead of flattering the queen and seeming to seek her advice as Disraeli did, Gladstone lectured her on all manner of things, including her duties as monarch. The difficulty was also in part political. As Gladstone aged he became, at least to the queen, increasingly radical, attacking the House of Lords, advocating home rule for Ireland, and proposing social and political reforms. Victoria in 1880 was so upset with "the People's William" that she considered abdicating rather than accepting as her prime minister "that *half-mad fire-brand.*"

Gladstone and Victoria also differed on the function of monarchy. As Bagehot observed in 1867, the constitution was divided into two parts—the "dignified," headed by the queen, and the "efficient," headed by her prime minister. Victoria had no intention of being a "dignified" rubber stamp, particularly for Gladstone. Albert had taught her the virtues of hard work; she spent long hours familiarizing herself with the details of government, expecting to be consulted on the decisions taken by "her" ministers. Gladstone had a different view of her duties. Following one of Victoria's many complaints involving political appointments, he exploded: "I think this intolerable. It is by courtesy only that these appointments are made known to H. M." To Gladstone, monarchy was a revered and valuable part of the constitution, but its usefulness was symbolic. He frequently urged Victoria to become more visible to the public, performing such functions as opening Parliament. Victoria viewed this advice as insulting to a woman of her age and impor-

Source: Philip Guedalla, *The Queen and Mr. Gladstone,* 2 vols., London: Hodder & Stoughton, Ltd. 1993, I, 218, 227–228, II, 90, 161, 220, 273–274, 286, 405.

tance. The conflict continued past Gladstone's death in 1898; when her son, the future Edward VII (1901–1910), agreed to be a pallbearer, Victoria expressed her displeasure.

Victoria's letters to Gladstone are on permanent loan to the British Library. The originals of Gladstone's letters to the queen are in the Royal Archives at Windsor Castle.

OSBORNE. *Jan.* 30. 1870.

The Queen has waited till *within* 10 *days* of the Opening of Parliament to give her final decision as to her doing so in person or not. She hardly thinks that Mr. Gladstone *can expect* any decision but what she must give:—viz: that it is *totally out of the question* that the Queen c^{LD}*undertake* it.—

After such repeated severe suffering w^h has weakened & shaken her v^y much & w^h obliges her to take the v^y g^{rest} care when she goes out like *sitting backwards* when she drives & covering her face & hands with the endless wraps— besides avoiding excitement & fatigue,—it w^{ld} be *madness* to expose herself to the fatigue of a journey up in this severe weather & to the g^t agitation & excitement of going to open Parl^t & above *all* to the *totally unavoidable* exposure to Cold Drafts & *heat.*

Till these attacks showed themselves since the 2nd of Jany the Queen had *seriously* intended to try & make the effort of doing so;—tho' this g^t tendency to neuralgia w^h has hung about her for the last year & $^1/_2$—but almost incessantly ever since Aug:—made her apprehensive that she might be unable to undertake it.

OSBORNE. *May* 6. 1870.

. . . The circumstances respecting the Bill to give women the same position as men with respect to Parliamentary franchise gives her an opportunity to observe that she had for some time past wished to call Mr. Gladstone's attention to the mad & utterly demoralizing movement of the present day to place women in the same position as to professions—as *men;*—& amongst others, in the *Medical Line.* . . .

The Queen is a woman herself—& knows what an anomaly her *own* position is:—but that can be reconciled with reason & propriety tho' it is a terribly difficult & trying one. But to tear away all the barriers w^h surround a woman, & to propose that they sh^{ld} study with *men*—things w^h c^{ld} not be named before them—certainly not *in a mixed* audience—w^{ld} be to introduce a total disregard of what must be considered as belonging to the rules & principles of morality.

The Queen feels so strongly upon this dangerous & unchristian & unnatural *cry* & movement of "woman's rights,"—in w^h she knows Mr. Gladstone *agrees;* (as he sent her that excellent Pamphlet by a Lady) that she is most anxious that Mr. Gladstone & others sh^{ld} take some steps to check this alarming danger & to make whatever use they can of her name.

She sends the letters w^h speak for themselves.

Let woman be what God intended; a helpmate for a man—but with totally different duties & vocations.

WINDSOR CASTLE. *April* 27. 1880.

The Queen acknowledges Mr. Gladstone's 2 letters just rec^d. She does not wish to object—if she can, to any persons who he submits to her as Members of the Government but she regrets to *see* the names of such very advanced Radicals as Mr. Chamberlain & Sir C. Dilke. It will alarm moderate Liberals as well as Conservatives & she cannot think will add to the harmony of the Cabinet. Before agreeing to either the Queen w^{ld} wish to feel *sure* that Mr. Chamberlain has never spoken disrespectfully of the Throne or expressed openly Republican principles.—The Queen must also ask, before she consents to Sir C. Dilke's appt to the office of Under Sec^y for Foreign Affairs that he sh^{ld} give a written explanation, or make one in Parlt. on the subject of his very offensive Speeches on the Civil List & Royal family. . . .

BALMORAL CASTLE. *May* 25. 1881.

The Queen has to thank Mr. Gladstone for a very kind letter on the occasion of her now somewhat ancient birthday.

The aff^{te} loyalty of her subjects is vy gratifying to her.—Her constant object, which only increases with years—is the welfare, prosperity, honour & glory of her dear Country.—

But the work & anxiety weigh heavily on her unsustained by the strong arm & loving advice of Him who now 19 $^1/_2$ years ago was taken to a higher & better World!

WINDSOR CASTLE. *Dec.* 12. 1882.

. . . She asked Ld. Hartington to speak to Mr. Gladstone on the subject of the proposed changes in the Gov^t & the addition of Ld Derby & Sir C. Dilke.

The Queen must again refer to the Speeches of Sir C. Dilke w^h though spoken ten years ago, contain statements w^h have never been withdrawn. Mr. Gladstone in then replying lamented his Republican tendencies—& Sir C. Dilke *avowed* his Anti Monachical principles.—

Does he still maintain these views? If so, he *cannot* be a *Minister* in the Govt of a *Monarchy.*

Has he changed his principles? If so, there *can* be *no difficulty* in *avowing* it *publicly.*

BALMORAL CASTLE. *June* 5. 1884.

. . . She cannot alter her *decided* opinion that to put *any* limit to our occupation of Egypt—as vy *fatal* mistake. But to lessen the 5 years *even*—when the state of Egypt is such that one cannot at all foresee any speedy improvement (in wh. case other Powers w^{ld} *inevitably* step in)—w^{ld} be most *shortsighted* & truckling to insolent France, & have the vy worst effect & results. —*One year*—if a g^t object is to be obtained (it might be yielded) but *not more* & the Queen will *not* give *her consent* to it.

How *often & often* on many questions within the last few years have her warnings been disregarded & alas! (when too late) justified!—

Let this not happen again now!

WINDSOR CASTLE. *July* 15. 1884.

The Queen thanks Mr. Gladstone for his lctter rec^d this mor^g.

She is sorry that she *cannot* agree with him in his opinion of the House of Lords w^h has rendered such important services to the Nation & w^h at this moment is believed to represent the true feeling of the Country. The House of Lords is in no way opposed to the *people.*

The existence of an independent body of men acting solely for the good of the Country & free from the terror w^h forces so many Commoners to vote against their consciences, is an element of strength in the state & a guarantee for its welfare & freedom.—

To protect the Moderate Men from being swamped by extreme partizans as the Peers now desire to do, is an object in which in itself, Mr. Gladstone himself concurs, & the Queen cannot therefore, understand why this legitimatc act of theirs is to expose them to the storm which noisy agitators for *their own* ends are preparing to raise against the House of Lords.

Many most useful measures for the benefit of the *people at large,* w^h had taken a long time to pass in the House of Commons, passed the House of the Lords at once!

The Queen fears that the passions once roused by an imaginary grievance will not be easily quelled but will threaten the existence of the Monarchy & the stability of the Empire itself!

Those who do not do *all* in their power to prevent such wild & senseless passion from being raised incur a frightful responsibility!. . .

BUCKINGHAM PALACE. *May* 6. 1886.

The Queen is anxious before leaving for Windsor to repeat to Mr. Gladstone what she tried to express but w^h she thinks perhaps she did not do vy clearly— viz: that her silence on the momentous Irish measures which *he* thinks it *his duty* to bring forward—does not imply her *approval* of or *acquiescence in* thcm.— Like so many of Mr. Gladstone's best friends—& faithful followers—& so many of the best & wisest statesmen, the Queen can *only* see danger to the Empire in the course he is pursuing.

The Queen writes this with pain as she always *wished to be able* to *give* her Prime Minister her *full support,* but it is *impossible* for her to do so, when the Union of the Empire is in danger of disintegration & serious disturbance. . . .

46
Punch (1868–1879). The Modern Political Cartoon

Punch, or *The London Charivari,* born on July 17, 1841, filled the journalistic void between the solid, respectable publications such as *The Times* and the *Edinburgh Review* and the transient, nearly pornographic radical papers so popular in the 1830s. *Punch* found a middle ground by being critical but also humorous, reforming but never bitter or crude, sophisticated but still attractive to a broad spectrum of the population. Its title came from Punchinello, the hump-backed figure in the Punch and Judy puppet shows, who ostensibly became the editor of the new weekly. The subtitle, "Charivari," meaning a babel of noise, referred to a popular Parisian magazine that was the model for *Punch.* In its early years, *Punch* was viewed as a radical, reforming journal. In about 1850, however, it began to shed its partisan biases, becoming by the 1870s a respectable, but still irreverent, middle-class publication. The secret of its success was probably its ability to change and reflect the dominant attitudes of successive generations, a process that made *Punch* a national institution until its demise on April 8, 1992.

Perhaps the most famous feature of *Punch* was the cartoon, adopted by the editors as an effective weapon against people and institutions' taking themselves too seriously. Thus was continued an English tradition developed by Hogarth (1697–1764) and George Cruikshank (1792–1878). Through its cartoons, *Punch* popularized Britannia, Johnny Bull, Columbia, Dr. Punch, and, of course, the British Lion (see doc. 64). In the following cartoons from the Disraeli-Gladstone era, neither political party nor England itself was spared the satire that is the stock-in-trade of the cartoonist. The *Alabama* claims dispute, taken seriously by both Britain and the United States, is ridiculed (Plate A). In the 1870s, both the Conservative program of Disraeli (Plate B) and Gladstone's Liberal platform (Plate C) were regarded with more than a little skepticism. In a more serious vein, Disraeli's eastern policy of 1878 is viewed with considerable apprehension (Plate D). The last cartoon (Plate E) criticizes the partisanship of both party leaders. By studying the cartoons of a popular journal, the historian can learn how an event was viewed by the public, which may be more important than a knowledge of the event itself.

Source: Punch, LIV (1868), 51; LXIII (1872), 5; LXXVII (1879), 271; LXXIV (1878), 19; LXXV (1878), 55.

"HOITY-TOITY!!!"

MRS. BRITANNIA. "HOITY-TOITY! WHAT'S ALL THIS FUSS ABOUT?"
JOHNNY BULL. "IT'S COUSIN COLUMBIA, MA, AND SHE SAYS I BROKE HER SHIPS, AND I DIDN'T—
AND I WANT TO BE FRIENDS—AND SHE'S A CROSS THING—AND WANTS TO HAVE IT ALL HER OWN
WAY!"

PLATE A
(*Punch,* February 1, 1868.)

PLATE B
(*Punch,* July 6, 1872.)

THE CONSERVATIVE PROGRAMME.

"DEPUTATION BELOW, SIR—WANT TO KNOW THE CONSERVATIVE PROGRAMME."
RT. HON. BEN. DIZ. "EH?—OH!—AH!—YES!—QUITE SO! TELL THEM, MY GOOD ABERCORN, WITH MY
COMPLIMENTS, THAT WE PROPOSE TO RELY ON THE SUBLIME INSTINCTS OF AN ANCIENT PEOPLE!!"
[*See Speech at Crystal Palace.*]

THE COLOSSUS OF WORDS.

PLATE C
(*Punch,* December 13, 1879.)

PLATE D
(*Punch,* January 19, 1878.)

ON THE DIZZY BRINK.

Lord B. "JUST A LEETLE NEARER THE EDGE?"
Britannia. "NOT AN INCH FURTHER. I'M A GOOD DEAL NEARER THAN IS PLEASANT ALREADY!"

A BAD EXAMPLE.

Dr. Punch. "WHAT'S ALL THIS?   YOU, THE TWO HEAD BOYS OF THE SCHOOL, THROWING MUD!
YOU OUGHT TO BE ASHAMED OF YOURSELVES!"

PLATE E
(*Punch,* August 10, 1878.)

Benjamin Disraeli, Crystal Palace Speech (1872). The New Imperialism

Benjamin Disraeli, earl of Beaconsfield (1804–1881), prime minister in 1868 and again from 1874 to 1880, is often considered the founder of the modern Conservative party. His career reflected the political changes produced by the social and political tensions in Victorian England. Born a Jew, Disraeli was distrusted early in life because of his "dandyism," his social and literary indiscretions, and his brilliant but undisciplined oratory. When Robert Peel (1788–1850) repealed the Corn Law and split the Conservative party in 1846, Disraeli was catapulted to political prominence as the spokesman of the otherwise leaderless country squires. Even then he remained an outsider, more tolerated than trusted. Not until 1868 did he become prime minister. As he described it, he had "climbed to the top of the greasy pole." Within a year, the Conservatives were swept from power by the urban classes, recently enfranchised by the Reform Act of 1867. Despite his disappointment and advanced age, Disraeli strengthened the party machinery and formulated "conservative" policies that enabled his party to survive in an increasingly democratic era: the preservation of traditional British institutions, the improvement of the working and living conditions of the lower classes, and the maintenance and strengthening of the empire.

Disraeli developed these policies in his Crystal Palace Speech of June 24, 1872, stressing his belief in and concern for the British Empire. Traditionally, this speech has been viewed as one of several indications in the 1870s of renewed British interest in imperial expansion and consolidation, a reaction to the supposedly "separatist" policies of Gladstone's Liberal government. Disraeli is seen as a new prophet of imperialism, instilling in the British attitudes that contributed to the "partition" of Africa in the 1880s and 1890s and to Joseph Chamberlain's imperial federation and imperial preference at the turn of the century. To many historians, however, this view of the Crystal Palace Speech is an oversimplification. Disraeli never developed these ideas in detail. When he became prime minister again in 1874, he remained indifferent to the prac-

Source: W. F. Monypenny and George Earl Buckle, *The Life of Benjamin Disraeli, Earl of Beaconsfield,* 6 vols., New York: The Macmillan Company, 1920, V, 194–196.

tical problems facing the empire. In fact, it can be argued that colonial nationalism made his theories incapable of implementation. Disraeli, who had earlier attacked the colonies as a "millstone" around Britain's neck, nevertheless saw the political utility of associating the concept of empire with the Conservative party.

If you look to the history of this country since the advent of Liberalism—forty years ago—you will find that there has been no effort so continuous, so subtle, supported by so much energy, and carried on with so much ability and acumen, as the attempts of Liberalism to effect the disintegration of the Empire of England. And, gentlemen, of all its efforts, this is the one which has been the nearest to success. Statesmen of the highest character, writers of the most distinguished ability, the most organised and efficient means, have been employed in this endeavour. It has been proved to all of us that we have lost money by our Colonies. It has been shown with precise, with mathematical demonstration, that there never was a jewel in the Crown of England that was so truly costly as the possession of India. How often has it been suggested that we should at once emancipate ourselves from this incubus! Well, that result was nearly accomplished. When those subtle views were adopted by the country under the plausible plea of granting self-government to the Colonies, I confess that I myself thought that the tie was broken. Not that I for one object to self-government; I cannot conceive how our distant Colonies can have their affairs administered except by self-government.

But self-government, in my opinion, when it was conceded, ought to have been conceded as part of a great policy of Imperial consolidation. It ought to have been accompanied by an Imperial tariff, by securities for the people of England for the enjoyment of the unappropriated lands which belonged to the Sovereign as their trustee, and by a military code which should have precisely defined the means and the responsibilities by which the Colonies should be defended, and by which, if necessary, this country should call for aid from the Colonies themselves. It ought, further, to have been accompanied by the institution of some representative council in the metropolis, which would have brought the Colonies into constant and continuous relations with the Home Government. All this, however, was omitted because those who advised that policy—and I believe their convictions were sincere—looked upon the Colonies of England, looked even upon our connection with India, as a burden upon this country; viewing everything in a financial aspect, and totally passing by those moral and political considerations which make nations great, and by the influence of which alone men are distinguished from animals.

Well, what has been the result of this attempt during the reign of Liberalism for the disintegration of the Empire? It has entirely failed. But how has it failed? Through the sympathy of the Colonies for the Mother Country. They have decided that the Empire shall not be destroyed; and in my opinion no Minister in this country will do his duty who neglects any opportunity of reconstructing as much as possible our Colonial Empire, and of responding to those distant sympathies which may become the source of incalculable strength and happiness to this land.

The issue is not a mean one. It is whether you will be content to be a comfortable England, modelled and moulded upon Continental principles and meeting in due course an inevitable fate, or whether you will be a great country, an Imperial country, a country where your sons, when they rise, rise to paramount positions, and obtain not merely the esteem of their countrymen, but command the respect of the world.

48
Gilbert and Sullivan, *H.M.S. Pinafore* (1878) and *Iolanthe* (1882)

Few things are so typically or idiosyncratically English as the comic operas of Gilbert and Sullivan. As with many of life's charms, however, they were partly the product of life's failures and frustrations. Arthur Seymour Sullivan (1842–1900) wanted to, and did, write serious music, but occasionally he got distracted,writing the music for several hymns, including "Onward Christian Soldiers," and becoming entangled with William Schwenck Gilbert (1836–1911), a failed attorney, with a talent for writing humorous and even ridiculous lyrics. Their first collaboration, in 1871, was a failure, but Richard D'Oyly Carte (1844–1901) recognized their collective genius, which he managed and promoted for the next twenty years. Together they produced thirteen operas, beginning with *Trial by Jury* in 1875. To accommodate their productions, Carte in 1881 built the Savoy Theatre, the first such facility to be lighted entirely by electricity.

Probably the most successful of the Savoy operas was *H.M.S. Pinafore; or The Lass That Loved a Sailor,* which opened on May 25, 1878, and ran for 571 performances. Small summer audiences threatened an early closing, but after Sullivan conducted orchestral

Source: Leslie Ayre, *The Gilbert & Sullivan Companion,* New York: Dodd, Mead & Company, 1972, pp. 153–54, 172–73, 183. Reprinted with the permission of Virgin Publishing, Ltd., London.

adaptations of some of its music at Covent Garden, "The audience, England, and the Anglo-Saxon world went bananas in that order." *Pinafore* was a satire of grand opera, the English class structure, the Royal Navy, and, as seen below, the means of gaining promotion to the highest rank. W. H. Smith, First Lord of the Admiralty from 1877 to 1880, a bookseller before he was a politician, was soon referred to, even by Prime Minister Disraeli, as "Pinafore Smith."

In *Iolanthe; or The Peer and the Peri* (1882) Gilbert turned his satire on the Lord Chancellor, whose duties in his Chancery Court included finding suitable husbands for orphaned heiresses. He also poked fun at Parliament, especially the House of Lords, where he suggested that dukes be appointed on the basis of competitive examination. Prime Minister Gladstone and the Prince of Wales attended opening night.

The theater-going public loved the good fun of the Savoy operas. They were a "burlesque in long clothes," where Victorian propriety was not offended and where a young man could take his parents without embarrassment. Official Britain was uncertain how to react. Not surprisingly, Sullivan was given a knighthood for his beautiful music in 1883, but Gilbert and his lyrics had to wait until 1907.

H.M.S. Pinafore; or The Lass That Loved a Sailor

To loud cheers and the accompaniment of a drum roll, the dapper figure of Sir Joseph appears, with his cousin Hebe. With interruptions from his lively relatives, he expounds:

> I am the monarch of the sea,
> The ruler of the Queen's Navee,
> Whose praise Great Britain loudly chants.
> (And we are his sisters and his cousins and his aunts!
> When at anchor here I ride,
> My bosom swells with pride,
> And I snap my fingers at a foeman's taunts;
> (And so do his sisters and his cousins and his aunts!
> But when the breezes blow,
> I generally go below,
> And seek the seclusion that a cabin grants!
> (And so do his sisters and his cousins and his aunts!
> His sisters and his cousins,
> Whom he reckons up by dozens,
> And his aunts!)

Sir Joseph then obliges with an account of the unusual manner in which he
reached the high office in which he finds himself:

> When I was a lad I served a term
> As office boy to an Attorney's firm.
> I cleaned the windows and swept the floor,
> And I polished up the handle of the big front door.
> I polished up that handle so carefullee
> That now I am the Ruler of the Queen's Navee!
>
> As office boy I made such a mark
> That they gave me the post of a junior clerk.
> I served the writs with a smile so bland,
> And I copied all the letters in a big round hand—
> I copied all the letters in a hand so free,
> That now I am the Ruler of the Queen's Navee!
>
> In serving writs I made such a name
> That an articled clerk I soon became;
> I wore clean collars and a brand-new suit
> For the pass examinations of the Institute.
> That pass examination did so well for me,
> That now I am the Ruler of the Queen's Navee!
>
> Of legal knowledge I acquired such a grip
> That they took me into the partnership.
> And that junior partnership I ween
> Was the only ship that I ever had seen.
> That kind of ship so suited me,
> That now I am the Ruler of the Queen's Navee!
>
> I grew so rich that I was sent
> By a pocket borough into Parliament.
> I always voted at my party's call,
> And I never thought of thinking for myself at all.
> I thought so little, they rewarded me
> By making me the Ruler of the Queen's Navee!
>
> Now landsmen all, whoever you may be,
> If you want to rise to the top of the tree,
> If your soul isn't fettered to an office stool,
> Be careful to be guided by the golden rule—
> Stick close to your desks and never go to sea,
> And you all may be Rulers of the Queen's Navee!

Iolanthe; or *The Peer and the Peri*

The Lord Chancellor comes in, attended by his train-bearer, and explains some
of the difficulties of being responsible for attractive Wards in Chancery:

> The Law is the true embodiment
> Of everything that's excellent.
> It has no kind of fault or flaw,
> And I, my Lords, embody the Law.
> The constitutional guardian I
> Of pretty young Wards in Chancery,
> All very agreeable girls—and none
> Are over the age of twenty-one.
> A pleasant occupation for
> A rather susceptible Chancellor!
>
> But though the compliment implied
> Inflates me with legitimate pride,
> It nevertheless can't be denied
> That it has its inconvenient side.
> For I'm not so old, and not so plain,
> And I'm quite prepared to marry again,
> But there'd be the deuce to pay in the Lords
> If I fell in love with one of my Wards!
> Which rather tries my temper, for
> I'm *such* a susceptible Chancellor!
>
> And every one who'd marry a Ward
> Must come to me for my accord,
> And in my court I sit all day,
> Giving agreeable girls away,
> With one for him—and one for he—
> And one for you—and one for ye—
> And one for thou—and one for thee—
> But never, oh, never a one for me!
> Which is exasperating for
> A highly susceptible Chancellor!

Lord Mountararat expresses his annoyance at Strephon's introduction of a Bill
to throw the Peerage open to competitive examination. He insists that the House
of Peers does quite nicely as it is:

> When Britain really ruled the waves—
> (In good Queen Bess's time)
> The House of Peers made no pretence

To intellectual eminence,
Or scholarship sublime;
Yet Britain won her proudest bays
In good Queen Bess's glorious days!

When Wellington thrashed Bonaparte,
As every child can tell,
The House of Peers, throughout the war,
Did nothing in particular,
And did it very well:
Yet Britain set the world ablaze
In good King George's glorious days!

And while the House of Peers withholds
Its legislative hand,
And noble statesmen do not itch
To interfere with matters which
They do not understand,
As bright will shine Great Britain's rays
As in King George's glorious days!

49

William Ewart Gladstone, Speech in Commons (1886). Irish Home Rule

The Act of Union of 1800, binding Ireland and Great Britain together as a political unit, was from the beginning unacceptable to many Irish. Daniel O'Connell (1775–1847), even after he had achieved Catholic emancipation in 1829, continued to work for repeal of the Act of Union. Such political agitation, interrupted in the 1840s by the horrors of the potato famine, was by the 1860s again becoming a fact of Irish life. The first statesman in Britain to recognize the legitimacy of Ireland's complaint was William Ewart Gladstone (1809–1898). On learning that his Liberal party had won the election of 1868 and that he would become prime minister, he asserted, "My mission is to pacify Ireland."

In 1869, Gladstone disestablished the Church of Ireland. His land acts of 1870 and 1881 attempted, with limited success, to deal with the problem of English absentee landlords and oppressed Irish tenants. By 1886, when he became prime minister for a third time, protest in Ireland had become so violent and Irish obstruction in the House of Commons so annoying that he concluded the only solution was to give Ireland its own parliament for local affairs. Introducing his Home Rule Bill on April 8, Gladstone applied to Ireland the Liberal Party's traditional policy toward other countries: they should be allowed to conduct their own affairs.

Gladstone's bill failed in the House of Commons because of opposition from the Conservatives and also from the Liberal Unionists, the 93 Liberals who supported the union of Britain and Ireland. Lord Randolph Churchill, a Conservative who decided to play "the Orange card," insisted with some foresight that "Ulster will fight, " and then opined that "Ulster will be right." Seven years later, in 1893, Gladstone attempted a second Home Rule Bill, this time defeated in the House of Lords. A third bill was introduced in 1912, after the Lords' power to defeat it had been destroyed by the Parliament Act of 1911. When its implementation was delayed by World War I, if not by Protestant Ulster's readiness to resist, the Catholic south also prepared to fight. The Easter Rebellion of 1916 in Dublin and the division of Ireland in 1921 set the stage for later conflict.

Source: Hansard's Parliamentary Debates, Third Series, CCCIV (1886), 1080–1085.

Gladstone's Irish policy, by which he risked his own political career and the tenure of his political party, is often cited as the courageous stance of a statesman acting on principle rather than on political expediency. Or was it, on the other hand, the pursuit of an unrealistic objective, doomed from the beginning to failure and not worth the political turmoil it caused?

I do not deny the general good intentions of Parliament on a variety of great and conspicuous occasions, and its desire to pass good laws for Ireland. But let me say that, in order to work out the purposes of government, there is something more in this world occasionally required than even the passing of good laws. It is sometimes requisite not only that good laws should be passed, but also that they should be passed by the proper persons. The passing of many good laws is not enough in cases where the strong permanent instincts of the people, their distinctive marks of character, the situation and history of the country require not only that these laws should be good, but that they should proceed from a congenial and native source, and besides being good laws should be their own laws. . . .

The principle that I am laying down I am not laying down exceptionally for Ireland. It is the very principle upon which, within my recollection, to the immense advantage of the country, we have not only altered, but revolutionized our method of governing the Colonies. I had the honour to hold Office in the Colonial Department—perhaps I ought to be ashamed to confess it—51 years ago. At that time the Colonies were governed from Downing Street. It is true that some of them had Legislative Assemblies; but with these we were always in conflict. We were always fed with information by what was termed the British Party in those Colonies. A clique of gentlemen constituted themselves the British Party; and the non-British Party, which was sometimes called the "Disloyal Party," was composed of the enormous majority of the population. We had continual shocks, continual debates, and continual conflicts. All that has changed. England tried to pass good laws for the Colonies at that period; but the Colonies said—"We do not want your good laws; we want our own." We admitted the reasonableness of that principle, and it is now coming home to us from across the seas. We have to consider whether it is applicable to the case of Ireland. Do not let us disguise this from ourselves. We stand face to face with what is termed Irish nationality. Irish nationality vents itself in the demand for local autonomy, or separate and complete self-government in Irish, not in Imperial, affairs. Is this an evil in itself? Is it a thing that we should view with horror or apprehension? Is it a thing which we ought to reject or accept only with a wry face, or ought we to wait until some painful and sad necessity is incumbent upon the country, like the necessity of 1780 or the necessity of 1793? Sir, I hold that it is not. . . .

I hold that there is such a thing as local patriotism, which, in itself, is not bad, but good. The Welshman is full of local patriotism—the Scotchman is full of local patriotism; the Scotch nationality is as strong as it ever was, and should the occasion arise—which I believe it never can—it will be as ready to assert itself as in the days of Bannockburn. I do not believe that that local patriotism is an evil. I believe it is stronger in Ireland even than in Scotland. Englishmen are eminently English; Scotchmen are profoundly Scotch; and, if I read Irish history aright, misfortune and calamity have wedded her sons to her soil. The Irishman is more profoundly Irish; but it does not follow that, because his local patriotism is keen, he is incapable of Imperial patriotism. . . . Take the case of the Irish soldier and of the Irish Constabulary. Have you a braver or a more loyal man in your Army than the Irishman, who has shared every danger with his Scotch and English comrades, and who has never been behind them, when confronted by peril, for the sake of the honour and safety of his Empire? Compare this case with that of an ordinary Irishman in Ireland. The Irish soldier has voluntarily placed himself under military law, which is to him a self-chosen law, and he is exempted from that difficulty which works upon the population in Ireland—namely, that they are governed by a law which they do not feel has sprung from the soil. . . .

However this may be, we are sensible that we have taken an important decision—our choice has been made. It has not been made without thought; it has been made in the full knowledge that trial and difficulty may confront us on our path. We have no right to say that Ireland, through her constitutionally-chosen Representatives, will accept the plan I offer. Whether it will be so I do not know—I have no title to assume it; but if Ireland does not cheerfully accept it, it is impossible for us to attempt to force upon her what is intended to be a boon; nor can we possibly press England and Scotland to accord to Ireland what she does not heartily welcome and embrace. There are difficulties; but I rely upon the patriotism and sagacity of this House; I rely on the effects of free and full discussion; and I rely more than all upon the just and generous sentiments of the two British nations. . . . I ask that we should apply to Ireland that happy experience which we have gained in England and in Scotland, where the course of generations has now taught us, not as a dream or a theory, but as practice and as life, that the best and surest foundation we can find to build upon is the foundation afforded by the affections, the convictions, and the will of the nation; and it is thus, by the decree of the Almighty, that we may be enabled to secure at once the social peace, the fame, the power, and the permanence of the Empire.

50
Sidney Webb, "The Historic Basis of Socialism," *Fabian Essays* (1889)

The outstanding political fact of the late nineteenth century was the new democratic electorate created by the reform acts of 1867 and 1884. The traditional political parties—the Liberals (formerly Whigs) and the Conservatives (formerly Tories)—attempted to marshal the new voters but, in fact, offered little of tangible benefit to them. Walter Bagehot's prediction that politicians would seek to outbid one another for popular support was not immediately realized. The Liberals, at first championing laissez-faire individualism and then preoccupied with Ireland, had little time or inclination to cater to the needs of the new working-class electorate. The Conservatives, although occasionally advocating paternalistic Tory Democracy, were more interested in maintaining the *status quo* at home and in defending the British Empire

This political neglect and the anxiety caused by the "Great Depression" of the late nineteenth century led some to search for more radical solutions. Socialism, espoused in a utopian form by Robert Owen (1771–1858) in the 1820s and 1830s, was made scientific and more resolute by Karl Marx (1818–1883), who after 1849 lived in London and wrote, from his desk in the British Museum, his revolutionary masterpiece, *Das Kapital*. Such ideas, however, seemed to many people either too utopian and impractical or, as with those of Marx, too violent and un-English.

The Fabian Society, organized in 1884, was one of several socialist groups formed about the same time. It was unique in its respectability, disavowing revolutionary means and attracting as members notable intellectuals such as the historian Sidney Webb (1859–1947) and the playwright George Bernard Shaw (1856–1950). It took its name from the Roman general Quintus Fabius Maximus, who had bested Hannibal by refusing a direct confrontation, confident that by being patient and prepared the victory would ultimately be his. Thus, the Fabians stressed teaching, speaking to any group that would listen, preaching that socialistic cooperation was destined peacefully and constitutionally to re-

Source: George Bernard Shaw, et al., *Fabian Essays,* sixth edition, introduction by Asa Briggs, London: George Allen & Unwin, Ltd., 1962, pp. 64, 66–67, 90–93. Reprinted by permission of the Fabian Society.

place capitalistic competitiveness: the "economic side of the democratic ideal is, in fact, Socialism."

The following selection, originally a speech by Sidney Webb, is filled with typically Fabian ideas. It and seven other essays by other Fabians were edited by Shaw and published in 1889. These *Fabian Essays* did much to establish the authority of the Society and to publicize its ideals. In 1900 the Fabians joined with other socialist groups and labor unions to form the Labour Representation Committee, which in 1906 became the Labour party.

Socialism is by this time a wave surging throughout all Europe; and for want of a grasp of the series of apparently unconnected events by which and with which it has been for two generations rapidly coming upon us—for want, in short, of knowledge of its intellectual history, we in England today see our political leaders in a general attitude of astonishment at the changing face of current politics; both great parties drifting vaguely before a nameless undercurrent which they fail utterly to recognize or understand. With some dim impression that Socialism is one of the Utopian dreams they remember to have heard comfortably disposed of in their academic youth as the impossible ideal of Humanity-intoxicated Frenchmen, they go their ways through the nineteenth century as a countryman blunders through Cheapside. . . .

In the present Socialist movement . . . two streams are united: advocates of social reconstruction have learnt the lesson of Democracy, and know that it is through the slow and gradual turning of the popular mind to new principles that social reorganization bit by bit comes. All students of society who are abreast of their time, Socialists as well as Individualists, realize that important organic changes can only be (1) democratic, and thus acceptable to a majority of the people, and prepared for in the minds of all; (2) gradual, and thus causing no dislocation, however rapid may be the rate of progress; (3) not regarded as immoral by the mass of the people, and thus not subjectively demoralizing to them; and (4) in this country at any rate, constitutional and peaceful. Socialists may therefore be quite at one with Radicals in their political methods. Radicals, on the other hand, are perforce realizing that mere political levelling is insufficient to save a State from anarchy and despair. Both sections have been driven to recognize that the root of the difficulty is economic; and there is every day a wider consensus that the inevitable outcome of Democracy is the control by the people themselves, not only of their own political organization, but, through that, also of the main instruments of wealth production; the gradual substitution of organized co-operation for the anarchy of the competitive struggle; and the consequent recovery, in the only possible way, of what John Stuart Mill calls "the enormous share which the possessors of the instruments of industry are able to take from the produce." The economic side of the democratic ideal is, in fact, Socialism itself. . . .

We must abandon the self-conceit of imagining that we are independent units, and bend our jealous minds, absorbed in their own cultivation, to this subjection to the higher end, the Common Weal. Accordingly, conscious "direct adaptation" steadily supplants the unconscious and wasteful "indirect adaptation" of the earlier form of the struggle for existence; and with every advance in sociological knowledge Man is seen to assume more and more, not only the mastery of "things," but also a conscious control over social destiny itself.

This new scientific conception of the Social Organism has put completely out of countenance the cherished principles of the Political Economist and the Philosophic Radical. . . .

The result of this development of Sociology is to compel a revision of the relative importance of liberty and equality as principles to be kept in view in social administration. In Bentham's celebrated "ends" to be aimed at in a civil code, liberty stands predominant over equality, on the ground that full equality can be maintained only by the loss of security for the fruits of labour. That exposition remains as true as ever; but the question for decision remains, how much liberty? Economic analysis has destroyed the value of the old criterion of respect for the equal liberty of others. Bentham, whose economics were weak, paid no attention to the perpetual tribute on the fruits of others' labour which full private property in land inevitably creates. In his view liberty and security to property meant that every worker should be free to obtain the full result of his own labour; and there appeared no inconsistency between them. The political economist now knows that with free competition and private property in land and capital, no individual can possibly obtain the full result of his own labour. The student of industrial development, moreover, finds it steadily more and more impossible to trace what is precisely the result of each separate man's toil. Complete rights of liberty and property necessarily involve, for example, the spoliation of the Irish cottier tenant for the benefit of Lord Clanricarde. What then becomes of the Benthamic principle of the greatest happiness of the greatest number? When the Benthamite comes to understand the Law of Rent, which of the two will he abandon? For he cannot escape the lesson of the century, taught alike by the economists, the statesmen, and the "practical men," that complete individual liberty, with unrestrained private ownership of the instruments of wealth production, is irreconcilable with the common weal. The free struggle for existence among ourselves menaces our survival as a healthy and permanent social organism. Evolution, Professor Huxley declares, is the substitution of consciously regulated co-ordination among the units of each organism, for blind anarchic competition. Thirty years ago Herbert Spencer demonstrated the incompatibility of full private property in land with the modern democratic State; and almost every economist now preaches the same doctrine. The Radical is rapidly arriving, from practical experience, at similar conclusions; and the steady increase of the Government regulation of private enterprise, the growth of municipal administration, and the rapid shifting of the burden of taxation directly to rent and interest, mark in treble lines the statesman's unconscious abandonment of the old Individualism, and our irresistible glide into collectivist Socialism.

It was inevitable that the Democracy should learn this lesson. With the masses painfully conscious of the failure of Individualism to create a decent social life for four-fifths of the people, it might have been foreseen that Individualism could not survive their advent to political power. If private property in land and capital necessarily keeps the many workers permanently poor (through no fault of their own) in order to make the few idlers rich (from no merit of their own), private property in land and capital will inevitably go the way of the feudalism which it superseded. The economic analysis confirms the rough generalization of the suffering people. The history of industrial evolution points to the same result; and for two generations the world's chief ethical teachers have been urging the same lesson. No wonder the heavens of Individualism are rolling up before our eyes like a scroll and even the Bishops believe and tremble. . . .

Every increase in the political power of the proletariat will most surely be used by them for their economic and social protection. In England, at any rate, the history of the century serves at once as their guide and their justification.

51
Charles Booth, *Life and Labour of the People of London* (1889)

Charles Booth's seventeen-volume *Life and Labour* is one of the most important sources on life in late Victorian London. It was used to support many of the social reforms introduced into England at the turn of the century. Booth (1840–1916) was an unlikely candidate for such a momentous and pioneering sociological undertaking. Born to comfort, he devoted his early life to his successful shipping business. Not until he had become middle-aged and wealthy did he commit himself to his great survey, a decision that is still something of a mystery. Most likely his natural curiosity was reinforced by a desire to prove that the socialists were exaggerating the extent of urban poverty. He concluded that they were not.

Booth's study is composed of several different parts. Much is simply a detailed description of various London neighborhoods (as in this selection on Parker Street), the industries of London, and the habits and morals of the different social classes. He also attempted to offer solutions to the problems he observed. Like Smiles, he remained a defender of capitalism and considered "self-reliance" the key to progress in most areas. As a result, Beatrice Potter, one of his early associates, deserted him and embraced the Fabian socialism of her future husband, Sidney Webb. Booth, perhaps simply aware of the social implications of democracy, was more willing than Smiles to grant government a limited role in solving obvious social problems. For example, he was an early and strong advocate of old-age pensions, begun in Britain in 1908.

Life and Labour came out piecemeal between 1889 and 1903. When completed it consisted of four volumes on poverty, five volumes on London industry, seven volumes on religious influences, and a *Final Volume* containing his conclusions.

This street differs in some respects from Shelton Street, and, bad as Shelton Street is, Parker Street touches a little lower level. In Shelton Street the rooms

Source: Charles Booth's London, edited by Albert Fried and Richard M. Elman, New York: Pantheon Books, 1968, pp. 70–71, 74–75, 190–191, 197, 199, 202, 334–335. Copyright (c) 1968 by Albert Fried and Richard M. Elman. Reprinted by permission of Pantheon Books, a division of Random House, Inc.

were not taken by the night, but by the week. In Parker Street it was not unusual to let by the night, so that any man and woman who had met could find accommodation. . . .

No. 2, Parker Street has two entrances, the one being numbered at 159, Drury Lane. One of the parlour floors is used for the sale of coal and coke, and the room over for living in. . . . In one of those rooms there was at one time a Mrs. Carter, a woman with a fiery temper, almost fit to commit murder, and her husband has been in prison for ill-using her. She was, however, a clean, hard-working woman. These people were at times very poor. On the second floor to the right there were a man and woman (English) who had lived unmarried for fourteen years. There were no children; the room clean, with a few comforts. In the other room lived another pair in the same fashion; the woman very unhappy, brutally treated by the man, whom she says she would leave if she knew how else to get a living. Such cases are not uncommon. The man was a drunkard. On the third floor lived an old woman and her son, Irish, who declined to be visited by a Protestant missionary. . . .

No. 24 is let in furnished apartments. It was in the occupation of a Mr. Holden, a quiet man who died about a year ago, and his widow carries on the business. The characters occupying the rooms are very low indeed; one of them, a girl of eighteen, mentioned that she had been confirmed by a Bishop but had been a b—— sight worse since. About two or three years ago a woman was found dead in the parlour of this house; she appeared to have been strangled. . . .

No. 1 on the north side, at the corner of Drury Lane, does not really belong to Parker Street at all. The shop entrance is in Drury Lane, the house only enters from Parker Street, and with its inhabitants, who in position and appearance are much above the dwellers in Parker Street, we need not concern ourselves. Nos. 3 to 5 are warehouses. No. 7 has been pulled down. . . . The whole house for eleven years past was noted for poverty, dirt, and drink, and deaths were at one time so frequent in it that it got a bad name for "ill-luck." . . .

Drinking habits and the disorderliness resulting from them could not but be continually mentioned in the course of the long walks taken in all parts of London day after day with the picked police officers who were permitted to assist us during the revision of our maps; and we had the advantage of discussing these and other cognate subjects with their divisional superiors. . . .

Whether the people drink less or not, the police are practically agreed in saying that they are much less rowdy than formerly: "Totally different people to what they were thirty-three years ago," said one who joined the force then; an improvement which he claims has extended also to publicans and the police themselves, of whom the latter are now an almost entirely sober body of men, while the former are much more respectable and steady, and for the most part careful as to the conduct of their houses. . . .

Upon the connection of poverty, or at any rate the poverty that seeks charitable relief, with drink, the statements are uncompromising. A Wesleyan minister, referring to claims on their relief fund, stated that in almost every application the necessity was traced ultimately to drink on the part of man or wife "or both." A Congregationalist says that "he came to London believing that the influence of drink was much exaggerated, but has been convinced that it is at the root of all the poverty and distress with which they come into contact; with every case of distress that is relieved they always find afterwards that drink has been the cause of leakage." A Church of England vicar speaks of it as "the great trouble; the main cause of all the poverty. In almost every application for relief there is a history of drink." He began with a determination not to help when either parent was a drunkard, but has found this impossible. Apart from drunkenness he emphasized the fearful extravagance in drink. . . . And a relieving officer of an adjoining Union confirms this, saying that "though there is less rowdiness, the general habits of drinking have not decreased," and that in his experience "in all applications for relief, except from widows, cripples, and the aged, the ultimate, if not immediate cause of poverty is drink." . . .

From the religious point of view it is remarked that teetotalism is apt to become a cult of its own, of a rather narrow kind, and it is added that "those who yield to the seductions of temperance are sometimes too much bitten by the idea of saving." But carping such as this leaves untouched the great main fact to which we have endless testimony, that "Christian people are nearly all temperate and thrifty," and the better in every way for being so. . . .

Improvement must be sought, first of all, in the deepening of the sentiment of Individual Responsibility. This sentiment rests no doubt upon right feeling, but is subject to stimulation by the opinion of others, and may finally be enforced by law. Of these three, public opinion seems to me to be the most lax. The expectation of evil, the attributing of bad motives, and the ready acceptance of a low standard constitute the first difficulty we have to meet. Cynicism is accounted so clever that men pretend to be worse than they are rather than be thought fools. Clear views of right and wrong in matters of daily action, however firmly they may be rooted in the hearts of men, seldom find utterance; and when this polite rule is broken some surprise is always felt. . . .

It would seem inevitable that the sense of duty must be weakened by the loss of the habit of judging and of the experience of being judged, as well as by laxity, but nevertheless I venture to assert that it is maintained at a far higher level than is generally thought or claimed. Thus legal enactment, if carefully aimed and measured, becomes doubly and trebly valuable, serving first to check the evil-doer, and secondly to awaken the individual conscience, while it also, by impressing an undeniable seal of condemnation, crystallizes the looseness of public opinion as to any particular offence. Legislation can never go far beyond the sanction of existing public opinion, but may yet lead the way, and in many cases has done so.

52
Rudyard Kipling, "Recessional" (1897)

Rudyard Kipling (1865–1936) is usually regarded as the high priest of British Imperialism. Born in India, he became a journalist, writing a number of popular short stories about India and the army. In 1889 he settled in England, where he continued to develop the imperial theme, producing such widely read works as *Barrack-Room Ballads* (1892), the *Jungle Books* (1894–1895), and *Captains Courageous* (1897). These works reflected the imperial spirit that pervaded Britain in the late nineteenth century.

Kipling was, however, always suspicious of Britain's jingo imperialism. For one thing, British power had been purchased at a great price.

> If blood be the price of admiralty,
> Lord God, we ha' paid in full!

More important, he believed in an older, humanitarian imperialism. Power implied duty and responsibility; Britain must rule for the benefit of the "lesser breeds without the Law," a belief developed most forcefully in his "White Man's Burden" (1899). Loving India as he did and respecting the "Fuzzy-Wuzzy," who "bruk a British square," Kipling regretted the arrogance bred of power and the contempt bred of familiarity. His concern was the same as that of Queen Victoria when she wrote, "Coloured races should be treated with every kindness and affection, as brothers, not—as, alas, Englishmen too often do."

It was in this somber mood that Kipling approached the Diamond Jubilee of 1897 commemorating Victoria's sixty years on the throne. The resulting pageantry was to many British an opportunity for self-congratulation, and even of boastfulness. "Recessional," perhaps Kipling's greatest poem, struck a melancholy note during the joyous proceedings, warning of the danger of becoming "drunk with sight of power," and drawing a comparison of Britain's empire with those of Nineveh and Tyre. Only he, the imperialist, could have written such lines and not lost public respect. His warning was apt; two years later the Boer War began. This

Source: Rudyard Kipling, *The Five Nations*, London: Methuen and Co., 1903, pp. 214–215.

messy and morally dubious conflict produced a reaction not only against the aggressive imperialism of Joseph Chamberlain and Alfred Milner but also against the literature of Kipling himself. When he received the Nobel Prize for literature in 1907, his literary career was largely over.

RECESSIONAL
(1897)

God of our fathers, known of old,
    Lord of our far-flung battle-line,
Beneath whose awful Hand we hold
    Dominion over palm and pine—
Lord God of Hosts, be with us yet,
Lest we forget—lest we forget!

The tumult and the shouting dies;
    The captains and the kings depart:
Still stands Thine ancient sacrifice,
    An humble and a contrite heart.
Lord God of Hosts, be with us yet,
Lest we forget—lest we forget!

Far-called, our navies melt away;
    On dune and headland sinks the fire:
Lo, all our pomp of yesterday
    Is one with Nineveh and Tyre!
Judge of the Nations, spare us yet,
Lest we forget—lest we forget!

If, drunk with sight of power, we loose
    Wild tongues that have not Thee in awe,
Such boastings as the Gentiles use,
    Or lesser breeds without the Law—
Lord God of Hosts, be with us yet,
Lest we forget—lest we forget!

For heathen heart that puts her trust
    In reeking tube and iron shard,
All valiant dust that builds on dust,
    And guarding, calls not Thee to guard,
For frantic boast and foolish word—
Thy Mercy on Thy People, Lord!

                    Amen.

53
Eyre Crowe, Memorandum (1907). England and Germany

Britain's world position was eroded in the late nineteenth century by the creation of the German Empire (1871), the industrialization of Europe and the United States, the growth of colonial nationalism, and the division of Europe in the 1880s and 1890s into two alliance systems. Nevertheless, Britain remained reluctant to make formal diplomatic commitments, preferring instead the freedom of her traditional "splendid isolation." By the turn of the century, this policy appeared increasingly unrealistic. The Boer War (1899 1902) revealed that Britain had few, if any, friends in Europe, and, as Germany began to build a powerful navy, Britain realized that she could no longer support an independent foreign policy. Her emergence from diplomatic isolation was signaled by the Anglo-Japanese Treaty of 1902 and, more importantly, by the *Entente Cordiale* with France in 1904, a "friendly understanding" backed up by a series of colonial agreements. This *entente* was seen by many as anti-German, especially when Britain sided with France in the Moroccan Crisis of 1905 to 1906.

Eyre Crowe (1864–1925), who entered the Foreign Office in 1885, observed this change in foreign policy at close quarters. In early 1907 he wrote a long memorandum justifying Britain's support of France. He portrayed this action as a reflection of Britain's traditional foreign policy, the use of sea power to maintain freedom of commerce and the balance of power. If Britain appeared anti-German, it was only because Germany currently represented the greatest threat to this balance of power. It is also apparent that Crowe opposed "appeasement"; peace could best be maintained by resisting German demands. His memorandum provoked controversy within the Foreign Office, some of his colleagues arguing that he was overly suspicious of German intentions. Nevertheless, Sir Edward Grey (1862–1933), the foreign secretary, found his analysis "most valuable." As Germany's challenge to British naval supremacy intensified, Crowe's views increasingly prevailed with-

Source: G. P. Gooch and Harold Temperley, eds., *British Documents on the Origins of the War, 1898–1914*, Vol. III: *The Testing of the Entente 1904–6*, London: His Majesty's Stationery Office, 1928, pp. 402–403, 414–416, 419–420. Reprinted by permission of the Controller of Her Britannic Majesty's Stationery Office.

in the Foreign Office, contributing ultimately to Britain's support of France in 1914.

Crowe's secret memorandum, distributed only to select members of the cabinet, was deposited in the Public Record Office. It was made public only in 1928, when the British government published a large collection of official documents designed to explain and justify Britain's pre-World War I diplomacy.

The general character of England's foreign policy is determined by the immutable conditions of her geographical situation on the ocean flank of Europe as an island State with vast oversea colonies and dependencies, whose existence and survival as an independent community are inseparably bound up with the possession of preponderant sea power. . . . Its formidable character makes itself felt the more directly that a maritime State is, in the literal sense of the word, the neighbour of every country accessible by sea. It would, therefore, be but natural that the power of a State supreme at sea should inspire universal jealousy and fear, and be ever exposed to the danger of being overthrown by a general combination of the world. Against such a combination no single nation could in the long run stand, least of all a small island kingdom not possessed of the military strength of a people trained to arms, and dependent for its food supply on oversea commerce. The danger can in practice only be averted—and history shows that it has been so averted—on condition that the national policy of the insular and naval State is so directed as to harmonize with the general desires and ideals common to all mankind, and more particularly that it is closely identified with the primary and vital interests of a majority, or as many as possible, of the other nations. Now, the first interest of all countries is the preservation of national independence. It follows that England, more than any other non-insular Power, has a direct and positive interest in the maintenance of the independence of nations, and therefore must be the natural enemy of any country threatening the independence of others, and the natural protector of the weaker communities.

Second only to the ideal of independence, nations have always cherished the right of free intercourse and trade in the world's markets, and in proportion as England champions the principle of the largest measure of general freedom of commerce, she undoubtedly strengthens her hold on the interested friendship of other nations, at least to the extent of making them feel less apprehensive of naval supremacy in the hands of a free trade England than they would in the face of a predominant protectionist Power. This is an aspect of the free trade question which is apt to be overlooked. It has been well said that every country, if it had the option, would, of course, prefer itself to hold the power of supremacy at sea, but that, this choice being excluded, it would rather see England hold that power than any other State.

History shows that the danger threatening the independence of this or that nation has generally arisen, at least in part, out of the momentary predominance of a neighbouring State at once militarily powerful, economically efficient, and ambitious to extend its frontiers or spread its influence, the danger being directly proportionate to the degree of its power and efficiency, and to the spontaneity or "inevitableness" of its ambitions. The only check on the abuse of political predominance derived from such a position has always consisted in the opposition of an equally formidable rival, or of a combination of several countries forming leagues of defence. The equilibrium established by such a grouping of forces is technically known as the balance of power, and it has become almost an historical truism to identify England's secular policy with the maintenance of this balance by throwing her weight now in this scale and now in that, but ever on the side opposed to the political dictatorship of the strongest single State or group at a given time.

If this view of British policy is correct, the opposition into which England must inevitably be driven to any country aspiring to such a dictatorship assumes almost the form of a law of nature. . . .

By applying this general law to a particular case, the attempt might be made to ascertain whether, at a given time, some powerful and ambitious State is or is not in a position of natural and necessary enmity towards England; and the present position of Germany might, perhaps, be so tested. Any such investigation must take the shape of an inquiry as to whether Germany is, in fact, aiming at a political hegemony with the object of promoting purely German schemes of expansion, and establishing a German primacy in the world of international politics at the cost and to the detriment of other nations. . . .

The immediate object of the present inquiry was to ascertain whether there is any real and natural ground for opposition between England and Germany. It has been shown that such opposition has, in fact, existed in an ample measure for a long period, but that it has been caused by an entirely one-sided aggressiveness, and that on the part of England the most conciliatory disposition has been coupled with never-failing readiness to purchase the resumption of friendly relations by concession after concession.

It might be deduced that the antagonism is too deeply rooted in the relative position of the two countries to allow of its being bridged over by the kind of temporary expedients to which England has so long and so patiently resorted. On this view of the case it would have to be assumed that Germany is deliberately following a policy which is essentially opposed to vital British interests, and that an armed conflict cannot in the long run be averted, except by England either sacrificing those interests, with the result that she would lose her position as an independent Great Power, or making herself too strong to give Germany the chance of succeeding in a war. This is the opinion of those who see in the whole trend of Germany's policy conclusive evidence that she is consciously aiming at the establishment of a German hegemony, at first in Europe, and eventually in the world. . . .

It might be suggested that the great German design is in reality no more than the expression of a vague, confused, and unpractical statesmanship, not fully realizing its own drift. A charitable critic might add, by way of explanation, that the well-known qualities of mind and temperament distinguishing for good or for evil the present Ruler of Germany may not improbably be largely responsible for the erratic, domineering, and often frankly aggressive spirit which is recognizable at present in every branch of German public life, not merely in the region of foreign policy; and that this spirit has called forth those manifestations of discontent and alarm both at home and abroad with which the world is becoming familiar: that, in fact, Germany does not really know what she is driving at, and that all her excursions and alarums, all her underhand intrigues do not contribute to the steady working out of a well conceived and relentlessly followed system of policy, because they do not really form part of any such system. This is an hypothesis not flattering to the German Government, and it must be admitted that much might be urged against its validity. But it remains true that on this hypothesis also most of the facts of the present situation could be explained. . . .

If, merely by way of analogy and illustration, a comparison not intended to be either literally exact or disrespectful be permitted, the action of Germany towards this country since 1890 might be likened not inappropriately to that of a professional blackmailer, whose extortions are wrung from his victims by the threat of some vague and dreadful consequences in case of a refusal. To give way to the blackmailer's menaces enriches him, but it has long been proved by uniform experience that, although this may secure for the victim temporary peace, it is certain to lead to renewed molestation and higher demands after ever-shortening periods of amicable forbearance. The blackmailer's trade is generally ruined by the first resolute stand made against his exactions and the determination rather to face all risks of a possibly disagreeable situation than to continue in the path of endless concessions. But, failing such determination, it is more than probable that the relations between the two parties will grow steadily worse.

54
Sir Robert Baden-Powell, *Scouting for Boys* (1908)

Robert Stephenson Smyth Baden–Powell (1857–1941) was one of the great educators of modern times, to this day touching the lives of countless millions of boys and girls around the world. Schooled at Charterhouse, he entered the army and, as a specialist in reconnaissance, participated in several African campaigns. His military fame rested, however, on his heroic defense of Mafeking during the Boer War (1899–1902). Returning to England in 1904 a major general, he was surprised to discover that his military manual, *Aids in Scouting,* was being used in some schools to promote initiative and self-reliance. Adapting the "game of scout" to peacetime, he held a trial camp, organized a few patrols, and viewed with amazement the rapid implementation of his ideas. In 1909, over 11,000 Scouts rallied at Crystal Palace. The next year Baden-Powell resigned his commission, convinced by R. B. Haldane, the secretary of state for war, that he could best serve the army through Scouting.

Scouting's purposes, illustrated in Baden-Powell's 1908 *Scouting for Boys. A Handbook for Instruction in Good Citizenship,* were diverse, reflecting British concerns in the prewar era. Dismayed at the poor physiques of army recruits and impressed by the camp traditions of such earlier groups as the Children's Fresh Air Mission, Baden-Powell sought through vigorous outdoor activities to strengthen the bodies of Britain's youth. There was also a military dimension, reflected in the Chief Scout's emphasis on rifle training and his conviction that Scouts would play a major role in any European war. He strove to extend to Britain's poor the benefits of the sporting activities of the English public schools. Patrol spirit and troop competitions would teach self-reliance and "the essential virtue of sportsmanship." Finally, the Scouts would through merit badges and Empire Day activities learn imperial patriotism, a neglected part of the curricula of British schools.

The objectives of the Scouts and the Girl Guides, formed in

Source: R. S. S. Baden-Powell, *Scouting for Boys. A Handbook for Instruction in Good Citizenship,* London: Horace Cox, 1908, Reprinted by C. Arthur Pearson Ltd., 1957, pp. 12–13, 21, 28–30, 49–51. Copyright of The Scout Association, London. Reproduced by permission.

1909 to prevent the girls from infiltrating and destroying the manliness of Scouting, guaranteed criticism. The imperialism and military training fostered by Scouting made a mockery of Baden-Powell's ideal of "peace scouting." Furthermore, by aiming his work at "moral defectives" and those who were "mentally and physically defective," he appeared to deny a place to law-abiding and healthy middle-class youth and their parents. Finally, the movement's nondenominationalism and emphasis on manliness upset many. Baden-Powell's assertion that boys were not required "to come and be good" but only "to come and be men," seemed to make Scouting a religion unto itself. By the 1920s, however, Scouting's internationalism, its religious emphasis, and its growing middle-class orientation had begun to give the movement its modern characteristics.

SCOUTS' WORK

I SUPPOSE every British boy wants to help his country in some way or other.

There is a way, by which he can do so easily, and that is by becoming a scout.

A scout, as you know, is generally a soldier who is chosen for his cleverness and pluck to go out in front of an army in war to find out where the enemy are, and report to the commander all about them.

But, besides war scouts, there are also peace scouts, *i.e.,* men who in peace time carry out work which requires the same kind of abilities. These are the frontiersmen of all parts of our Empire. The "trappers" of North America, hunters of Central Africa, the British pioneers, explorers, and missionaries over Asia and all the wild parts of the world, the bushmen and drovers of Australia, the constabulary of North-West Canada and of South Africa—all are peace scouts, real *men* in every sense of the word, and thoroughly up in scout craft, *i.e.,* they understand living out in the jungles, and they can find their way anywhere, are able to read meaning from the smallest signs and foot-tracks; they know how to look after their health when far away from any doctors, are strong and plucky, and ready to face any danger, and always keen to help each other. They are accustomed to take their lives in their hands, and to fling them down without hesitation if they can help their country by doing so.

They give up everything, their personal comforts and desires, in order to get their work done. They do not do all this for their own amusement, but because it is their duty to their King, fellow-countrymen, or employers. . . .

The following subjects are what you have to know about to pass the test as a scout:—. . .

PATRIOTISM.—You belong to the Great British Empire, one of the greatest empires that has ever existed in the world. . . .

From this little island of Great Britain have sprung colonies all over the world, Australia, New Zealand, South Africa, India, Canada.

Almost every race, every kind of man, black, white, or yellow, in the world furnishes subjects of King Edward VII.

This vast empire did not grow of itself out of nothing; it was made by your forefathers by dint of hard work and hard fighting, at the sacrifice of their lives—that is, by their hearty patriotism.

People say that we have no patriotism nowadays, and that therefore our empire will fall to pieces like the great Roman empire did, because its citizens became selfish and lazy, and only cared for amusements. I am not so sure about that. I am sure that if you boys will keep the good of your country in your eyes *above everything else* she will go on all right. But if you don't do this there is very great danger, because we have many enemies abroad, and they are growing daily stronger and stronger.

Therefore, in all that you do, remember to think of your country first; don't spend the whole of your time and money on games and tuck shops merely to amuse *yourself,* but think first how you can be of use in helping your empire, and when you have done that you can justly and honestly sit down and enjoy yourself in your own way.

"Country first, self second," should be your motto. Probably, if you ask yourself truly, you will find you have at present got them just the other way about.

I hope if it is so that you will from this moment put yourself right and remain so always. Patriot first, player second. Don't be content, like the Romans were, and some people now are, to pay other people to play your football or to fight your battles for you. Do something yourself to help in keeping the flag flying. . . .

THE SCOUT LAW.

1 A SCOUT'S HONOUR IS TO BE TRUSTED. . . .

2 A SCOUT IS LOYAL to the King, and to his officers, and to his country, and to his employers. He must stick to them through thick and thin against anyone who is their enemy, or who even talks badly of them.

3 A SCOUT'S DUTY IS TO BE USEFUL AND TO HELP OTHERS. . . .

4 A SCOUT IS A FRIEND TO ALL, AND A BROTHER TO EVERY OTHER SCOUT, NO MATTER TO WHAT SOCIAL CLASS THE OTHER BELONGS. . . . A scout must never be a SNOB. A snob is one who looks down upon another because he is poorer, or who is poor and resents another because he is rich. A scout accepts the other man as he finds him, and makes the best of him. . . .

5 A SCOUT IS COURTEOUS: That is, he is polite to all—but especially to women and children and old people and invalids, cripples, etc. And he must not take any reward for being helpful or courteous.

6 A SCOUT IS A FRIEND TO ANIMALS. . . .

7 A SCOUT OBEYS ORDERS of his patrol leader or scout master without question. Even if he gets an order he does not like he must do as soldiers and sailors do, he must carry it out all the same *because it is his duty;* and after he has done it he can come and state any reasons against it: but he must carry out the order at once. That is discipline.

8 A SCOUT SMILES AND WHISTLES under all circumstances. When he gets an order he should obey it cheerily and readily, not in a slow, hang-dog sort of way.
Scouts never grouse at hardships, nor whine at each other, nor swear when put out. . . .

9 A SCOUT IS THRIFTY, that is, he saves every penny he can, and puts it into the bank, so that he may have money to keep himself when out of work, and thus not make himself a burden to others; or that he may have money to give away to others when they need it.

55
David Lloyd George, Campaign Speech (1910). Attack on the House of Lords

The Liberal party of William Ewart Gladstone, standing for laissez-faire individualism and economy in government, had by 1910 been transformed. Much of the middle class, frightened by Gladstone's Irish policy, transferred its allegiance to the Conservatives. Increasingly, the Liberal party was led by men appealing to the interests of the lower classes. This new posture was personified by David Lloyd George (1863–1945), who spoke with the fire and moral fervor of his Welsh nonconformist background, abhorring aristocratic privilege and demanding social and economic justice for the poor. Achieving national prominence by his outspoken opposition to the Boer War, he became in 1905 a member of the new Liberal government, first as president of the Board of Trade and then in 1908 as chancellor of the exchequer.

Lloyd George championed social welfare legislation, but his greatest domestic achievement was his Budget of 1909 and the resulting reform of the House of Lords. The budget was controversial not only because of its size, necessary to fund new welfare programs and the naval race with Germany, but because it increased the tax on the wealthy by a graduated income tax and death duties on land. When the Conservative-dominated House of Lords, which had already rejected several Liberal bills, now, on doubtful constitutional grounds, rejected the budget also, the lines of battle were drawn. The election of January 1910, a referendum on the budget, narrowly returned the Liberals to power. The Lords bowed to the wishes of the electorate and passed the budget, but it then killed the Parliament Bill, which limited its ability to reject legislation to a suspensive veto, thirty days for money bills and two years for other legislation. In December 1910, there was another election, this one on the issue of the Parliament Bill. The Liberals and their Labour and Irish allies were again successful, and the Lords in 1911 accepted the Parliament Act, although the king, as in 1832, had to threaten to create additional peers.

In defending the Parliament Bill to the working-class voters of

Source: The Times, November 22, 1910, p. 8. Reproduced from *The Times* by permission.

London at Mile-end-road on November 21, 1910, Lloyd George was in his element. From *The Times* report, one sees his unabashed radicalism and the popular reaction to his fiery and emotional oratory. From his success in inaugurating the budget and the reform of the House of Lords, Lloyd George gained in stature with the Liberal party and, of course, with the electorate. This victory, however, was the last for the Liberal party. Dependent on the support of Labour and the Irish, it was burdened with political debts that could not easily be paid. Its last, best excuse for not enacting all it had promised—rejection in the House of Lords—had, by its own hand, been destroyed. The unhappy sequel to the events of 1909 to 1911 has been described as "The Strange Death of Liberal England."

MR. LLOYD GEORGE AT MILE-END

Attack on the Peers

Mr. Lloyd George last night addressed a meeting of 5,000 men at the Paragon Music Hall, Mile-end-road. His speech was intended to mark the opening of the Liberal election campaign in the Tower Hamlets, and the interest which had been aroused by the announcement of his visit was shown by the great crowd outside the hall who clamoured in vain to be admitted to its already over-burdened balconies and boxes.

The Chancellor of the Exchequer, as he recalled at the beginning of his speech, had opened his first campaign against the Lords in the neighbouring district of Limehouse. That was 18 months ago, but it seemed to be fresh in the minds of his audience, who greeted his references to his former speech with a cheer of encouragement and invitation to further exploits in the same field. The great majority of his hearers had clearly come to hear another Limehouse speech, and Mr. Lloyd George did not disappoint them. They were restless and unenthusiastic while he was detailing the merits of his Budget, . . . but they became keenly attentive and fiercely demonstrative when he began a violent attack upon the aristocracy. . . . A few of his supporters on the platform winced at the tone of these remarks, . . . but it was greatly to the liking of the "East-enders," as the chairman, Mr. B. S. Straus, called the audience, and Mr. Lloyd George was enthusiastically cheered when, at the end of an hour and a half, he sat down.

The meeting was several times interrupted by the intervention and immediate ejection, mercilessly carried out, of a number of male supporters of woman suffrage. The only other disturber of the meeting was a Socialist with a message to deliver.

Mr. Lloyd George's Speech

Mr. Lloyd George said: . . . I came here to talk to you tonight about the grave issue which has arisen out of a series of events which culminated in the rejection of that Budget. . . . The government needed money for the defence of the country. . . . We also needed money for the purpose of great schemes of social reform long promised, long promised by both parties—much too long deferred. (Cheers.) That was our need. No one denied it. How did we meet it? We met it by taxing great incomes, great fortunes, and the luxuries of all classes. That was our proposal. We sent it to the House of Lords. What did they demand? That great wealth should be spared, that we should pass luxuries by untaxed and un-tolled, and the money squandered on luxuries also, and that we should impose the burden on the bread and meat of the people. (Cries of "Shame.") What was our answer? We said not an ounce would be taken out of the necessaries of life of the people. (Cheers.) Then the Lords said, "Out with your Budget then." (More cries of "Shame.") And we have come here to ask you to help us to put them out. (Cheers.)

Success of the Budget

The Budget . . . has been in operation six months. Some resolutions have been in operation 18 months. Out of the money from the Budget we voted 20 millions last year and this, out of the new taxes, to raise the old people above need. Twenty millions! What more have we done? They talk as if we had done nothing for the Navy. Why, out of the money raised by that very abused Budget we have spent ten millions more upon building ships and upon the equipment of the Navy, and we have found every penny of it. But that is not all. We are going to bring in an additional 200,000 poor old people who are now branded with the stain of pauperism. We are going to make them State pensioners—like the dukes. . . .

The Imaginary Trip to Australia

Let [the Lords] take a trip to Australia to persuade the Australians to set up a House of Lords on our plan. Well now, let us go there with them. Now we go to Australia, . . . and before we landed we would ask, "Have you a Second Chamber here?" and they would say, "Yes." Then we would say, "We will stay the night." (Laughter.) "Would you mind telling us how it is composed and of what class of people?" "Oh," they would say, "just the class of people you see all around you. It is elected by all the people, male and female, who are of age." "But," our Tariff Reform friends would say, "surely you give more votes to the owners of property than to a mere man who works for his living?" And they would say, "No; here we want to be governed by souls not sods." (Cheers.) Then our Tory friends would say, "Is life safe here?" "Absolutely," they would be told. "Is property secure?" "Quite." "Can a man safely bring his capital to this country?" and the Australian would say, "From all I hear it would be much safer here than it would be in many quarters in the City of London." "Well, then," we would say to them, "Mind you, we are a mission to convert the heathen to the principles of an hereditary Chamber." (Laughter.) . . . "Ah! what shall Australia do to be saved? Give us an aristocracy." "How are we to get one?" they would say. "Nothing easier in the world. I will tell you how we got ours. I will give you our oldest and most ancient stock, and consequently our best, because aristocracy is like cheese—the older it is (Voice,—"The more it stinks.") (Laughter) the higher it becomes.

Family Origins

Now I will tell you how we got our first and best quality. A few shiploads of French filibusters came over from the coast of Normandy. They killed all the owners of property they could lay their hands on. (Laughter.) Having done so, they levied for their own uses death duties of 100 per cent. upon the rest. (Laughter.) Unfortunately their descendants ever since have been cutting each other's throats and there are very few of them left. Consequently they are very rare and very costly, and I need hardly assure you that such a common and vulgar doctrine as the survival of the fittest does not apply to them." (Laughter.) Now that is how we started. And we would say to the Australians:—"Have you anything like that?" And they would say:—"Well, stop a minute. We had a few years ago bushrangers (cheers); but we must inform you that they only stole cattle." "Oh," we say, "cattle won't do; it must be land, and that on a large scale." "Well," says the Australian, "it really doesn't matter. We hanged the last of them a short time ago before they had an opportunity of founding a family. Have you anything else?" (Laughter.) "Well, let's give you our second quality. Our second quality arose in this way. We had a great religious Reformation in this country and we had a certain number of people who took advantage of it to appropriate to their own uses land and buildings which had been consecrated to feed the needy and to attend the sick. (Shame.) . . . And they are the people whose descendants hurl at us the epithets of robbers, thieves, spoliators, because we dare put a tax of a halfpenny upon the land they purloined. . . . I would . . . say, "Have you anything to match that?" and they would say, "We have never been quite as bad as that in our worst days in this country." "Well then," I would say, "I am afraid we cannot help you. We have given you our two best qualities. We might go on and spread out a few more of those goods—the peerages created to ennoble the indiscretions of kings. (Laughter.) We could go on, but it is hopeless. Don't you think you could found an aristocracy out of something of that sort?" They would say, "Here, rather than be governed by men like that we would have a Senate of Kangaroos." (Loud laughter and cheers.) . . .

"A Ludicrous Assembly"

It is no use going to the Colonies: there is no country in the world that would look at our Second Chamber. It is a ludicrous Assembly. Had it not been for the fact that for centuries the British-race has somehow got accustomed to them, their sense of humour would not tolerate them for half an hour. They may have been useful hundreds of years ago, but it must have been before my time, and it is no use trying to tinker at reform. They are past it. (Laughter.) Their system is just like the sort of thing I saw in London when they first introduced the electric trams—it is just like running an old horse tram and the electric cars on the same track. It ends in blocking the traffic. It is true the Tory Party now are doing their very best to put life into the old horse. (Laughter.) They are fitting up electric wires to his tail just to make him go for a time. . . . Well, on humanitarian principles I am opposed to cruelty to animals (Laughter), and I would turn the poor old thing to grass and convert his old tram into a cucumber frame.

56
Emmeline Pankhurst, *My Own Story* (1914). The Suffragette Movement

Women in nineteenth-century Britain made steady progress toward achieving equality with men. Divorce was obtainable at law after 1857. Oxford and Cambridge began to admit women in the 1870s, and employment opportunities for women began to improve about the same time. In 1893, Parliament gave married women the same property rights as single women, freeing them from economic dependence on their husbands. Politically, women meeting the property qualifications could vote in some local elections and, by the 1890s, even hold office. At the end of the century, however, women could still not vote in parliamentary elections, a restriction increasingly viewed as an anolmaly in "democratic" Britain. The Women's Social and Political Union (WSPU), founded in 1903, undertook to win this fundamental right. Led by Mrs. Emmeline Pankhurst (1858–1928), the widow of a radical labor leader, and her two daughters, Sylvia and Christabel, the WSPU attempted peacefully to persuade the

Source: Emmeline Pankhurst, *My Own Story*, New York: Kraus Reprint Co., 1971, pp. 116, 280–283, 306–307.

Liberals to sponsor the necessary legislation. When this failed, the Pankhursts turned to "guerrilla warfare," as described in the selection from Mrs. Pankhurst's autobiography.

The Pankhursts, like most British revolutionaries, portrayed themselves as acting within established tradition. The Americans had rebelled to save their freedom; Englishmen had used force to obtain their political rights. And now, "the argument of broken glass," said Emmeline Pankhurst, "is the most valuable argument in modern politics." Not everyone accepted this logic, and the violence of the WSPU perhaps delayed women's suffrage. Some suffragettes lost sight of their objective—the right to vote. The "rapture of battle" became more important than victory. By 1913, the moderate Sylvia had split from her mother and sister, who were turning to arson and bombing. World War I ended the movement; suffragettes could now hate the "Huns." In 1918, following the war, Parliament enfranchised women over thirty, those who were mature and responsible and, in numbers, insufficient to outvote the men.

Now we had reached a point where we had to choose between two alternatives. We had exhausted argument. Therefore either we had to give up our agitation altogether, as the suffragists of the eighties virtually had done, or else we must act, and go on acting, until the selfishness and the obstinacy of the Government was broken down, or the Government themselves destroyed. Until forced to do so, the Government, we perceived, would never give women the vote.

We realised the truth of John Bright's words, spoken while the reform bill of 1867 was being agitated. Parliament, John Bright then declared, had never been hearty for any reform. The Reform Act of 1832 had been wrested by force from the Government of that day, and now before another, he said, could be carried, the agitators would have to fill the streets with people from Charing Cross to Westminster Abbey. . . .

We had tried every other measure, as I am sure that I have demonstrated to my readers, and our years of work and suffering and sacrifice had taught us that the Government would not yield to right and justice, what the majority of members of the House of Commons admitted was right and justice, but that the Government would, as other governments invariably do, yield to expediency. Now our task was to show the Government that it was expedient to yield to the women's just demands. In order to do that we had to make England and every department of English life insecure and unsafe. We had to make English law a failure and the courts farce comedy theatres; we had to discredit the Government and Parliament in the eyes of the world; we had to spoil English sports, hurt business, destroy valuable property, demoralise the world of society, shame the churches, upset the whole orderly conduct of life—

That is, we had to do as much of this guerilla warfare as the people of England would tolerate. When they came to the point of saying to the Government: "Stop this, in the only way it can be stopped, by giving the women of England representation," then we should extinguish our torch.

Americans, of all people, ought to see the logic of our reasoning. There is one piece of American oratory, beloved of schoolboys, which has often been quoted from militant platforms. In a speech now included among the classics of the English language your great statesman, Patrick Henry, summed up the causes that led to the American Revolution. He said: "We have petitioned, we have remonstrated, we have supplicated, we have prostrated ourselves at the foot of the throne, and it has all been in vain. We must fight—I repeat it, sir, we must fight."

Patrick Henry, remember was advocating killing people, as well as destroying private property, as the proper means of securing the political freedom of men. The Suffragettes have not done that, and they never will. In fact the moving spirit of militancy is deep and abiding reverence for human life. In the latter course of our agitation I have been called upon to discuss our policies with many eminent men, politicians, literary men, barristers, scientists, clergymen. One of the last named, a high dignitary of the Church of England, told me that while he was a convinced suffragist, he found it impossible to justify our doing wrong that right might follow. I said to him: "We are not doing wrong—we are doing right in our use of revolutionary methods against private property. It is our work to restore thereby true values, to emphasise the value of human rights against property rights. You are well aware, sir, that property has assumed a value in the eyes of men, and in the eyes of the law, that it ought never to claim. It is placed above all human values. The lives and health and happiness, and even the virtue of women and children—that is to say, the race itself—are being ruthlessly sacrificed to the god of property every day of the world."

To this my reverend friend agreed, and I said: "If we women are wrong in destroying private property in order that human values may be restored, then I say, in all reverence, that it was wrong for the Founder of Christianity to destroy private property, as He did when He lashed the money changers out of the Temple and when He drove the Gaderene swine into the sea."

It was absolutely in this spirit that our women went forth to war. In the first month of guerilla warfare an enormous amount of property was damaged and destroyed. On January 31st a number of putting greens were burned with acids; on February 7th and 8th telegraph and telephone wires were cut in several places and for some hours all communication between London and Glasgow were suspended; a few days later windows in various of London's smartest clubs were broken, and the orchid houses at Kew were wrecked and many valuable blooms destroyed by cold. The jewel room at the Tower of London was invaded and a showcase broken. The residence of H. R. H. Prince Christian and Lambeth Palace, seat of the Archbishop of Canterbury, were visited and had windows broken. The refreshment house in Regents Park was burned to the ground on February 12th and on February 18th a country house which was being built at Walton-on-the-Hill for Mr. Lloyd-George was partially destroyed, a bomb having been exploded in the early morning before the arrival of the workmen. A hat pin and a hair pin picked up near the house—coupled with the fact that care had been taken not to endanger any lives—led the police to believe that the deed had been done by women enemies of Mr. Lloyd-George. Four days later I was arrested and brought up in Epsom police court, where I was charged with having "counselled and procured" the persons who did the damage. Admitted to bail for the night, I appeared next morning in court, where the case was fully reviewed. Speeches of mine were read, one speech, made at a meeting held on January 22nd, in which I called for volunteers to act with me in a particular engagement; and another, made the day after the explosion, in which I publicly accepted responsibility for all militant acts done in the past, and even for what had been done at Walton. At the conclusion of the hearing I was committed for trial at the May Assizes at Guildford. Bail would be allowed, it was stated, if I would agree to give the usual undertaking to refrain from all militancy or incitement to militancy. . . .

That struggle is not a pleasant one to recall. Every possible means of breaking down my resolution was resorted to. The daintiest and most tempting food was placed in my cell. All sorts of arguments were brought to bear against me— the futility of resisting the Cat and Mouse Act, the wickedness of risking suicide—I shall not attempt to record all the arguments. They fell against a blank wall of consciousness, for my thoughts were all very far away from Holloway and all its torments. I knew, what afterwards I learned as a fact, that my imprisonment was followed by the greatest revolutionary outbreak that had been witnessed in England since 1832. From one end of the island to the other the beacons of the women's revolution blazed night and day. Many country houses—all unoccupied—were fired, the grand stand of Ayr race course was burned to the ground, a bomb was exploded in Oxted Station, London, blowing out walls and windows, some empty railroad carriages were blown up, the glass of thirteen famous paintings in the Manchester Art Gallery were smashed with hammers— these are simply random specimens of the general outbreak of secret guerilla warfare waged by women to whose liberties every other approach had been barricaded by the Liberal Government of free England. The only answer of the Government was the closing of the British Museum, the National Gallery, Windsor Castle, and other tourist resorts. As for the result on the people of England, that was exactly what we had anticipated. The public were thrown into a state of emotion of insecurity and frightened expectancy. Not yet did they show themselves ready to demand of the Government that the outrages be stopped in the only way they could be stopped—by giving votes to women. I knew that it would be so. Lying in my lonely cell in Holloway, racked with pain, oppressed with increasing weakness, depressed with the heavy responsibility of unknown happenings, I was sadly aware that we were but approaching a far goal. The end, though certain, was still distant. Patience, and still more patience, faith and still more faith, well, we had called upon these souls' help before and it was certain that they would not fail us at this greatest crisis of all.

57
Wilfred Owen, Poems (1917–1918). The Western Front

World War I was a traumatic experience. The initial enthusiasm evaporated quickly among the machine guns, heavy artillery, and mustard gas—the harsh realities of trench warfare. Exhilaration turned to a sullen acceptance of a conflict that led not to victory but military stalemate and lengthy casualty lists. This despair produced the poetry of Robert Graves, Siegfried Sassoon, and Wilfred Owen. Earlier wars had inspired poets, but most had been non-combatants concerned with glorifying the deeds of their nations' warriors. The best poetry of World War I was written, however, by those who fought, and in some cases died, in the trenches. It reflected a questioning of the morality and utility of war, an attitude that survived the war and became the pacifism of the 1920s and 1930s.

Wilfred Owen (1893–1918) owed both his fame and his death to World War I. In 1915 he volunteered as a private in the Artists' Rifles and fought in France for three years. He was seriously wounded in 1917 but recovered and became a company commander. He was killed in action on November 4, 1918, one week before the armistice. Because his best poetry was written between August 1917 and September 1918, his literary fame was posthumous. His poetry reflects the cynicism, anger, and frustration of the men who were sent to die on the Western Front.

Source: Wilfred Owen, *Collected Poems.* Copyright Chatto & Windus Ltd., 1946, © 1963. Reprinted by permission of New Directions Publishing Corporation, Chatto and Windus Ltd., and the Estate of Harold Owen.

THE PARABLE OF THE OLD MAN AND THE YOUNG

So Abram rose, and clave the wood, and went,
And took the fire with him, and a knife.
And as they sojourned both of them together,
Isaac the first-born spake and said, My Father,
Behold the preparations, fire and iron,
But where the lamb for this burnt-offering?
Then Abram bound the youth with belts and straps,
And builded parapets and trenches there,
And stretched forth the knife to slay his son.
When lo! an angel called him out of heaven,
Saying, Lay not thy hand upon the lad,
Neither do anything to him. Behold,
A ram, caught in a thicket by its horns;
Offer the Ram of Pride instead of him.
But the old man would not so, but slew his son,
And half the seed of Europe, one by one.

SPRING OFFENSIVE

Halted against the shade of a last hill,
They fed, and lying easy, were at ease
And, finding comfortable chests and knees,
Carelessly slept. But many there stood still
To face the stark, blank sky beyond the ridge,
Knowing their feet had come to the end of the world.

Marvelling they stood, and watched the long grass swirled
By the May breeze, murmurous with wasp and midge,
For though the summer oozed into their veins
Like an injected drug for their bodies' pains,
Sharp on their souls hung the imminent line of grass,
Fearfully flashed the sky's mysterious glass.

•   •   •

So, soon they topped the hill, and raced together
Over an open stretch of herb and heather
Exposed. And instantly the whole sky burned
With fury against them; earth set sudden cups
In thousands for their blood; and the green slope
Chasmed and steepened sheer to infinite space.

Of them who running on that last high place
Leapt to swift unseen bullets, or went up
On the hot blast and fury of hell's upsurge,

Or plunged and fell away past this world's verge,
Some say God caught them even before they fell.

But what say such as from existence' brink
Ventured but drave too swift to sink,
The few who rushed in the body to enter hell,
And there out-fiending all its fiends and flames
With superhuman inhumanities,
Long-famous glories, immemorial shames—
And crawling slowly back, have by degrees
Regained cool peaceful air in wonder—
Why speak not they of comrades that went under?

SOLDIER'S DREAM

I dreamed kind Jesus fouled the big-gun gears;
And caused a permanent stoppage in all bolts;
And buckled with a smile Mausers and Colts;
And rusted every bayonet with His tears.

And there were no more bombs, of ours or Theirs,
Not even an old flint-lock, nor even a pikel.
But God was vexed, and gave all power to Michael;
And when I woke he'd seen to our repairs.

Plate A
Battle of Passchendaele (from the Imperial War Museum; courtesy of Camera Press, Ltd., London).

58
Marie Carmichael Stopes, *Married Love* (1918)

Marie Carmichael Stopes (1880–1958) was one of the most remarkable and controversial women of her time. Her father was a
brewer and an architect of breweries but was always more interested in archeology than economic success. Her Scottish mother,
eleven years older than her father, was a Shakespearean scholar
and a Suffragette. Educated at home until she was twelve and then
in public schools, Stopes became an academic achiever first at the
University of London, and then at Munich, where she received a
doctorate in 1904. She had a distinguished career at the University
of Manchester as a paleobotanist studying coal. She also wrote poetry and plays and many books on sex and marriage.

Stopes was not lucky in her relationships. She had first a long
platonic affair with a Japanese professor she met while studying at
Munich and then an unhappy three-year marriage that ended in an
annulment. Then in 1918, at the age of 37 and, she declared, still
a virgin, she blissfully married Humphrey Verdon Roe, a World
War I pilot who had become wealthy manufacturing Avro air-
planes. Roe's money and moral support assisted Marie in pursuing
her interest in the problems of sex in marriage. With Roe's encouragement, she opened Britain's first birth-control clinic in London
in 1921. Her libel suit against one of her critics, finally lost in the
House of Lords in 1924, ensured her notoriety but publicized and
benefited her cause.

*Married Love: A New Contribution to the Solution of Sex
Difficulties* was an instant best-seller, quickly going through many
editions. "Dedicated to young husbands and all those who are be-
trothed in love," it was partly a scientific treatise on human sexual-
ity and partly a romantic paean to happy marriages. That there
were so few happy marriages, Stopes believed, was due to human,
chiefly male, ignorance. Other animals knew by instinct how to
run their private lives, but humans had to be taught. The heart of
the book dealt with the physiological aspects of human sexual relations, but Stopes was also concerned that the wife be as free as

Source: Marie Carmichael Stopes, *Married Love: A New Contribution to the Solution of
Sex Difficulties*, Tenth Edition, Revised, London: G. P. Putnam's Sons, Ltd., 1922, pp.
31–35.

the husband to develop all aspects of her life and that the marriage be a true partnership of equals. On the one hand, her book was evidence of a new openness regarding subjects that were once thought to be improper for public discussion. On the other, it was, just as much as the more respectable plea of Virginia Woolf for *A Room of One's Own* (1929), a platform for the promotion of the equality of women. The passage below is taken from the second chapter, entitled "The Broken Joy."

Dreaming of happiness, feeling that at last they have each found the one who will give eternal understanding and tenderness, the young man and maiden marry.

At first, in the time generally called the honeymoon, the unaccustomed freedom and the sweetness of the relation often does bring real happiness. How long does it last? Too often a far shorter time than is generally acknowledged.

In the first joy of their union it is hidden from the two young people that they know little or nothing about the fundamental laws of each other's being. Much of the sex-attraction (not only among human beings, but even throughout the whole world of living creatures) depends upon the differences between the two that pair; and probably taking them all unawares, those very differences which drew them together now begin to work their undoing.

But so long as the first illusion that each understands the other is supported by the thrilling delight of ever-fresh discoveries, the sensations lived through are so rapid and so joyous that the lovers do not realise that there is no firm foundation of real mutual knowledge beneath their feet. While even the happiest pair may know of divergencies about religion, politics, social custom, and opinions on things in general, these, with goodwill, patience, and intelligence on either side, can be ultimately adjusted, because in all such things there is a common meeting ground for the two. Human beings, while differing widely about every conceivable subject in such human relations, have at least *thought* about them, threshed them out, and discussed them openly for generations.

But about the much more fundamental and vital problems of sex, there is a lack of knowledge so abysmal and so universal that its mists and shadowy darkness have affected even the few who lead us, and who are prosecuting research in these subjects. And the two young people begin to suffer from fundamental divergencies, before perhaps they realise that such exist, and with little prospect of ever gaining a rational explanation of them.

Nearly all those whose own happiness seems to be dimmed or broken count themselves exceptions, and comfort themselves with the thought of some of their friends, who, they feel sure, have attained the happiness which they themselves have missed.

It is generally supposed that happy people, like happy nations, have no history

—they are silent about their own affairs. Those who talk about their marriage are generally those who have missed the happiness they expected. True as this may be in general, it is not permanently and profoundly true, and there are people who are reckoned, and still reckon themselves, happy, but who yet unawares reveal the secret disappointment which clouds their inward peace.

Leaving out of account *"femmes incomprises"* and all the innumerable neurotic, super-sensitive, and slightly abnormal people, it still remains an astonishing and tragic fact that *so* large a proportion of marriages lose their early bloom and are to some extent unhappy.

For years many men and women have confided to me the secrets of their lives; and of all the innumerable marriages of which the inner circumstances are known to me, there are tragically few which approach even humanly attainable joy.

Many of those considered by the world, by the relatives, *even by the loved and loving partner,* to be perfectly happy marriages, are secretly shadowed to the more sensitive of the pair.

Where the bride is, as are so many of our educated girls, composed of virgin sweetness shut in ignorance, the man is often the first to create "the rift within the lute"; but his suffering begins almost simultaneously with hers. The surface freedom of our women has not materially altered, cannot materially alter, the pristine purity of a girl of our northern race. She generally has neither the theoretical knowledge nor the spontaneous physical development which might give the capacity even to imagine the basic facts of physical marriage, and her bridegroom may shock her without knowing that he was doing so. Then, unconscious of the nature, and even perhaps of the existence of his fault, he is bewildered and pained by her inarticulate pain.

Yet I think, nevertheless, it is true that in the early days of marriage the young man is often even more sensitive, more romantic, more easily pained about all ordinary things, and he enters marriage hoping for an even higher degree of spiritual and bodily unity than does the girl or the woman. But the man is more quickly blunted, more swiftly rendered cynical, and is readier to look upon happiness as a Utopian dream than is his mate.

On the other hand, the woman is slower to realise disappointment, and more often by the sex-life of marriage is of the two the more *profoundly* wounded, with a slow corrosive wound that eats into her very being and warps all her life.

Perfect happiness is a unity composed of a myriad essences; and this one supreme thing is exposed to the attacks of countless destructive factors.

59
The Balfour Report (1926).
From Empire to Commonwealth

John Stuart Mill in the nineteenth century defined Great Britain as "the Power which, of all in existence, best understands liberty." If this premise is accepted, the evolution of Britain's nineteenth-century empire into the twentieth-century Commonwealth of Nations becomes a natural, inevitable process. Following the introduction of responsible government in the 1840s and 1850s, the colonies of white settlement asserted increasing control over their own affairs, including commerce and, to a more limited extent, foreign policy. Their participation in World War I and in the postwar deliberations at Versailles gave the dominions a new standing in the international community. Their new, practical independence was registered by their membership in the League of Nations.

There remained in the 1920s, however, constitutional difficulties connected with "dominion status." Most important, the Colonial Laws Validity Act (1865) declared void any colonial statute conflicting with a British law extended to the colony. Furthermore, the British Parliament retained the theoretical power to pass legislation affecting the dominions. The Imperial Conference of 1926, therefore, appointed the Inter-Imperial Relations Committee to clarify the status of the dominions and named Lord Balfour (1848–1930), the former British prime minister, as its chairman.

The Balfour Report, although recognized as an important statement of principle, was typically British in its ambiguity and flexibility. It firmly stated that Britain and the dominions were "freely associated" "autonomous communities." It also stated the obvious, that in the areas of defense and foreign policy "the major share of responsibility" would continue to rest with Britain. But, if the dominions were autonomous, what held the British Commonwealth together? Was it simply a semimystical "unity in diversity" as Stanley Baldwin, the prime minister, described it? It was apparent that this "piece of Scottish, Balfourian metaphysics" did not actually give the dominions legal independence. To do that, the British

Source: "Report of the Inter-Imperial Relations Committee," Cmd. 2768, pp. 14–15, 20, 22, 25–26, *Parliamentary Papers*, 1926, XI. Reprinted by permission of the Controller of Her Britannic Majesty's Stationery Office.

Parliament in the Statute of Westminster (1931) repealed the
Colonial Laws Validity Act and forbade Britain to legislate for a
dominion without its consent. A dominion could now, if it chose,
legislate itself out of the British Commonwealth, as Ireland immediately began to do. Later, the Statute of Westminster made it possible for the colonies in Asia and Africa to aspire to independence
and yet remain within the Commonwealth.

II. STATUS OF GREAT BRITAIN AND THE DOMINIONS

The Committee are of opinion that nothing would be gained by attempting to lay
down a Constitution for the British Empire. Its widely scattered parts have very
different characteristics, very different histories, and are at very different stages
of evolution; while, considered as a whole, it defies classification and bears no
real resemblance to any other political organisation which now exists or has ever
yet been tried.

There is, however, one most important element in it which, from a strictly
constitutional point of view, has now, as regards all vital matters, reached its full
development—we refer to the group of self-governing communities composed
of Great Britain and the Dominions. Their position and mutual relation may be
readily defined. *They are autonomous Communities within the British Empire,
equal in status, in no way subordinate one to another in any aspect of their domestic or external affairs, though united by a common allegiance to the Crown,
and freely associated as members of the British Commonwealth of Nations.*

A foreigner endeavouring to understand the true character of the British
Empire by the aid of this formula alone would be tempted to think that it was devised rather to make mutual interference impossible than to make mutual co-
operation easy.

Such a criticism, however, completely ignores the historic situation. The
rapid evolution of the Oversea Dominions during the last fifty years has involved many complicated adjustments of old political machinery to changing
conditions. The tendency towards equality of status was both right and inevitable. Geographical and other conditions made this impossible of attainment
by the way of federation. The only alternative was by the way of autonomy: and
along this road it has been steadily sought. Every self-governing member of the
Empire is now the master of its destiny. In fact, if not always in form, it is subject to no compulsion whatever. . . .

Equality of status, so far as Britain and the Dominions are concerned, is thus
the root principle governing our Inter-Imperial Relations. But the principles of
equality and similarity, appropriate to *status,* do not universally extend to function. Here we require something more than immutable dogmas. For example, to
deal with questions of diplomacy and questions of defence, we require also flex-

ible machinery—machinery which can, from time to time, be adapted to the changing circumstances of the world. . . .

V. RELATIONS WITH FOREIGN COUNTRIES

It was agreed in 1923 that any of the Governments of the Empire contemplating the negotiation of a treaty should give due consideration to its possible effect upon other Governments and should take steps to inform Governments likely to be interested of its intention. . . .

When a Government has received information of the intention of any other Government to conduct negotiations, it is incumbent upon it to indicate its attitude with reasonable promptitude. So long as the initiating Government receives no adverse comments and so long as its policy involves no active obligations on the part of the other Governments, it may proceed on the assumption that its policy is generally acceptable. It must, however, before taking any steps which might involve the other Governments in any active obligations, obtain their definite assent.

Where by the nature of the treaty it is desirable that it should be ratified on behalf of all the Governments of the Empire, the initiating Government may assume that a Government which has had full opportunity of indicating its attitude and has made no adverse comments will concur in the ratification of the treaty. In the case of a Government that prefers not to concur in the ratification of a treaty unless it has been signed by a plenipotentiary authorised to act on its behalf, it will advise the appointment of a plenipotentiary so to act. . . .

It was frankly recognized that in this sphere, as in the sphere of defence, the major share of responsibility rests now, and must for some time continue to rest, with His Majesty's Government in Great Britain. Nevertheless, practically all the Dominions are engaged to some extent, and some to a considerable extent, in the conduct of foreign relations, particularly those with foreign countries on their borders. A particular instance of this is the growing work in connection with the relations between Canada and the United States of America which has led to the necessity for the appointment of a Minister Plenipotentiary to represent the Canadian Government in Washington. We felt that the governing consideration underlying all discussions of this problem must be that neither Great Britain nor the Dominions could be committed to the acceptance of active obligations except with the definite assent of their own Governments.

The British Gazette (1926).
The General Strike

Following two years of economic prosperity after the Armistice in
1918, Britain encountered economic difficulties, including a permanent condition of unemployment. About 10 percent of the work
force was without jobs throughout the 1920s. Hardest hit were the
coal miners, whose industry had been artificially expanded by the
needs of World War I and then bolstered for a time by government
subsidies. A reduction in wages provoked the miners to strike on
April 26, 1926. This action was supported by the Trades Union Congress (TUC), which called a general, sympathetic strike on May 3.

The General Strike lasted only nine days. Although people sympathized with the plight of the miners, they viewed the strike as a
threat to constitutional authority and supported Prime Minister
Stanley Baldwin's refusal to bow to TUC demands. Abandoned by
the other unions, the miners, six months later, were forced to accept lower wages, longer hours, and increased unemployment.
The failure of the General Strike brought a realization that working
people had more to gain from a strong labor party than by direct
action.

One surprising characteristic of the General Strike was the
goodwill between the combatants; football matches between strik-
ers and police were hardly the prelude to revolution. In many
areas, the inconveniences and hardships produced by the strike
provoked a spirit of civic cooperation and gaiety. In fact, one of
Baldwin's major concerns was to restrain hotheads such as
Winston Churchill (1874–1965), the chancellor of the exchequer,
who wanted to call out the troops and suppress "the enemy."
Fortunately, Churchill was occupied by his new duties as editor of
The British Gazette, a government newspaper created to replace
the private papers, most of which had been closed by the strike.
Baldwin later boasted that this appointment was the "cleverest"
thing that he had ever done; otherwise Churchill "would have
wanted to shoot someone."

The British Gazette is an interesting piece of historical evidence, especially in view of the absence of other press accounts of

Source: The British Gazette, No. 1 (May 5, 1926), p. 1; No. 2 (May 6, 1926), p. 3.
Reprinted by permission of the Controller of Her Britannic Majesty's Stationery Office.

the General Strike. It made no pretense at objectivity and was more inflammatory in tone and style than the strike itself. It reflects Churchill's combative personality, a fighting spirit that seemed inappropriate in 1926 but an invaluable national asset in 1940.

FIRST DAY OF GREAT STRIKE. NOT SO COMPLETE AS HOPED BY ITS PROMOTERS. PREMIER'S AUDIENCE OF THE KING. MINERS AND THE GENERAL COUNCIL MEET AT HOUSE OF COMMONS.

The great strike began yesterday. There are already signs, however, that it is by no means so complete as its promoters hoped. There were far more trains running than was the case on the first day of the railway strike in 1919.

The King received the Prime Minister in audience at Buckingham Palace yesterday morning. . . .

Never-Ending Queue

The wooden huts in the courtyard of the Foreign Office were besieged yesterday by an eager crowd anxious to do their bit. In the never-ending queue were representatives of every walk of life fairly evenly divided between men and women.

Inside the huts the officials and their volunteer helpers had a hard time of it, with never a minute to look up from their work or to cease their relentless fire of questions. "What can you do? What are you willing to do?" The answer to the first part of the question was usually something to do with motors, and the answer to the second question was invariably "anything."

This overwhelming flood of willing volunteers provided an interesting study in types. Here was the obvious City man, the lady from Mayfair, the "charlady," and an extraordinary number of young girls. The younger men, who by the queue held a majority ranged from the bareheaded motor-bicycle type to the newsboy and the van boy.

A casual inquiry as to what one of the latter was willing to do met with a unanimous cry from everybody in the vicinity, "Anything." "That," remarked the patient policeman at the door, "is the right spirit, and the sort of spirit we have had here in large quantities for the last two days."

Outside in Downing-street, the Police managed to keep the roadway fairly clear, but in Whitehall half a dozen mounted men had their work cut out to keep the curious on the move. Everywhere, however, good temper prevailed. . . .

Londoners' Trek to Work

On foot, squeezed into cars, standing in vans, riding pillion, pedaling on cycles, swarming Citywards by every road and route, London came yesterday morning doggedly and cheerially to work.

Whoever has struggled along the choked highway to Epsom Downs on Derby Day may form a mental picture of the first day's strike pilgrimmage to the East of Temple Bar. The congestion was as bad, and the temper of the people was as good.

No newspaper came to many houses to tell whether the conflict had in the eleventh hour been averted, but to read the news one had only to look out of the window. The streets with their press of private vehicles, with their streams of walkers settled to a long and steady stride, and, with never a sign of red omnibus or clanging tram, told emphatically as print that the great general strike had begun.

Every thoroughfare was a one-way street—to London. The luxurious 1920 limousines and the drab and coughing relics of prewar motoring crept along side by side in the crowded fraternity of the road. At every crossing the police beckoned on the unending line, and their task was made easy, because every man and woman at the wheel drove with consideration and a new courtesy.

In the inevitable blocks and jams, conversation rose above the throbbing of the engines. "How long will it last?" "They say that the Government—" And there Englishmen are gathered together. "Was that Mr. Ford's first sample?" demanded a lorry driver stuck level with a sorry machine whose radiator oozed little rivulets. "Never mind," retorted the anxious owner, "it moves, and"—indicating three laughing girls in the back seat—"I've a better cargo than you."

[May 5, 1926]

THE NATIONAL ISSUE. *CONSTITUTION TO BE VINDICATED.* ASSAULT ON RIGHTS OF THE NATION. *UNION LEADERS' PERSONAL RESPONSIBILITY.*

Everyone must realize that, so far as the General Strike is concerned, there can be no question of compromise of any kind. Either the country will break the General Strike, or the General Strike will break the country.

Not only is the prosperity of the country gravely injured; not only is immense and increasing loss and suffering inflicted upon the whole mass of the people; but the foundations of the lawful Constitution of Great Britain are assailed.

His Majesty's Government will not flinch from the issue, and will use all the resources at their disposal and whatever measures may be necessary to secure in a decisive manner the authority of Parliamentary government.

The Prime Minister's message to *The British Gazette* expresses a decision from which there can be no withdrawal. All loyal citizens, without respect to party or class, should forthwith range themselves behind his Majesty's Government and Parliament in the task of defending in an exemplary fashion the deliberate and organized assault upon the rights and freedom of the nation. The stronger the rally of loyal and faithful men to the cause of Parliamentary government, the sooner will the victory be achieved and the shorter the period of waste and suffering.

Extremists' Pressure

No doubt it is true that the majority of the Trades Union leaders did not intend, when they launched the General Strike, to raise the constitutional issue. They drifted weakly forward under the pressure of more extreme men. Perhaps they thought that the Government would collapse and Parliament bow down before the threat of so much injury to the Commonwealth. But whatever they may have wished or thought, a national issue has been raised of supreme magnitude.

Moreover, the responsibility of these Trades Union leaders is grievous. It is also a personal responsibility. They made no attempt to consult by ballot those whom they claim to represent. They broke in many directions contracts and engagements to which their good name was pledged, and they yielded themselves to a course of action reckless, violent, and, but for the strength and good sense of the British nation, immeasurable in its possibilities.

It would be the manly course on their part, and one which they have a perfect right to take, to reconsider their action now that they can see into what deep and deepening waters it is daily carrying them. It is not yet too late.

But whatever they may do, the authority of Parliamentary government over any sectional combination must be vindicated. Every man and every woman must consider where duty lies, and, if duties seem to conflict, where the greater duty lies. The first of all duties, a duty greater than all others put together, is owed to the nation as a whole and to that system of democratic and representative Parliamentary government which has for so many generations been the mainstay of British progress and of British freedom.

[May 6, 1926]

61

Lord Birkenhead, Speech in Lords (1928). Equal Voting Rights for Women

The House of Lords remained, despite the Parliament Act of 1911, an important part of the constitution. Although it could no longer kill legislation outright, it could and did continue to make suggestions and to correct the oversights of the busy House of Commons. Ironically, the Lords had always been the less formal of the two houses in its proceedings and rules of debate. Its membership, continually augmented by the ennobling of successful men from many walks of life, invariably contained a number of capable and diligent statesmen.

Such a man was F. E. Smith (1872–1930), a successful barrister, a member of Parliament and the cabinet, and certainly one of the most intelligent men in Britain. In 1919, he was made lord chancellor and elevated to the peerage as baron, later earl of, Birkenhead. In the Lords his dramatic sarcasm and sense of humor were more appropriate and better appreciated than in the workaday House of Commons. In the speech below, which Birkenhead delivered on May 22, 1928, one can see the history of women's emancipation from the viewpoint of a witty but pragmatic male chauvinist. With the passage of this act, the Representation of the People (Equal Franchise) Act of 1928, women attained the same voter qualifications as men.

It is worth while going into the history of this matter. . . . It was in the year 1918, after the War, that the disaster took place. Had it not been for the War in my judgment we should have continued successfully to resist this measure for an indefinite period of time. But what happened? In that year, in which nearly everybody went mad, when the phrases of President Wilson and his predictions were translated into logical and mathematical conclusions, and we talked of self-determination when we made the Peace Treaty—it was in that year that a discussion arose as to the extension of the franchise. . . .

Let me describe to your Lordships how gradually, yet how inevitably, we descended the slippery slope. First of all, it was not proposed that women should

Source: The Parliamentary Debates (House of Lords), Fifth Series, LXXI (1928), 251–254.

be included. Then a member of the House of Commons, and an important one, said that whoever was included or was not included, it was quite impossible to exclude from the franchise the brave men who had supported our cause in the field. Although it is not a political or a philosophic certainty that a man who has supported your cause in the field is necessarily equally qualified to support your cause at the polls, that argument in the spirit of the moment was accepted with facile enthusiasm, and accordingly the soldiers were admitted, subject to the qualification of age and without reference to any other very rigorous examination. Then another member of the House arose and said: "If you are extending the franchise to our brave soldiers in recognition of their valour on the field how about our brave munition workers, many of whom would greatly have desired to serve in the field, but who were not allowed to do so because of the immensely greater services which they were rendering to the nation by their work in relation to munitions?" That argument, too, was difficult to resist when once you had yielded to the first. Then an insidious and subtle member of the House said: "How about our brave women munition workers?" and, having once on principle yielded to the first argument, it was absolutely impossible to resist the second. . . .

In those circumstances—preserving, as I made it plain to the House of Commons of that day in not opposing that Bill that I did preserve, all my old objections and prejudices—was I to say: "I will leave this Government because I am in a small minority in the House of Commons?" I have spent nearly the whole of my political life in giving wise advice to my fellow countrymen, which they have almost invariably disregarded, and if I had resigned every time that my wise and advantageous advice was rejected I should seldom, indeed, during that critical period have been in office. I, therefore, reasonably took the view, making a frank explanation to the House of Commons of the position in which I found myself, that it was my duty as Attorney-General to carry out the wishes of the Government; but I expressly made my advocacy of that Bill conditional upon my complete freedom to explain the circumstances in which I found myself at the moment as its paradoxical champion. I claim the same freedom to-night.

Let me for a moment discuss the real issue which is before this House. Nearly all the arguments that have been addressed to your Lordships have been arguments that would have been valuable, timely and relevant in the year 1919. I have not heard one argument in the course of debate which has the slightest value in the period which we have reached. . . . Suppose your Lordships took the grave and most unwise responsibility of rejecting this Bill to-night, what would happen at the next General Election? The Leader of the Labour Party, the Leader of the Liberal Party and the Leader of the Conservative Party would all go to the country and say: "We profoundly resent the attitude of the House of Lords and we all of us pledge ourselves to re-introduce this Bill at once the moment the Election has taken place." I picture Lord Banbury taking the field and informing the country that if he is returned to power it is his purpose to refuse to carry this Bill into law. These things are not done by members of this House without organisation, or Parties, or followings. When you are to attempt a prognosis of that which the country will do you must address yourselves to it in the spirit of practical politicians. Once you know that the Leaders of all the Parties and the organisations of all the Parties are deeply pledged to this change it is folly to make a recommendation to your Lordships which, if adopted, would cover this House with ridicule. We know that such a course could never be taken by an Assembly which, upon so many grave and critical occasions, has given evidence of prudence and sanity.

We have to-day to meet a new situation. I have made it plain that I did and do contemplate the results with anxiety, but let us realise that when once both Houses have affirmed as a matter of principle in the Preamble to the 1919 Act, as the noble and learned Lord upon the Woolsack reminded us, that men and women were to be equal, there was indeed a kind of hypocrisy and insincerity in relation to which we had little defence, when we put it off year after year and said that women of twenty-one are not as mature and not as sophisticated as men of twenty-one. Everyone of us in our hearts knows that a woman of twenty-one is far more mature and far more sophisticated than a man of twenty-one. The moment, therefore, you had settled the principle that women were to have votes at all it became a lost cause to argue that there should be differentiation between people of the same ages. . . . My recommendation to your Lordships is to go into the Lobby in favour of this Bill, if without enthusiasm yet in a spirit of resolute resignation.

62
John Maynard Keynes, "Can Lloyd George Do It?" (1929)

The general election of May 1929 focused on the problem of unemployment. The Conservatives, led by Prime Minister Stanley Baldwin (1867–1949), emphasized that 90 percent of the work force had jobs, and they adopted as their slogans "Trust Baldwin" and "Safety First." As evidence of economic progress, Baldwin cited the expanded broccoli exports to Europe. Although Labour believed in socialism and ending "the capitalist dictatorship," its leader, Ramsay MacDonald (1866–1937), was primarily concerned with appearing moderate and responsible. The most innovative program was that of the Liberal party, now reunited under the leadership of David Lloyd George (1863–1945). The Liberals' campaign manifesto, "We Can Conquer Unemployment," incorporated many of the ideas of John Maynard Keynes (1883–1946), one of Britain's leading economists.

Keynes, a Treasury official from 1915 to 1919, became famous because of his *Economic Consequences of the Peace* (1919), a violent attack on the Treaty of Versailles, which he felt would retard the revival of German and, hence, European prosperity. In 1925, he protested Britain's return to the gold standard by criticizing the chancellor of the exchequer in a pamphlet, "The Economic Consequences of Mr. Churchill." He proposed, unsuccessfully, to promote economic growth by means of government programs. His ideas struck a responsive chord in the fertile mind of Lloyd George, and Keynes became a part of the Liberal brain trust. Together with H. D. Henderson, a similar-minded colleague, Keynes wrote in 1929 a pamphlet in support of the Liberals: "Can Lloyd George Do It?"

Keynes advocated bold governmental experimentation in the field of economic planning and an end to blind, do-nothing reliance on the natural laws of laissez-faire economics. He supported Lloyd George's plan for government programs of public works, financed in part by deficit spending. This, he argued, was less costly than unemployment insurance and the unproductiveness of

Source: The Collected Writings of John Maynard Keynes, Vol. IX: *Essays in Persuasion*, London: Macmillan for the Royal Economic Society, 1972, pp. 92–93, 121–122, 124–125. Reprinted by permission of Professor E. A. G. Robinson and Lord Kahn, Executor of the Estate of Lord Keynes.

unemployed labor. Keynes's ideas were, as he stated, regarded by most as "extreme and reckless utterances," and, in the 1929 election, the Liberals received only 59 seats in the House of Commons. Although the Liberals and Lloyd George were dead, Keynes was not. Following the Wall Street Crash of late 1929, his ideas, most forcefully articulated in his *General Theory of Employment, Interest and Money* (1936), gradually gained acceptance, receiving their most complete test in the New Deal programs of President Franklin Roosevelt and in the wartime government of Winston Churchill.

Except for a brief recovery in 1924 before the return to the gold standard, one-tenth or more of the working population of this country have been unemployed for eight years–a fact unprecedented in our history. The number of insured persons counted by the Ministry of Labour as out of work has never been less than one million since the initiation of their statistics in 1923. Today (April 1929) 1,140,000 work people are unemployed.

This level of unemployment is costing us out of the Unemployment Fund a cash disbursement of about £50 million a year. This does not include poor relief. Since 1921 we have paid out to the unemployed in cash a sum of about £500 million—and have got literally nothing for it. This sum would have built a million houses; it is nearly double the whole of the accumulated savings of the Post Office Savings Bank; it would build a third of all the roads in the country; it far exceeds the total value of all the mines, of every description, which we possess; it would be enough to revolutionise the industrial equipment of the country; or to proceed from what is heavy to what is lighter, it would provide every third family in the country with a motor-car or would furnish a fund enough to allow the whole population to attend cinemas for nothing to the end of time.

But this is not nearly all the waste. There is the far greater loss to the unemployed themselves, represented by the difference between the dole and a full working wage, and by the loss of strength and morale. There is the loss in profits to employers and in taxation to the Chancellor of the Exchequer. There is the incalculable loss of retarding for a decade the economic progress of the whole country. . . .

It is important to know and appreciate these figures because they put the possible cost of Mr Lloyd George's schemes into its true perspective. He calculates that a development programme of £100 million a year will bring back 500,000 men into employment. *This expenditure is not large in proportion to the waste and loss accruing year by year* through unemployment. . . .

Nothing has been included in the programme which cannot be justified as worth doing for its own sake. Yet even if half of it were to be wasted, *we should still be better off.* Was there ever a stronger case for a little boldness, for taking a risk if there be one? . . . Our whole economic policy during recent years has been dominated by the preoccupation of the Treasury with their departmental problem of debt conversion. The less the government borrows, the better, they argue, are the chances of converting the national debt into loans carrying a lower rate of interest. In the interests of conversion, therefore, they have exerted themselves to curtail, as far as they can, all public borrowing, all capital expenditure by the State, no matter how productive and desirable in itself. We doubt if the general public has any idea how powerful, persistent, and far-reaching this influence has been.

To all well-laid schemes of progress and enterprise, they have (whenever they could) barred the door with, No! Now it is quite true that curtailing capital expenditures exerts some tendency towards lower interest rates for government loans. But it is no less true that it makes for increased unemployment and that it leaves the country with a pre-war outfit. . . . It is not an accident that the Conservative government have landed us in the mess where we find ourselves. It is the natural outcome of their philosophy:

> You must not press on with telephones or electricity, because this will raise the rate of interest.
>
> You must not hasten with roads or housing, because this will use up opportunities for employment which we may need in later years.
>
> You must not try to employ everyone, because this will cause inflation.
>
> You must not invest, because how can you know that it will pay?
>
> You must not do anything, because this will only mean that you can't do something else.
>
> Safety first! The policy of maintaining a million unemployed has now been pursued for eight years without disaster. Why risk a change?
>
> We will not promise more than we can perform. We, therefore, promise nothing.

This is what we are being fed with.

They are slogans of depression and decay—the timidities and obstructions and stupidities of a sinking administrative vitality.

Negation, restriction, inactivity—these are the government's watchwords. Under their leadership we have been forced to button up our waistcoats and compress our lungs. Fears and doubts and hypochondriac precautions are keeping us muffled up indoors. But we are not tottering to our graves. We are healthy children. We need the breath of life. There is nothing to be afraid of. On the contrary. The future holds in store for us far more wealth and economic freedom and possibilities of personal life than the past has ever offered.

There is no reason why we should not feel ourselves free to be bold, to be open, to experiment, to take action, to try the possibilities of things. And over against us, standing in the path, there is nothing but a few old gentlemen tightly buttoned-up in their frock coats, who only need to be treated with a little friendly disrespect and bowled over like ninepins.

Quite likely they will enjoy it themselves, when once they have got over the shock.

63
Winston S. Churchill, *My Early Life* (1930). The English Public School

Winston S. Churchill (1874–1965) was the dominant British political figure of the twentieth century. For an almost unbroken period of over sixty years, he sat in the House of Commons at Westminster, influencing that venerable institution if not by the power of his office then by the force of his personality and oratory. Nevertheless, his 1930 autobiography, *My Early Life: A Roving Commission,* reminds us that Churchill was a Victorian, a product of the attitudes and institutions of an earlier age.

Churchill was born at Blenheim Palace, the ancestral home of the dukes of Marlborough, the first son of Lord Randolph Churchill, the second surviving son of the seventh duke of Marlborough, and Jenny Jerome, the daughter of a wealthy American financier. Thus, Churchill was born to privilege, remaining the likely successor to the dukedom until 1897, when his cousin Sunny, the ninth duke, and his American wife, Consuelo Vanderbilt, produced an heir. It was natural that Winston experienced the traditional upbringing and education of the English elite. Not surprisingly, he had little contact with either parent. Though he may have seen his mother as "a fairy princess," she was to be loved "dearly—but at a distance." Nurturing was provided by his beloved nurse, Mrs. Everest, and by a "sinister figure" known as "the Governess."

Churchill's formal education consisted of two years at St. James's boarding school, and then almost five years at Harrow, after Eton the most exclusive of England's public schools, with no fewer than 56 Harrovians sitting in the House of Commons. In the selection below, Churchill described his experiences at both institutions. The English public school, in fact a private school catering to the privileged and wealthy, was a Victorian institution made famous by such educators as Dr. Thomas Arnold, headmaster of Rugby, and such novels as Thomas Hughes's *Tom Brown's Schooldays.* Churchill found the public school traditions—the

Source: Winston S. Churchill, *My Early Life: A Roving Commission,* New York: Charles Scribner's Sons, 1930, pp. 12–13, 15–24. Reprinted with the permission of Charles Scribner's Sons, an imprint of Macmillan Publishing Company from *My Early Life: A Roving Commission* by Winston Churchill. Copyright 1930 Charles Scribner's Sons; copyright renewed (c) 1958 Winston Churchill. Copyright the Estate of Sir Winston Churchill. Reproduced with permission of Curtis Brown Ltd., London.

flogging, the institutionalized hazing known as fagging, the emphasis on team sports, and the domination of the curriculum by the classics—most uncongenial. He particularly questioned the relevancy of his education, perhaps a typical complaint of students of any generation.

My Early Life was serialized in the *News Chronicle* before its publication in 1930. The reader must, of course, take care in accepting a middle-aged man's recollections of his childhood. Nevertheless, it is easy to agree with Churchill, a winner of a Nobel Prize for literature, that this brief, unpretentious offering was "the best book I ever wrote."

The Form Master's observations about punishment were by no means without their warrant at St. James's School. Flogging with the birch in accordance with the Eton fashion was a great feature in its curriculum. But I am sure no Eton boy, and certainly no Harrow boy of my day, ever received such a cruel flogging as this Headmaster was accustomed to inflict upon the little boys who were in his care and power. They exceeded in severity anything that would be tolerated in any of the Reformatories under the Home Office. My reading in later life has supplied me with some possible explanations of his temperament. Two or three times a month the whole school was marshalled in the Library, and one or more delinquents were haled off to an adjoining apartment by the two head boys, and there flogged until they bled freely, while the rest sat quaking, listening to their screams. This form of correction was strongly reinforced by frequent religious services of a somewhat High Church character in the chapel. . . .

How I hated this school, and what a life of anxiety I lived there for more than two years. I made very little progress at my lessons, and none at all at games. I counted the days and the hours to the end of every term, when I should return home from this hateful servitude and range my soldiers in line of battle on the nursery floor. The greatest pleasure I had in those days was reading. When I was nine and a half my father gave me *Treasure Island,* and I remember the delight with which I devoured it. My teachers saw me at once backward and precocious, reading books beyond my years and yet at the bottom of the Form. They were offended. They had large resources of compulsion at their disposal, but I was stubborn. . . .

I HAD scarcely passed my twelfth birthday when I entered the inhospitable regions of examinations, through which for the next seven years I was destined to journey. These examinations were a great trial to me. The subjects which were dearest to the examiners were almost invariably those I fancied least. I would have liked to have been examined in history, poetry and writing essays. The examiners, on the other hand, were partial to Latin and mathematics. And their will prevailed. Moreover, the questions which they asked on both these subjects were almost invariably those to which I was unable to suggest a satisfactory answer. I should have liked to be asked to say what I knew. They always tried to ask what I did not know. When I would have willingly displayed my knowledge, they sought to expose my ignorance. This sort of treatment had only one result: I did not do well in examinations.

This was especially true of my Entrance Examination to Harrow. . . . I was in due course placed in the third, or lowest, division of the Fourth, or bottom, Form. . . .

I continued in this unpretentious situation for nearly a year. However, by being so long in the lowest form I gained an immense advantage over the cleverer boys. They all went on to learn Latin and Greek and splendid things like that. But I was taught English. We were considered such dunces that we could learn only English. Mr. Somervell—a most delightful man, to whom my debt is great—was charged with the duty of teaching the stupidest boys the most disregarded thing—namely, to write mere English. He knew how to do it. He taught it as no one else has ever taught it. Not only did we learn English parsing thoroughly, but we also practised continually English analysis. Mr. Somervell had a system of his own. He took a fairly long sentence and broke it up into its components by means of black, red, blue and green inks. Subject, verb, object: Relative Clauses, Conditional Clauses, Conjunctive and Disjunctive Clauses! Each had its colour and its bracket. It was a kind of drill. We did it almost daily. As I remained in the Third Fourth (β) three times as long as anyone else, I had three times as much of it. I learned it thoroughly. Thus I got into my bones the essential structure of the ordinary British sentence—which is a noble thing. And when in after years my schoolfellows who had won prizes and distinction for writing such beautiful Latin poetry and pithy Greek epigrams had to come down again to common English, to earn their living or make their way, I did not feel myself at any disadvantage. Naturally I am biassed in favour of boys learning English. I would make them all learn English: and then I would let the clever ones learn Latin as an honour, and Greek as a treat. But the only thing I would whip them for would be for not knowing English. I would whip them hard for that. . . .

It was thought incongruous that while I apparently stagnated in the lowest form, I should gain a prize open to the whole school for reciting to the Headmaster twelve hundred lines of Macaulay's 'Lays of Ancient Rome' without making a single mistake. I also succeeded in passing the preliminary examination for the Army while still almost at the bottom of the school. This examination seemed to have called forth a very special effort on my part, for many boys far above me in the school failed in it. . . .

I was now embarked on a military career. This orientation was entirely due to my collection of soldiers. I had ultimately nearly fifteen hundred. They were all of one size, all British, and organised as an infantry division with a cavalry brigade. My brother Jack commanded the hostile army. But by a Treaty for the

Limitation of Armaments he was only allowed to have coloured troops, and they were not allowed to have artillery. Very important! . . .

Meanwhile I found an admirable method of learning my Latin translations. . . . I formed an alliance with a boy in the Sixth Form. He was very clever and could read Latin as easily as English. Caesar, Ovid, Virgil, Horace and even Martial's epigrams were all the same to him. My daily task was perhaps ten or fifteen lines. This would ordinarily have taken me an hour or an hour and a half to decipher, and then it would probably have been wrong. But my friend could in five minutes construe it for me word by word, and once I had seen it exposed, I remembered it firmly. My Sixth-Form friend for his part was almost as much troubled by the English essays he had to write for the Headmaster as I was by these Latin cross-word puzzles. We agreed together that he should tell me my Latin translations and that I should do his essays. The arrangement worked admirably. . . .

But even as a schoolboy I questioned the aptness of the Classics for the prime structure of our education. So they told me how Mr. Gladstone read Homer for fun, which I thought served him right; and that it would be a great pleasure to me in after life. When I seemed incredulous, they added that classics would be a help in writing or speaking English. They then pointed out the number of our modern words which are derived from the Latin or Greek. Apparently one could use these words much better, if one knew the exact source from which they had sprung. I was fain to admit a practical value. But now even this has been swept away. The foreigners and the Scotch have joined together to introduce a pronunciation of Latin which divorces it finally from the English tongue. . . . I am very conservative in all these things. I always spell the Czar, 'Czar.' As for the Revised version of the Bible and the alterations in the Prayer Book and especially the Marriage service, they are grievous.

64

The Times (1933). The Body-line Bowling Controversy

The British have always been a sporting people, one historian arguing that organized games "rank among England's leading contributions to world culture." Archery, bowls, hunting, shooting, prizefighting, croquet, and polo (from India) were all popular sports in the nineteenth century. The revival of horse racing (St. Leger, the Derby, and Ascot) and steeplechasing (the Grand National at Aintree) was assisted by the reforms of Lord George Bentinck and the introduction of handicapping. Golf, originally a "peculiarity of Scotsmen," was introduced into England in the 1860s and grew rapidly. Lawn tennis, patented in 1874, was regulated after 1877 by the Wimbledon All England Croquet and Lawn Tennis Club. Most significant in the long run was the development of "football," regularized by the Football Association (1863) and the Rugby Union (1871). "Association" football, or soccer, swept the world, becoming without question the premier sport of modern times. And then there was cricket.

Cricket, an old game, was already recognized as the national sport by the early nineteenth century. It was viewed as peculiarly English, because it developed qualities such as courage and grace, individualism and teamwork, sportsmanship and, of course, honesty. Cricket's popularity as a spectator sport was signaled by the opening of Lord's Cricket Ground in 1827 and the emergence of such cricketers as Alfred Mynn (1807–1861) and W. G. Grace (1848–1915), who became national heroes. Cricket was also a good export, especially to the colonies. In 1859, the All England XI journeyed to Canada and the United States. The first eleven to visit England was a team of Australian Aborigines in 1868. The first Test Match was between England and Australia in 1871. These matches, more than important sporting events, were a bond uniting the empire.

Because cricket was a gentlemanly sport, which taught fair play and respect for rules, there was dismay in both Britain and Australia at the bitterness and controversy produced in the 1932 to

Source: The Times, January 19, 1933, pp. 3, 12; January 20, 1933, p. 9; January 24, 1933, p. 10; March 1, 1933, p. 15. Reproduced from *The Times* by permission.

THE "LEAGUE THEORY."

Mr. Punch. "COME ALONG, LET'S REFER THIS LITTLE SQUABBLE TO GENEVA."

PLATE A
(Punch 1933).

1933 Test Matches. Douglas Jardine, the captain of the English team sponsored by the Marylebone Cricket Club (MCC), attempted to neutralize the strong Australian batsmen by instructing his premier bowler, Harold Larwood, to bowl on the leg side or, as the Australians claimed, at the batsman rather than the wicket. When in the second match two of Australia's best batsmen were carried from the field, the situation became explosive. The Australians regarded this body-line, or leg-theory, bowling as unsportsmanlike, as "not cricket." The resulting controversy can be judged from the sports pages of *The Times*. The problem was so serious that the dominions secretary called the MCC officials to Downing Street for a conference (see Plate A). Although the crisis was short-lived, the following year the British government took the precaution of insisting that Larwood be dropped from the English team.

THE THIRD TEST MATCH. ENGLAND'S WINNING POSITION. AUSTRALIA PROTEST AT LEG-THEORY.

England seems almost certain to beat Australia in the Third Test Match for, after scoring 412 in their second innings and leaving the Australians 532 to make in order to win, they succeeded in dismissing four of their best batsmen in the second innings for 120 before stumps were pulled up to-day. At the close of play Ponsford, Fingleton, McCabe, and Bradman were all out, and Woodfull and Richardson may be regarded as Australia's last hope, though Oldfield, if he is able to go in, which seems unlikely, is capable of a good performance. The wicket was still in excellent order when Australia went in a second time. On the form of this match the English team have proved themselves superior all round. . . .

The only bright feature of the match from the Australian point of view was Bradman's bright innings to-day. In a little over an hour he showed his best form. He hit the bowling hard at a critical period, and he made it look playable, which other Australians have hitherto failed to do. The crowd applauded heartily while Jardine kept his bowlers to the off theory, but when he reverted to leg theory against Bradman, who seemed to be getting the better of the bowling, they howled and hooted loudly. . . .

When Australia went in Larwood began bowling to an off-field. His first few opening overs were very fast and he completely beat Fingleton with his pace. Ponsford went in at the fall of the first wicket. He began well, but was out to a good stroke. Larwood had, so far taken two for one run. Larwood continued bowling to an orthodox field for a few overs, but, after Bradman had begun to score freely off him, he reverted to the leg theory. Woodfull and Bradman continued to make runs off Larwood and Bradman hit eight 4's and a 6 before he was caught and bowled by Verity.

The Australian Board of Control have cabled a protest against "body-line bowling" to the M.C.C., which is printed on p. 12.

[*The Times*, January 19, 1933]

"LEG-THEORY" BOWLING. AUSTRALIAN PROTEST.

The Australian Cricket Board of Control has sent the following telegram to the M.C.C.:

> Body-line bowling has assumed such proportions as to menace the best interests of the game, making the protection of his body by a batsman his main consideration. It is causing intensely bitter feeling between the players as well as injury to them. In our opinion it is unsportsmanlike. Unless it is stopped at once it is likely to upset the friendly relations existing between Australia and England. . . .

The M.C.C. received the telegram sent by the Australian Cricket Board of

Control on the subject of leg-theory bowling shortly before noon yesterday. It is not yet known when the matter will be discussed.

[*The Times,* January 19, 1933]

LEG BOWLING. OTHER DAYS AND OTHER GROUNDS.
"IS IT A BETTER GAME?"

To the Editor of *The Times*

SIR,

The discussion in your paper on "leg bowling" revives old memories and old desires. Pitches like billiard tables and spectators numbered in thousands make people forget what cricket used to be. Fifty years ago this new danger was a common incident of every match played outside the few places where grounds-men guarded the turf. Fast bowlers —*quorum parvissima pars fui*—were regarded as essential and were often, as I was, most erratic. I have often seen a ball pitch once and then bounce straight into the backstop's hands.

Nor were these bowling eccentricities confined to local grounds. I remember on one occasion the first ball of a match slung with immense violence straight at the big black beard of W. G. Grace. Did he object? Certainly not: he simply hit it out of the ground and waited for the next.

In the country there were some pitches renowned for their fiery qualities. On one of these I recall a game in which Ranjitsinhji took part. Two benches from the village school provided the grand stand and on these were seated the squire, the local doctor—whose patients were long-suffering and few—the publican, and some countrymen.

Ranjitsinhji was clean bowled by the village postman, who wore his official costume, and all the four innings were finished in the day. As for leg balls and head balls and body balls, they formed the feature of the match, which no one seemed more thoroughly to enjoy than Ranjitsinhji himself.

The world has been made smooth for the game and its lords, but is it a better game?

Yours faithfully,
BUCKMASTER

1, Porchester Terrace, W. 2.

[*The Times,* January 20, 1933]

M.C.C. REPLY TO AUSTRALIA.
"FULLEST CONFIDENCE" IN JARDINE.

The Committee of the M.C.C. met at Lord's yesterday to consider the message which they had received from the Australian Board of Control, . . . and replied:

"We, the Marylebone Cricket Club, deplore your cable. We deprecate your

opinion that there has been unsportsmanlike play. We have the fullest confidence in our captain, team, and managers, and we are convinced that they would
do nothing to infringe either the laws of cricket or the spirit of the game. We
have no evidence that our confidence has been misplaced. Much as we regret the
accidents to Woodfull and Oldfield, we understand that in neither case was the
bowler to blame. If the Australian Board of Control wish to propose a new law
or rule it shall receive our careful consideration in due course. We hope the situation is not now as serious as your cable would seem to indicate, but if it is such
as to jeopardize the good relations between English and Australian cricketers,
and you consider it desirable to cancel the remainder of the programme, we
would consent, but with great reluctance."

(Signed) FINDLAY, Secretary.
[*The Times*, January 24, 1933]

FIFTY-ONE FIFTY-ONE

In four out of five of this season's Test Matches between England and Australia
the English Captain has lost the toss; in four of the five he and his side have easily won the game. That, in brief, is the whole story of the struggle between the
two countries which ended yesterday on the Sydney ground. It is the outcome of
the indomitable will-power with which Jardine has played his part and managed
his team, and of the loyal and willing teamspirit with which, to a man, they re-
sponded. In the whole series of these matches, of which the Mother Country and
the Dominion have so far each won fifty-one, no English captain, however great
and distinguished, has been more in evidence as a controlling factor of the play.
He had under his command what is admittedly on this year's form the better of
the two sides—and he had Larwood. But if Woodfull and Bradman and the other
Australian batsmen found themselves up against an unfamiliar type of bowling,
the practice as well as the theory of which was not on the whole to their liking, it
is no less true that Larwood and his captain in particular have had to face a style
of criticism which they must have found at least as distasteful and nerveracking.

Happily that is all over now. Several of the Dominion batsmen have shown
that they can deal successfully with the bowling to which objections were
raised—a natural evolution of the bowler's art to cope with the modern predominance of the batsman, and largely due, as many think, to the batsman's own
fault—and time and reflection may perhaps lead its critics to question whether
the maintenance of their protest is worth while. For the moment England has the
better team, every member of which from first to last has good reason to be
proud of his share in England's victory. But by the law of averages Australia's
turn will come again. The two countries are now level in the number of matches
won, and for the good of the game and the enjoyment of the players on both
sides nothing must ever be allowed to interfere with the friendly feelings and
close rivalry that have bound them together so long.

[*The Times*, March 1, 1933]

65
Edward VIII, Radio Speech (1936).
The Abdication Crisis

The monarchy's decline in power was not accompanied by a drop in public interest in the royal family. This interest was heightened in late 1936, when monarchy became controversial for the first time since the republican criticism of Victoria in the 1860s. The issue was the right of the king, Edward VIII (January 20–December 11, 1936), to order his personal life as he saw fit. Specifically, Edward, a bachelor of 41, wanted to marry Mrs. Wallis Simpson, an American divorcee who had remarried. The news of the king's association with Mrs. Simpson was kept out of British papers, largely through the voluntary restraint of the editors. In October 1936 Mrs. Simpson was granted her divorce, making her marriage to Edward possible. Prime Minister Stanley Baldwin, concerned about the effect of such a marriage on the institution of monarchy, gave the king a simple choice: give up Mrs. Simpson or the throne. In early December the news broke in the press, creating a public sensation. The attempts to work out a compromise failed, and on December 11, 1936, Edward abdicated and with his bride went into exile.

Edward's abdication speech is interesting in two ways. First, it illustrates how Edward's personal crisis had been transformed into a constitutional issue. Edward's remark that earlier he had not been free to speak indicates that he, a good constitutional monarch, had accepted Baldwin's argument that the monarch's private and public lives could not be separated. In both areas the king must act on the advice of his ministers, and Baldwin had forbidden him as king to appeal for public support. Second, Edward's use of the BBC for his announcement reflects the obvious growth in the importance of the electronic news media, a development also of significance to the historian.

At long last I am able to say a few words of my own.

I have never wanted to withhold anything, but until now it has not been constitutionally possible for me to speak.

A few hours ago I discharged my last duty as King and Emperor, and now

Source: Edward, Duke of Windsor, *A King's Story: The Memoirs of the Duke of Windsor,* New York: G. P. Putnam's Sons, 1947, pp. 411–412.

that I have been succeeded by my brother, the Duke of York, my first words must be to declare my allegiance to him. This I do with all my heart.

You all know the reasons which have impelled me to renounce the Throne, but I want you to understand that in making up my mind I did not forget the Country or the Empire, which, as Prince of Wales and lately as King, I have for 25 years tried to serve.

But you must believe me when I tell you that I have found it impossible to carry the heavy burden of responsibility and to discharge my duties as King, as I wish to do, without the help and support of the woman I love, and I want you to know that the decision I have made has been mine, and mine alone. This was a thing I had to judge for myself. The other person most nearly concerned has tried, up to the last, to persuade me to take a different course. I have made this, the most serious decision of my life, only upon the single thought of what would in the end be best for all.

This decision has been made less difficult to me by the sure knowledge that my brother, with his long training in the public affairs of this Country and with his fine qualities, will be able to take my place forthwith without interruption or injury to the life and progress of the Empire, and he has one matchless blessing, enjoyed by so many of you, and not bestowed on me, a happy home with his wife and children.

During these hard days I have been comforted by my Mother and by my Family.

The Ministers of the Crown, and in particular Mr. Baldwin, the Prime Minister, have always treated me with full consideration. There has never been any constitutional difference between me and them and between me and Parliament. Bred in the constitutional tradition by my Father, I should never have allowed any such issue to arise.

Ever since I was Prince of Wales, and later on when I occupied the Throne, I have been treated with the greatest kindness by all classes wherever I have lived or journeyed throughout the Empire. For that I am very grateful.

I now quit altogether public affairs, and I lay down my burden. It may be some time before I return to my native land, but I shall always follow the fortunes of the British race and Empire with profound interest, and if, at any time in the future, I can be found of service to His Majesty in a private station, I shall not fail.

And now we all have a new King.

I wish Him, and you, His people, happiness and prosperity with all my heart.

God bless you all.

God Save The King.

66
George Orwell, *The Road to Wigan Pier* (1937). The Great Depression

Eric Arthur Blair (1903–1950), better known as George Orwell, was one of the most influential writers of this century. His two novels of political satire, *Animal Farm* (1945) and *Nineteen Eighty-Four* (1949), warned of the horrors of totalitarianism and added words and phrases to contemporary speech: "Newspeak," "Doublethink," "Big Brother is watching," and "All animals are equal but some animals are more equal than others."

Orwell was born in India, where his father was a middle-level civil servant superintending the opium trade. Raised and educated in England, he returned to the East, serving in the Indian Imperial Police in Burma from 1922 to 1927. He resigned this secure position, determined to become a writer. He described the life he saw and experienced in his first book, *Down and Out in Paris and London* (1933).

The turning point in Orwell's literary career came in 1936, when publisher Victor Gollancz and the Left Book Club commissioned him to write a book describing the condition of the unemployed in the economically depressed north of England. Orwell later described these observations, published in 1937 as *The Road to Wigan Pier*, as his first attempt "to make political writing into an art."

In the first part of the book, excerpted below, Orwell described the misery he observed and his abhorrence of the economic system which produced it. He sympathized with those unfortunates caught in the capitalistic web, especially the miners who spent their lives shoveling coal in a cramped black hell to enable others, like Orwell himself, to live comfortable lives as intellectuals. In the second part, which Gollancz had not wanted and which he tried in a long introduction to refute, Orwell described the dilemma of socialism. He saw it as the only remedy for the conditions he described and the only defense against the rising tide of fascism, but it seemed unable to gather people to its banner. The poor were absorbed with their own problems, and workers sought a modicum

Source: George Orwell, *The Road to Wigan Pier*, New York: Berkley Medallion Books published by The Berkley Publishing Company, 1961, pp. 28–29, 31–33, 41–42. Excerpts from *The Road to Wigan Pier* by George Orwell, reprinted by permission of Harcourt Brace Jovanovich, Inc., the estate of Sonia Brownell Orwell and Martin Secker & Warburg Ltd.

of quiet leisure. To the average person, the socialists appeared to attract "every fruit-juice drinker, nudist, sandal-wearer, sex-maniac, Quaker, 'Nature Cure' quack, pacifist and feminist in England." And Orwell, himself, was too much the individualist ever to feel comfortable with a system which necessarily stressed collective solutions at the expense of personal freedom.

On the day when there was a full chamber-pot under the breakfast table I decided to leave. The place was beginning to depress me. It was not only the dirt, the smells and the vile food, but the feeling of stagnant meaningless decay, of having got down into some subterranean place where people go creeping round and round, just like blackbeetles, in an endless muddle of slovened jobs and mean grievances. The most dreadful thing about people like the Brookers is the way they say the same things over and over again. It gives you the feeling that they are not real people at all, but a kind of ghost for ever rehearsing the same futile rigmarole. In the end Mrs. Brooker's self-pitying talk—always the same complaints, over and over, and always ending with the tremulous whine of "It does seem 'ard, don't it now?"—revolted me even more than her habit of wiping her mouth with bits of newspaper. But it is no use saying that people like the Brookers are just disgusting and trying to put them out of mind. For they exist in tens and hundreds of thousands; they are one of the characteristic by-products of the modern world. . . . It is a kind of duty to see and smell such places now and again, especially smell them, lest you should forget that they exist; though perhaps it is better not to stay there too long.

The train bore me away, through the monstrous scenery of slag-heaps, chimneys, piled scrap-iron, foul canals, paths of cindery mud criss-crossed by the prints of clogs. This was March, but the weather had been horribly cold and everywhere there were mounds of blackened snow. As we moved slowly through the outskirts of the town we passed row after row of little grey slum houses running at right angles to the embankment. At the back of one of the houses a young woman was kneeling on the stones, poking a stick up the leaden waste-pipe which ran from the sink inside and which I suppose was blocked. I had time to see everything about her—her sacking apron, her clumsy clogs, her arms reddened by the cold. She looked up as the train passed, and I was almost near enough to catch her eye. She had a round pale face, the usual exhausted face of the slum girl who is twenty-five and looks forty, thanks to miscarriages and drudgery; and it wore, for the second in which I saw it, the most desolate, hopeless expression I have ever seen. It struck me then that we are mistaken when we say that "It isn't the same for them as it would be for us," and that people bred in the slums can imagine nothing but the slums. For what I saw in her face was not the ignorant suffering of an animal. She knew well enough what was happening to her—understood as well as I did how dreadful a destiny it was to be kneeling there in the bitter cold, on the slimy stones of a slum backyard, poking a stick up a foul drain-pipe. . . .

OUR CIVILISATION . . . *is* founded on coal, more completely than one realises until one stops to think about it. The machines that keep us alive, and the machines that make the machines, are all directly or indirectly dependent upon coal. In the metabolism of the Western world the coal-miner is second in importance only to the man who ploughs the soil. . . .

When you go down a coal-mine it is important to try and get to the coal face when the "fillers" are at work. . . . The time to go there is when the machines arc roaring and the air is black with coal dust, and when you can actually see what the miners have to do. At those times the place is like hell, or at any rate like my own mental picture of hell. Most of the things one imagines in hell are there—heat, noise, confusion, darkness, foul air, and, above all, unbearably cramped space. Everything except the fire, for there is no fire down there except the feeble beams of Davy lamps and electric torches which scarcely penetrate the clouds of coal dust. . . .

The first impression of all, overmastering everything else for a while, is the frightful, deafening din from the conveyor belt which carries the coal away. You cannot see very far, because the fog of coal dust throws back the beam of your lamp, but you can see on either side of you the line of half-naked kneeling men, one to every four or five yards, driving their shovels under the fallen coal and flinging it swiftly over their left shoulders. They are feeding it on to the conveyor belt, a moving rubber belt a couple of feet wide which runs a yard or two behind them. . . .

It is impossible to watch the "fillers" at work without feeling a pang of envy for their toughness. It is a dreadful job that they do, an almost superhuman job by the standards of an ordinary person. For they arc not only shifting monstrous quantities of coal, they are also doing it in a position that doubles or trebles the work. They have got to remain kneeling all the while. . . . You can hardly tell by the look of them whether they are young or old. They may be any age up to sixty or even sixty-five, but when they are black and naked they all look alike. No one could do their work who had not a young man's body, and a figure fit for a guardsman at that; just a few pounds of extra flesh on the waist-line, and the constant bending would be impossible. You can never forget that spectacle once you have seen it—the line of bowed, kneeling figures, sooty black all over, driving their huge shovels under the coal with stupendous force and speed. They are on the job for seven and a half hours, theoretically without a break, for therc is no time "off." Actually they snatch a quarter of an hour or so at some time during the shift to eat the food they have brought with them, usually a hunk of bread and dripping and a bottle of cold tea. The first time I was watching the "fillers" at work I put my hand upon some dreadful slimy thing among the coal dust. It was a chewed quid of tobacco. Nearly all the miners chew tobacco, which is said to be good against thirst. . . .

It is not long since conditions in the mines were worse than they are now. There are still living a few very old women who in their youth have worked underground, with a harness round their waists and a chain that passed between their legs, crawling on all fours and dragging tubs of coal. They used to go on doing this even when they were pregnant. And even now, if coal could not be produced without pregnant women dragging it to and fro, I fancy we should let them do it rather than deprive ourselves of coal. But most of the time, of course, we should prefer to forget that they were doing it. It is so with all types of manual work; it keeps us alive, and we are oblivious of its existence. More than anyone else, perhaps, the miner can stand as the type of the manual worker, not only because his work is so exaggeratedly awful, but also because it is so vitally necessary and yet so remote from our experience, so invisible, as it were, that we are capable of forgetting it as we forget the blood in our veins. In a way it is even humiliating to watch coal-miners working. It raises in you a momentary doubt about your own status as an "intellectual" and a superior person generally. For it is brought home to you, at least while you are watching, that it is only because miners sweat their guts out that superior persons can remain superior. You and I and the editor of the *Times Lit. Supp.,* and the Nancy poets and the Archbishop of Canterbury and Comrade X, author of *Marxism for Infants*—all of us *really* owe the comparative decency of our lives to poor drudges underground, blackened to the eyes, with their throats full of coal dust, driving their shovels forward with arms and belly muscles of steel.

67
Neville Chamberlain, Speech in Commons (1938). The Munich Crisis

The British foreign policy of appeasement in the 1930s is today usually condemned as a policy of weakness and the sacrifice of moral principles in the face of danger. Appeasement's ineffectiveness is also taken as self-evident: aggressors whose initial demands are met simply increase their demands. The great appeaser was Neville Chamberlain (1869–1940), the prime minister from 1937 to 1940. He came to power, highly regarded for his success in dealing with domestic problems, just as public and parliamentary concern was shifting away from the depression and toward Hitler's Germany.

Chamberlain took pride in his rational approach to world problems. He believed that most disputes resulted from misunderstandings that could be settled by reasonable compromise. Indeed, this seemed the lesson of World War I. Like many in Britain, appalled by the cost of World War I, he listened sympathetically to Hitler's demands, believing that they often represented legitimate German grievances. He, therefore, supported active appeasement, the settlement of difficulties before they became crises. The great test of appeasement was the dispute between Czechoslovakia and Germany over the Sudetenland, an area of Czechoslovakia inhabited largely by Germans and desired by Hitler. In September 1938 Chamberlain made three trips to Germany, first agreeing to, and then at Munich helping to arrange the details of, the partition of Czechoslovakia.

In the Commons on October 3, 1938, Chamberlain defended his foreign policy, which he had already described as ensuring "peace for our time." Other members, however, including Winston Churchill, condemned Munich, arguing that it was a stain on British honor and would promote war rather than avert it. Following Hitler's dismemberment of the remainder of Czechoslovakia in March 1939 and the acknowledgment of the failure of appeasement, Britain's policy hardened. When Britain came to the defense of Poland in September 1939, the war was accepted by almost everyone as necessary and morally correct. Everything Chamberlain worked for had "crashed into ruins."

Source: Parliamentary Debates (House of Commons), Fifth Series, Vol. 339 (1938), pp. 41–42, 45, 47–49; Vol. 351 (1939), p. 292.

The Prime Minister (Mr. Chamberlain): . . . When the House met last Wednesday, we were all under the shadow of a great and imminent menace. War, in a form more stark and terrible than ever before, seemed to be staring us in the face. Before I sat down, a message had come which gave us new hope that peace might yet be saved, and to-day, only a few days after, we all meet in joy and thankfulness that the prayers of millions have been answered, and a cloud of anxiety has been lifted from our hearts. Upon the Members of the Cabinet the strain of the responsibility of these last few weeks has been almost overwhelming. Some of us, I have no doubt, will carry the mark of it for the rest of our days. . . .

Before I come to describe the Agreement which was signed at Munich in the small hours of Friday morning last, I would like to remind the House of two things which I think it is very essential not to forget when those terms are being considered. The first is this: We did not go there to decide whether the predominantly German areas in the Sudetenland should be passed over to the German Reich. That had been decided already. Czechoslovakia had accepted the Anglo-French proposals. What we had to consider was the method, the conditions and the time of the transfer of the territory. The second point to remember is that time was one of the essential factors. All the elements were present on the spot for the outbreak of a conflict which might have precipitated the catastrophe. We had populations inflamed to a high degree; we had extremists on both sides ready to work up and provoke incidents; we had considerable quantities of arms which were by no means confined to regularly organised forces. Therefore, it was essential that we should quickly reach a conclusion, so that this painful and difficult operation of transfer might be carried out at the earliest possible moment and concluded as soon as was consistent with orderly procedure, in order that we might avoid the possibility of something that might have rendered all our attempts at peaceful solution useless. . . .

Before giving a verdict upon this arrangement, we should do well to avoid describing it as a personal or a national triumph for anyone. The real triumph is that it has shown that representatives of four great Powers can find it possible to agree on a way of carrying out a difficult and delicate operation by discussion instead of by force of arms, and thereby they have averted a catastrophe which would have ended civilisation as we have known it. The relief that our escape from this great peril of war has, I think, everywhere been mingled in this country with a profound feeling of sympathy—[Hon. Members: "Shame."] I have nothing to be ashamed of. Let those who have, hang their heads. We must feel profound sympathy for a small and gallant nation in the hour of their national grief and loss. . . .

In my view the strongest force of all, one which grew and took fresh shapes and forms every day was the force not of any one individual, but was that unmistakable sense of unanimity among the peoples of the world that war somehow must be averted. The peoples of the British Empire were at one with those of Germany, of France and of Italy, and their anxiety, their intense desire for peace, pervaded the whole atmosphere of the conference, and I believe that that, and not threats, made possible the concessions that were made. I know the House will want to hear what I am sure it does not doubt, that throughout these discussions the Dominions, the Governments of the Dominions, have been kept in the closest touch with the march of events by telegraph and by personal contact, and I would like to say how greatly I was encouraged on each of the journeys I made to Germany by the knowledge that I went with the good wishes of the Governments of the Dominions. They shared all our anxieties and all our hopes. They rejoiced with us that peace was preserved, and with us they look forward to further efforts to consolidate what has been done.

Ever since I assumed my present office my main purpose has been to work for the pacification of Europe, for the removal of those suspicions and those animosities which have so long poisoned the air. The path which leads to appeasement is long and bristles with obstacles. The question of Czechoslovakia is the latest and perhaps the most dangerous. Now that we have got past it, I feel that it may be possible to make further progress along the road to sanity. . . .

In our relations with other countries everything depends upon there being sincerity and good will on both sides. I believe that there is sincerity and good will on both sides in this declaration. That is why to me its significance goes far beyond its actual words. If there is one lesson which we should learn from the events of these last weeks it is this, that lasting peace is not to be obtained by sitting still and waiting for it to come. It requires active, positive efforts to achieve it. No doubt I shall have plenty of critics who will say that I am guilty of facile optimism, and that I should disbelieve every word that is uttered by rulers of other great States in Europe. I am too much of a realist to believe that we are going to achieve our paradise in a day. We have only laid the foundations of peace. The superstructure is not even begun.

[October 3, 1938]

The Prime Minister (Mr. Chamberlain): This is a sad day for all of us, and to none is it sadder than to me. Everything that I have worked for, everything that I have hoped for, everything that I have believed in during my public life, has crashed into ruins. There is only one thing left for me to do; that is, to devote what strength and powers I have to forwarding the victory of the cause for which we have to sacrifice so much. I cannot tell what part I may be allowed to play myself; I trust I may live to see the day when Hitlerism has been destroyed and a liberated Europe has been re-established.

[September 3, 1939]

68

Winston Churchill, Speeches in Commons (1940). The Battle of Britain

Seldom have a man and his mission come together so dramatically or so happily for both as did Winston Churchill (1874–1965) and the salvation of Britain in May 1940. Churchill had already had a lifetime full of excitement, controversy, and frustration. As an intrepid young army officer and newspaper correspondent, he had been with the Malakand Field Force in India and with Lord Kitchener in the Sudan, a participant in the cavalry charge at Omdurman; captured by the Boers in South Africa, he had effected one of the most daring and lucky escapes in history. Elected to Parliament in 1900 and serving in several governments, he had pushed welfare legislation, taken the blame for the Dardanelles campaign, and in 1925 put Britain back on the gold standard. He was acknowledged to be talented and hardworking but equally erratic, daring, and pugnacious. During the 1930s he was out of power and out of favor. He warned of the danger of Germany's rearming and charged that at Munich Britain had "sustained a total and unmitigated defeat." But no one listened. Had he died before 1940, he would have been likened to his father, Lord Randolph, a brilliant failure.

Britain in 1940 was still suffering from the shock of World War I and from two decades of timid and unimaginative leadership. At first unwilling to prevent Germany from becoming powerful, she then seemed unable to stop the march of German aggression. Austria, Czechoslovakia, and Poland had been digested. Denmark and Norway were recent conquests. And on May 10, Holland, Belgium, and France were invaded. Under severe attack in Parliament, Neville Chamberlain resigned as prime minister, and Churchill was asked to form a national coalition government. In the dangerous months that followed, Churchill's speeches expressed Britain's resolve: "We shall never surrender." On May 13, he had just assumed power and was making his first address to Parliament as prime minister. On June 4, Britain's army had just

Source: The Parliamentary Debates (House of Commons), Fifth Series, Vol. 360 (1940), p. 1502; Vol. 361 (1940), pp. 795–796; Vol. 362 (1940), pp. 60–61; Vol. 364 (1940), p. 1170–1171.

been safely evacuated from the sands of Dunkirk, but the serious consequences of its expulsion, even the fall of France, were apparent. By June 18, France had fallen and Churchill was careful to point out the present danger to "the whole world, including the United States." On August 20, when the Battle of Britain was raging, he expanded the theme of British and American common interests. It was his own as well as Britain's "finest hour." Of his role, he later said that the lion's heart had been that of the British people; he had merely been allowed to give the lion's roar.

May 13, 1940

I would say to the House, as I said to those who have joined this Government: "I have nothing to offer but blood, toil, tears and sweat."

We have before us an ordeal of the most grievous kind. We have before us many, many long months of struggle and of suffering. You ask, what is our policy? I will say: It is to wage war, by sea, land and air, with all our might and with all the strength that God can give us; to wage war against a monstrous tyranny, never surpassed in the dark, lamentable catalogue of human crime. That is our policy. You ask, what is our aim? I can answer in one word: It is victory, victory at all costs, victory in spite of all terror, victory, however long and hard the road may be; for without victory, there is no survival. Let that be realised; no survival for the British Empire, no survival for all that the British Empire has stood for, no survival for the urge and impulse of the ages, that mankind will move forward towards its goal. But I take up my task with buoyancy and hope. I feel sure that our cause will not be suffered to fail among men. At this time I feel entitled to claim the aid of all, and I say, "Come then, let us go forward together with our united strength."

June 4, 1940

I have, myself, full confidence that if all do their duty, if nothing is neglected, and if the best arrangements are made, as they are being made, we shall prove ourselves once again able to defend our island home, to ride out the storm of war, and to outlive the menace of tyranny, if necessary for years, if necessary alone. At any rate, that is what we are going to try to do. That is the resolve of His Majesty's Government—every man of them. That is the will of Parliament and the nation. The British Empire and the French Republic, linked together in their cause and in their need, will defend to the death their native soil, aiding each other like good comrades to the utmost of their strength. Even though large tracts of Europe and many old and famous States have fallen or may fall into the grip of the Gestapo and all the odious apparatus of Nazi rule, we shall not flag or fail. We shall go on to the end. We shall fight in France, we shall fight on the seas and oceans, we shall fight with growing confidence and growing strength in the air, we shall defend our island, whatever the cost may be. We shall fight on the beaches, we shall fight on the landing grounds, we shall fight in the fields and in the streets, we shall fight in the hills; we shall never surrender, and even if, which I do not for a moment believe, this island or a large part of it were subjugated and starving, then our Empire beyond the seas, armed and guarded by the British Fleet, would carry on the struggle, until, in God's good time, the new world, with all its power and might, steps forth to the rescue and the liberation of the old.

June 18, 1940

What General Weygand called the "Battle of France" is over. I expect that the battle of Britain is about to begin. Upon this battle depends the survival of Christian civilisation. Upon it depends our own British life and the long continuity of our institutions and our Empire. The whole fury and might of the enemy must very soon be turned on us. Hitler knows that he will have to break us in this island or lose the war. If we can stand up to him all Europe may be free, and the life of the world may move forward into broad, sunlit uplands; but if we fail then the whole world, including the United States, and all that we have known and cared for, will sink into the abyss of a new dark age made more sinister, and perhaps more prolonged, by the lights of a perverted science. Let us therefore brace ourselves to our duty and so bear ourselves that if the British Commonwealth and Empire lasts for a thousand years men will still say, "This was their finest hour."

August 20, 1940

We have to think not only for ourselves but for the lasting security of the cause and principles for which we are fighting and of the long future of the British Commonwealth of Nations. Some months ago we came to the conclusion that the interests of the United States and of the British Empire both required that the United States should have facilities for the naval and air defence of the Western hemisphere against the attack of a Nazi power which might have acquired temporary but lengthy control of a large part of Western Europe and its formidable resources. We had therefore decided spontaneously, and without being asked or offered any inducement, to inform the Government of the United States that we would be glad to place such defence facilities at their disposal by leasing suitable sites in our Transatlantic possessions for their greater security against the unmeasured dangers of the future. The principle of association of interests for common purposes between Great Britain and the United States had developed even before the war. Various agreements had been reached about certain small islands in the Pacific Ocean which had become important as air fueling points. In all this line of thought we found ourselves in very close harmony with the Government of Canada.

Presently we learned that anxiety was also felt in the United States about the air and naval defence of their Atlantic seaboard, and President Roosevelt has recently made it clear that he would like to discuss with us, and with the Dominion of Canada and with Newfoundland, the development of American naval and air facilities in Newfoundland and in the West Indies. There is, of course, no question of any transference of sovereignty—that has never been suggested—or of any action being taken, without the consent or against the wishes of the various Colonies concerned, but for our part, His Majesty's Government are entirely willing to accord defence facilities to the United States on a 99 years' leasehold basis, and we feel sure that our interests no less than theirs, and the interests of the Colonies themselves and of Canada and Newfoundland will be served thereby. These are important steps. Undoubtedly this process means that these two great organisations of the English-speaking democracies, the British Empire and the United States, will have to be somewhat mixed up together in some of their affairs for mutual and general advantage. For my own part, looking out upon the future, I do not view the process with any misgivings. I could not stop it if I wished; no one can stop it. Like the Mississippi, it just keeps rolling along. Let it roll. Let it roll on full flood, inexorable, irresistible, benignant, to broader lands and better days.

The Atlantic Charter (1941).
Churchill and the United States

World War II united the two principal parts of the English-speaking community in a crusade against Nazism. This cooperation was reinforced by the nine wartime meetings between Winston Churchill and Franklin Roosevelt, the first on August 9 to 12, 1941, aboard H.M.S. *Prince of Wales* in Placentia Bay, Newfoundland. Britain's position was then precarious—the Battle of Britain had been a costly victory; her new ally, Russia, was in precipitous retreat, Egypt was threatened by Rommel's Afrika Korps; and, finally, the Battle of the Atlantic against German U-boats was in danger of being lost.

The Atlantic Charter, issued on August 14, 1941, is a perplexing document. It was not the purpose of the meeting, which was largely a discussion of Lend-Lease and war strategy. Nor was it an official document, one historian describing it as "nothing more than a press release." Only later was it accepted as a statement of the war objectives of the Grand Alliance formed after Pearl Harbor. Despite its general principles and flowery rhetoric, harking back to Wilson's "Fourteen Points" and, more recently, to Roosevelt's "Four Freedoms," the Atlantic Charter was a compromise of important differences between the two powers. Article 4, for example, sought to reconcile the British Empire's system of economic preference with the American demand for "access, on equal terms" to world markets. And, article 8, hinting at an Anglo-American peacekeeping force after the war, was a subtle attempt by Churchill to ensure continuing American participation in world affairs.

The Atlantic Charter was a symbolic victory for Churchill. America was now committed, in principle, to the "final destruction of Nazi tyranny." A more substantial assurance came on December 8, 1941, when the United States declared war not only on Japan but also on Germany. Of the latter event Churchill later wrote: "We had won the war. England would live. . . . Once again in our long island history we should emerge, however mauled or mutilated, safe and victorious. We should not be wiped out. Our history would not come to an end. . . . Being saturated

Source: The Times, August 15, 1941, p. 4. Reproduced from *The Times* by permission.

and satiated with emotion and sensation, I went to bed and slept the sleep of the saved and thankful."

MR. CHURCHILL MEETS THE PRESIDENT. THREE DAYS OF CONFERENCE AT SEA. JOINT DECLARATION OF PEACE AIMS. "FREEDOM FROM FEAR AND WANT." NEW SURVEY OF MUNITIONS SUPPLY.

After three days of secret conference at sea Mr. Churchill and Mr. Roosevelt have drawn up a joint declaration of principles upon which a better world should be based "after the final destruction of Nazi tyranny."

Mr. Attlee's Broadcast

Agreed Statement on the Meeting

The announcement of Mr. Churchill's meeting with Mr. Roosevelt and of their joint declaration of peace aims was made by Mr. Attlee, Lord Privy Seal and Deputy Prime Minister, in a special broadcast from Downing Street yesterday afternoon. He said:

"I have come to tell you about an important meeting between the President of the United States and the Prime Minister which has taken place and of a Declaration of Principles which has been agreed between them. Here is the statement which they have agreed to issue:

'The President of the United States and the Prime Minister, Mr. Churchill, representing his Majesty's Government in the United Kingdom, have met at sea.

'They have been accompanied by officials of their two Governments, including high-ranking officers of their military, naval, and air services.

'The whole problem of the supply of munitions of war, as provided by the Lease-Lend Act, for the armed forces of the United States and for those countries actively engaged in resisting aggression has been further examined.

'Lord Beaverbrook, Minister of Supply of the British Government, has joined in these conferences. He is going to proceed to Washington to discuss further details with appropriate officials of the United States Government. These conferences will also cover the supply problem of the Soviet Union.

'The President and the Prime Minister have had several conferences. They have considered the dangers to world civilization arising from the policy of military domination by conquest upon which the Hitlerite Government of Germany and other Governments associated therewith have embarked, and have made clear the steps which their countries are respectively taking for their safety in facing these dangers.'

Eight Points

reed upon the following joint declaration: . . .

countries seek no aggrandisement, territorial or other.

'Second, they desire to see no territorial changes that do not accord with the freely expressed wishes of the peoples concerned.

'*Third,* they respect the right of all peoples to choose the form of Government under which they will live; and they wish to see sovereign rights and self-government restored to those who have been forcibly deprived of them.

'*Fourth,* they will endeavour, with due respect for their existing obligations, to further enjoyment by all States, great or small, victor or vanquished, of access, on equal terms, to the trade and to the raw materials of the world which are needed for their economic prosperity.

'*Fifth,* they desire to bring about the fullest collaboration between all nations in the economic field, with the object of securing for all improved labour standards, economic advancement, and social security.

'*Sixth,* after the final destruction of Nazi tyranny, they hope to see established a peace which will afford to all nations the means of dwelling in safety within their own boundaries, and which will afford assurance that all the men in all the lands may live out their lives in freedom from fear and want.

'*Seventh,* such a peace should enable all men to traverse the high seas and oceans without hindrance.

'*Eighth,* they believe all of the nations of the world, for realistic as well as spiritual reasons, must come to the abandonment of the use of force. Since no future peace can be maintained if land, sea, or air armaments continue to be employed by nations which threaten, or may threaten, aggression outside of theirß frontiers, they believe, pending the establishment of a wider and permanent system of general security, that the disarmament of such nations is essential. They will likewise aid and encourage all other practicable measures which will lighten for peace-loving peoples the crushing burden of armament.'"

70
The Beveridge Report (1942).
Program for the Welfare State

Even while the Battle of Britain hung in the balance, Britons were thinking ahead to postwar reconstruction. They were determined to avoid the failure following World War I to make good the pledge that Britain should be a land "fit for heroes to live in." The community of danger and sacrifice and the expanded government powers necessitated by total war made more acceptable the idea that government planning should extend beyond the restoration of peace. Thus, a number of government commissions were appointed to investigate anticipated postwar problems. The most important, chaired by Sir William Beveridge (1879–1963), dealt with "Social Insurance and Allied Services." The Beveridge Report, presented to Parliament and published in December 1942, contained goals far more meaningful to the average Briton than the generalities of the Atlantic Charter.

The report asserted that Britain's aim should be "the abolition of want." Britain should have a "comprehensive policy of social progress," for the elimination of "Disease, Ignorance, Squalor and Idleness." Required were a comprehensive and compulsory scheme of insurance to replace the present array of specialized programs and a system of "children's allowances" to adjust earning power to family needs. The proposal was not that the state should assume complete responsibility for all needs. Rather there should be a cooperative venture of individuals and government working together. All subjects would be equal in the insurance premiums they paid and in the benefits they received.

The report met with immediate acclaim in Britain and abroad, everywhere that is except in the British government. In the crisis year of 1942, it was not surprising that Churchill was absorbed with the conduct of the war and not with the problems of peace and reconstruction. Although he later spoke in favor of an insurance scheme that would provide security for all "from the cradle to the grave," his attitude toward the report remained cool and uncommitted. The Labour party, however, was quick to endorse the report and eagerly awaited the postwar election. When the elec-

Source: *Social Insurance and Allied Services: Report by Sir William Beveridge* (Cmd. 6404), London: His Majesty's Stationery Office, 1942, pp. 5–9.

tion came in 1945, the voters remembered the offenses of the Conservative-dominated governments between the wars and the failure of Churchill to accept the challenge of the Beveridge Report. Instead of honoring the hero for his triumphs in war, they looked to the Labour party, whose election slogan invited, "Let us face the future."

1. The Inter-departmental Committee on Social Insurance and Allied Services were appointed in June, 1941, by the Minister without Portfolio, then responsible for the consideration of reconstruction problems. The terms of reference required the Committee "to undertake, with special reference to the inter-relation of the schemes, a survey of the existing national schemes of social insurance and allied services, including workmen's compensation and to make recommendations." The first duty of the Committee was to survey, the second to recommend. . . .

2. The schemes of social insurance and allied services which the Inter-departmental Committee have been called on to survey have grown piece-meal. Apart from the Poor Law, which dates from the time of Elizabeth, the schemes surveyed are the product of the last 45 years beginning with the Workmen's Compensation Act, 1897. . . . Together with this growth of social insurance and impinging on it at many points have gone developments of medical treatment, particularly in hospitals and other institutions; developments of services devoted to the welfare of children, in school and before it; and a vast growth of voluntary provision for death and other contingencies, made by persons of the insured classes through Industrial Life Offices, Friendly Societies and Trade Unions.

3. In all this change and development, each problem has been dealt with separately, with little or no reference to allied problems. The first task of the Committee has been to attempt for the first time a comprehensive survey of the whole field of social insurance and allied services, to show just what provision is now made and how it is made for many different forms of need. . . . The picture presented is impressive in two ways. First, it shows that provision for most of the many varieties of need through interruption of earnings and other causes that may arise in modern industrial communities has already been made in Britain on a scale not surpassed and hardly rivalled in any other country of the world. In one respect only of the first importance, namely limitation of medical service, both in the range of treatment which is provided as of right and in respect of the classes of persons for whom it is provided, does Britain's achievement fall seriously short of what has been accomplished elsewhere; it falls short also in its provision for cash benefit for maternity and funerals and through the defects of its system for workmen's compensation. In all other fields British provision for security, in adequacy of amount and in comprehensiveness, will stand

comparison with that of any other country; few countries will stand comparison with Britain. Second, social insurance and the allied services, as they exist today, are conducted by a complex of disconnected administrative organs, proceeding on different principles, doing invaluable service but at a cost in money and trouble and anomalous treatment of identical problems for which there is no justification. In a system of social security better on the whole than can be found in almost any other country there are serious deficiencies which call for remedy.

6. In proceeding from this first comprehensive survey of social insurance to the next task—of making recommendations—three guiding principles may be laid down at the outset.

7. The first principle is that any proposals for the future, while they should use to the full the experience gathered in the past, should not be restricted by consideration of sectional interests established in the obtaining of that experience. Now, when the war is abolishing landmarks of every kind, is the opportunity for using experience in a clear field. A revolutionary moment in the world's history is a time for revolutions, not for patching.

8. The second principle is that organisation of social insurance should be treated as one part only of a comprehensive policy of social progress. Social insurance fully developed may provide income security; it is an attack upon Want. But Want is one only of five giants on the road of reconstruction and in some ways the easiest to attack. The others are Disease, Ignorance, Squalor and Idleness.

9. The third principle is that social security must be achieved by co-operation, between the State and the individual. The State should offer security for service and contribution. The State in organising security should not stifle incentive, opportunity, responsibility; in establishing a national minimum, it should leave room and encouragement for voluntary action by each individual to provide more than that minimum for himself and his family.

10. The Plan for Social Security set out in this Report is built upon these principles. It uses experience but is not tied by experience. It is put forward as a limited contribution to a wider social policy, though as something that could be achieved now without waiting for the whole of that policy. It is, first and foremost, a plan of insurance—of giving in return for contributions benefits up to subsistence level, as of right and without means test, so that individuals may build freely upon it.

11. The work of the Inter-departmental Committee began with a review of existing schemes of social insurance and allied services. The Plan for Social Security, with which that work ends, starts from a diagnosis of want. . . . [This is] the main conclusion to be drawn from these surveys: abolition of want requires a double re-distribution of income, through social insurance and by family needs.

12. Abolition of want requires, first, improvement of State insurance, that is to say provision against interruption and loss of earning power. . . .

13. Abolition of want requires, second, adjustment of incomes, in periods of earning as well as in interruption of earning, to family needs, that is to say in one form or another it requires allowances for children. . . .

14. By a double re-distribution of income through social insurance and children's allowances, want, as defined in the social surveys, could have been abolished in Britain before the present war. . . . The income available to the British people was ample for such a purpose. The Plan for Social Security set out in . . . this Report takes abolition of want after this war as its aim. It includes as its main method compulsory social insurance, with national assistance and voluntary insurance as subsidiary methods. It assumes allowances for dependent children, as part of its background. The plan assumes also establishment of comprehensive health and rehabilitation services and maintenance of employment, that is to say avoidance of mass unemployment, as necessary conditions of success in social insurance.

17. The main feature of the Plan for Social Security is a scheme of social insurance against interruption and destruction of earning power and for special expenditure arising at birth, marriage or death. The scheme embodies six fundamental principles: flat rate of subsistence benefit; flat rate of contribution; unification of administrative responsibility; adequacy of benefit; comprehensiveness; and classification. . . . Based on them and in combination with national assistance and voluntary insurance as subsidiary methods, the aim of the Plan for Social Security is to make want under any circumstances unnecessary.

71
Letters to *The Times* (1946). The National Health Service

Following its decisive victory in the general election of 1945, the Labour party, led by Clement Attlee (1883–1967), set out to redeem its pledge to build a "Socialist Commonwealth." Several basic industries, totaling about 20 percent of the British economy, were nationalized and placed under the control of public corporations. Of more interest to the public was Labour's implementation of the Beveridge Report. The twin pillars of the new welfare state were the National Insurance Act (1946) and the National Health Service Act (1948). The former, supported in principle by all three parties, consolidated earlier legislation dealing with benefits for illness, unemployment, and disability, embracing "not certain occupations and income groups, but the entire population." New assistance was also provided for the aged, widowed, orphaned, and pregnant. More controversial was the National Health Service Act.

The need for a national health service, providing free, voluntary medical and dental treatment for all was never a matter of real debate. The British Medical Association (BMA) had accepted the principle in the 1930s. The Conservatives also conceded the need for, as one member stated, "a national, comprehensive, 100 per cent health service." The debate centered primarily on control of the new medical system. Aneurin Bevan, the fiery minister of health, insisted that it be run by a government agency responsible to Parliament. The BMA argued that a government-controlled bureaucracy would make medicine a salaried profession and destroy initiative. The intimate, voluntary doctor-patient relationship so essential to good medical treatment would thus be weakened. The government prevailed. The National Health Service, which went into effect on July 5, 1948, however, preserved freedom of choice for both doctors and patients. Within a year, 95 percent of the British public was enrolled in the plan; the doctors soon followed.

Something of the nature of the controversy surrounding nationalized medicine can be seen in the letters to *The Times* below.

Source: The Times, April 2, 1946, p. 5; April 17, 1946, p. 5; April 20, 1946, p. 5; April 23, 1946, p. 5. Letter from G. Bernard Shaw reprinted with permission of the Society of Authors on behalf of the Bernard Shaw Estate.

To the Editor of *The Times*

April 2, 1946

SIR,

The monstrosity of the present system of private practice in medicine is that it gives the doctors a vested interest in disease which they are defending desperately. We, the victims, support them because we want doctors of our own friendly choice and not strangers planted on us by the State.

The solution is simple. In Sweden, the most civilised country in western Europe, the private doctor is paid an agreed fee for keeping the family well throughout the year. He gains nothing and has more to do when there is illness in the family. He loses nothing and has less work when all is well.

My Swedish acquaintances have found no difficulty in inducing English doctors to make this arrangement. Why not make it obligatory, and abolish payment by the job ruthlessly?

Faithfully,
G. BERNARD SHAW,
Ayot St. Lawrence, Welwyn,
Hertfordshire.

To the Editor of *The Times*

April 17, 1946

SIR,

It is stated in the leading article in *The Times* of April 11 that the statement of the council of the B. M. A. contains no issues which justify "talk of a fight for medical freedom." While it is true that the selections made from the council's report may justify this comment, the parts to which no reference is made contain ample evidence of the council's views on the fundamental issues of public and professional freedom. . . .

For the medical profession to be converted into a technical branch of government would be disastrous both to medicine and the public. The doctor's primary loyalty and responsibility should be to his patient. He should be free to act, to speak, and to write unhampered by interference from above. The doctor should be the patient's doctor and not the Government's doctor. A whole-time salaried service is inconsistent with free choice of doctor. It would tend to impose a uniformity in a form of work in which initiative and originality are essential. It would tend to bureaucratize a human service. It would destroy a proper incentive, the relationship between remuneration and the amount and value of work done or responsibility accepted. It might tend to replace competition for patients by competition to avoid them.

The Government's proposals in their present form mean that the general practitioner in the future, no longer owning the goodwill of his practice, will be al-

lowed to practice in the public service in the area of his choice only with the permission of a committee appointed by the Minister. He will, as the Minister has
informed the negotiating committee of the profession, be remunerated under a
system which provides that a substantial part of his income will be salary. In the
council's view these proposals do lead to the general practitioner becoming the
full-time salaried servant of the State. . . .

> Yours faithfully,
> CHARLES HILL, Secretary,
> British Medical Association
> Havistock Square, W.C.1,

To the Editor of *The Times*

April 20, 1946

SIR,

In his letter published on April 17 Dr. Charles Hill wholly fails to substanti-
ate his disagreement with your view that there are no issues in the statement of
the B.M.A. which justify "talk of a fight for medical freedom."

Dr. Hill writes: "The doctor's primary loyalty and responsibility should be to
his patient. . . . The doctor should be the patient's doctor and not the
Government's doctor." We agree, but consider the implied antithesis fallacious.
The antithesis of the doctor dominated by the Government is the doctor dominated by the necessity of earning a living in a commercial market into which he
has probably sunk most of his capital. This Bill does not imperil the relationship
between doctor and patient. It reconciles the economic needs of the doctor with
the medical needs of the patient—and this must be for the benefit of all. The patient is free to choose his own doctor under the service, and their relationship is
the same as before except that the doctor's remuneration comes from public
funds.

Dr. Hill further states that a doctor will be able to practise in the area of his
choice "only with the permission of a committee appointed by the Minister." He
does not mention that it will be mainly professional in character and that it will
not be able to withhold permission on any ground other than that "there are already enough doctors practising in the public service in the area in question."
Without this provision, the Minister could not ensure the proper distribution of
doctors in accordance with the needs of the community. In the past the miners,
who needed doctors most, had the fewest and lowest-paid doctors of all. We are
glad that the Minister provides for the health of Merthyr Tydfil as well as that of
Maidenhead.

Doctors will be free to practise outside the service wherever they like.
Doctors practising under the service can take private patients outside it provided
that such patients are not on their lists as public patients or on the lists of their

partners in a health centre. It is a misuse of language for Dr. Hill to allege that the scheme may "lead to the general practitioner becoming the full-time salaried servant of the State." . . .

We do not deny that there are risks inherent in every far-reaching venture of social reform. It is the business of all of us, including doctors and members of Parliament, to minimize them by vigilance and wise administration. Dr. Hill has not produced one valid argument to show that any part of the scheme is inconsistent with a sound professional ethic. In these circumstances we are entitled to ask whether the B.M.A. is to join us in the battle for public health or to discredit itself by continuing to cry "Wolf."

We are, Sir, your obedient servants,

RAYMOND BLACKBURN,
JOHN FREEMAN,
WILLIAM WELLS
House of Commons, April 18

To the Editor of *The Times*

April 23, 1946

SIR,

In your leading article "Doctors and the Bill" which the secretary of the B.M.A. stigmatizes as partial, you refer to the emergency fund. As a long-standing member of the B.M.A., belonging to no other political body, may I mention that this £100,000, together with a further £100,000 from the National Insurance Defence Trust, comes in part from subscriptions of many members who are completely out of sympathy with the policy of the leaders of the B.M.A.? The latter are in the main elderly men firmly entrenched in secure positions who resent any innovation likely to disturb them. They make great play through the secretary of the B.M.A. with freedom of choice. What chance has a young doctor lacking capital to settle in a practice of his own choosing? Similarly, where large blocks of patients are bought and sold, what price freedom of choice for the patient?

Yours faithfully,
WILFRED KILROE
116, Kenley Road,
Merton Park, S.W. 19

72
Sir Anthony Eden, Speech on BBC (1956). The Suez Crisis

Britain's role in Hitler's defeat confirmed in most people's minds her standing as a world power. The euphoria of victory and her long tradition as a great power made it difficult for the British to recognize, let alone to accept, her decline after 1945, a decline occasioned by economic difficulties, American military dominance, and colonial nationalism.

Events in the Middle East demonstrated the erosion of British power. Although Britain gave up her mandates over Transjordan in 1946 and Palestine in 1948, her ownership and military control of the Suez Canal seemed to guarantee her dominance in the area. Nevertheless, in 1954 British troops were withdrawn from the canal zone in the face of demands by Colonel Gamal Abdel Nasser, the new Egyptian president. Due to the cancellation of American and British financial support for Egypt's proposed Aswan Dam, Nasser seized the canal. Following unsatisfactory negotiations, Prime Minister Sir Anthony Eden (1897–1977) approved a British, French, and Israeli attack on Egypt. On the evening of November 3, 1956, the day British troops landed in Egypt, Eden appealed for public support on BBC radio and television. Reprinted below is part of his speech as it appeared in *The Listener,* a weekly publication summarizing the major broadcasts carried on BBC.

Eden attempted to justify Britain's assertion of power independent of the United Nations, the Commonwealth, and, more importantly, the United States. Nasser, whom Eden characterized elsewhere as a "megalomaniacal dictator," was portrayed as a new Hitler. Eden, a critic of appeasement in the 1930s, argued that Nasser must learn the lesson that Hitler had not been taught. The situation in 1956 was different, however. The United States joined the Soviet Union in the UN to denounce Britain, and most of the Commonwealth nations disagreed with British policy. A Canadian remarked that hearing of Britain's invasion was "like finding a beloved uncle arrested for rape." Nehru of India could not think of "a grosser case of naked aggression." British public opinion was divided, and Eden eventually resigned from office. The lesson of

Source: The Listener, LVI, 735–736 (November 8, 1956). By permission of Lord Avon.

Suez was clear: Britain's policy had failed because she lacked the independent power needed to carry it out. The Suez Crisis of 1956 ended Britain's lingering illusions of world power.

I know that you would wish me, as Prime Minister, to talk to you tonight on the problem which is in everybody's mind; and to tell you what has happened, what the Government has done, and why it has done it. . . .

As a Government we have had to wrestle with the problem of what action we should take. So have our French friends. The burden of that decision was tremendous but inescapable. In the depths of our conviction we decided that here was the beginning of a forest fire, of immense danger to peace. We decided that we must act, and act quickly.

What should we do? We put the matter to the Security Council. Should we have left it to them? Should we have been content to wait to see whether they would act? How long would this have taken? And where would the forest fire have spread in the meantime? Would words have been enough? What we did was to take police action at once: action to end the fighting and to separate the armies. We acted swiftly and reported to the Security Council, and I believe that before long it will become apparent to everybody that we acted rightly and wisely.

Our friends inside the Commonwealth, and outside, could not in the very nature of things be consulted in time. You just cannot have immediate action and extensive consultation as well. But our friends are coming—as Australia and New Zealand have already done and I believe that Canada and the United States will soon come—to see that we acted with courage and speed, to deal with a situation which just could not wait.

There are two things I would ask you never to forget. We cannot allow—we could not allow—a conflict in the Middle East to spread; our survival as a nation depends on oil and nearly three-quarters of our oil comes from that part of the world. . . .

The other reflection is this. It is a personal one. All my life I have been a man of peace, working for peace, striving for peace, negotiating for peace. I have been a League of Nations man and a United Nations man, and I am still the same man, with the same convictions, the same devotion to peace. I could not be other, even if I wished, but I am utterly convinced that the action we have taken is right.

Over the years I have seen, as many of you have, the mood of peace at any price: many of you will remember that mood in our own country and how we paid for it. Between the wars we saw things happening which we felt were adding to the danger of a great world war. Should we have acted swiftly to deal with them—even though it meant the use of force? Or should we have hoped for the best, and gone on hoping and talking—as in fact we did?

There are times for courage, times for action—and this is one of them—in the interests of peace. I do hope we have learned our lesson. Our passionate love of peace, our intense loathing of war, have often held us back from using force even at times when we knew in our heads, if not in our hearts, that its use was in the interest of peace. And I believe with all my heart and head—for both are needed—that this is a time for action, effective and swift. Yes, even by the use of some force in order to prevent the forest fire from spreading—to prevent the horror and devastation of a larger war.

The Government knew, and they regretted it, that this action would shock and hurt some people: the bombing of military targets, and military targets only; it is better to destroy machines on the ground than let them destroy people from the air. We had to think of our troops and of the inhabitants of the towns and villages. After all, it was our duty to act and act swiftly, for only by such action could we secure peace. . . .

So finally, my friends, what are we seeking to do? First and foremost, to stop the fighting, to separate the armies, and to make sure that there is no more fighting. We have stepped in because the United Nations could not do so in time. If the United Nations will take over the police action we shall welcome it. Indeed, we proposed that course to them. And police action means not only to end the fighting now but also to bring a lasting peace to an area which for ten years has lived, or tried to live, under the constant threat of war.

73

Harold Macmillan, Speech to the Parliament of the Union of South Africa (1960). "The Wind Of Change"

Harold Macmillan, Conservative prime minister from 1957 to 1963, was the dominant political figure in Britain between Clement Attlee (1945–1951) and Margaret Thatcher (1979–1990). He was born into a prominent publishing family. In the title of the first volume of his autobiography, he described the First World War as his own "Winds of Change." He was wounded three times and forced to endure an entire day in no-man's-land with a shattered pelvis, reading Aeschylus. After the war, he turned to politics, and from the very beginning he tried to be a moderating force within his party. His 1938 book, *The Middle Way,* characteristically called for Conservatives to avoid extremist policies and to recognize government's role in solving economic and social problems.

As prime minister, "Super Mac" had considerable success in such domestic areas as housing, education, and consumer income. Under his leadership the Conservatives accepted many aspects of the welfare state, such as the National Health Service, and the concept of a mixed economy, part socialist and part capitalist. In retrospect, however, Macmillan's most lasting achievement may well have been his success in persuading the Conservatives, long the party of empire, to accept colonial nationalism and the resulting decolonization of the British Empire. India, Pakistan, Ceylon, and Burma had already received independence, but from Attlee's Labour government. Seeing no alternative, Macmillan committed the Conservatives to accepting independence for Britain's African colonies.

The Wind of Change Speech, Macmillan's most famous oration, had little to do with British colonial policy: by 1960, most Britons accepted colonial self-determination. Ghana (1957) was already independent, and Nigeria (1960), Tanganyika (1961), Uganda (1962), and Kenya (1963) were well on the way. Rather, Macmillan attempted to persuade the government of South Africa,

Source: Address by the R. Hon. Harold Macmillan, Prime Minister of the United Kingdom. Printed on the Authority of Mr. Speaker, Parliament of the Union of South Africa, Printed by Cape Times, Ltd., Parow, 1960, pp. 5–10, 13–14.

in the light of "the wind of change blowing through this Continent," to rethink its policy of apartheid, the segregation of the races. This institutional racism, strengthened after the defeat of the more moderate Jan Smuts in 1948, threatened not only peace in South Africa but the very existence of the Commonwealth of Nations. In one sense, the Wind of Change Speech was a failure. H. F. Verwoerd and his Nationalist party, offended by Macmillan's remarks, strengthened apartheid and, as the new Republic of South Africa, withdrew from the Commonwealth in 1961. In a larger sense, however, Macmillan won. Once South Africa was gone, it was possible for the Commonwealth to survive and grow as a voluntary, multiracial organization.

It is a great privilege to be invited to address the Members of both Houses of Parliament in the Union of South Africa. It is a unique privilege to do so in 1960, just half a century after the Parliament of the Union came to birth. . . . At such a time it is natural and right that you should pause to take stock of your position—to look back at what you have achieved, and to look forward to what lies ahead.

In the fifty years of their nationhood the people of South Africa have built a strong economy founded on a healthy agriculture and thriving and resilient industries.

During my visit I have been able to see something of your mining industry on which the prosperity of your country is so firmly based. . . .

I have seen too the fine cities of Pretoria and Bloemfontein.

This afternoon I hope to see something of your wine growing industry, which so far I have only admired as a consumer. . . .

As I have travelled round the Union, I have found everywhere, as I expected, a deep preoccupation with what is happening in the rest of the African continent. I understand and sympathise with your interest in these events and your anxiety about them. . . .

In the twentieth century, and especially since the end of the war, the processes which gave birth to the nation states of Europe have been repeated all over the world. We have seen the awakening of national consciousness in peoples who have for centuries lived in dependence on some other power.

Fifteen years ago this movement spread through Asia. Many countries there, of different races and civilisations, pressed their claim to an independent national life. To-day the same thing is happening in Africa.

The most striking of all the impressions I have formed since I left London a month ago is of the strength of this African national consciousness. In different places it may take different forms. But it is happening everywhere. The wind of change is blowing through this Continent.

Whether we like it or not, this growth of national consciousness is a political fact. We must all accept it as a fact. Our national policies must take account of it.

Of course you understand this better than anyone. You are sprung from Europe, the home of nationalism. And here in Africa you have yourselves created a free nation, a new nation. Indeed in the history of our times yours will be recorded as the first of the African nationalisms. And this tide of national consciousness which is now rising in Africa is a fact for which you and we and the other nations of the Western world are ultimately responsible. . . .

It is a basic principle of our modern Commonwealth that we respect each other's sovereignty in matters of internal policy. At the same time we must recognise that, in this shrinking world in which we live to-day, the internal policies of one nation may have effects outside it. We may sometimes be tempted to say to each other "Mind your own business." But in these days I would myself expand the old saying so that it runs "Mind your own business, of course, but mind how it affects my business too."

If I may be very frank, I will venture now to say this. What Governments and Parliaments in the United Kingdom *have* done since the last war in according independence to India, Pakistan, Ceylon, Malaya and Ghana, and what they *will* do for Nigeria and other countries now nearing independence—all this, though we must and do take full and sole responsibility for it, we do in the belief that it is the only way to establish the future of the Commonwealth and of the free world on sound foundations.

All this, of course, is of deep and close concern to you. For nothing we do in this small world can be done in a corner and remain hidden. . . .

I am well aware of the peculiar nature of the problems with which you are faced here in the Union. I know the differences between your situation and that of many other States in Africa.

You have here some three million people of European origin. This country is their home. It has been their home for hundreds of years. They have no other. The same is broadly true of Europeans in Central and East Africa.

Of course, in most other States those who have come from Europe have only come to work, to spend their working life, to contribute their skills, perhaps to teach, perhaps to administer and then go home. . . .

The problems to which you as members of the Union Parliament have to address yourselves are therefore very different from those which face the Parliaments of countries of homogeneous nations. Of course, I realize that these are difficult, hard, sometimes baffling problems. And, therefore, it would be surprising if your interpretation of your duty did not sometimes produce different results from ours, in terms of Government policies and actions.

As a fellow member of the Commonwealth we always try and, I think, we have succeeded, in giving to South Africa our full support and encouragement, but I hope you won't mind my saying frankly that there are some aspects of your policies which make it impossible for us to do this without being false to our own deep convictions about the political destinies of free men to which in our own territories we are trying to give effect.

I think therefore that we ought as friends to face together—without seeking, I trust, to apportion praise or blame—the fact that in the world of to-day this difference of outlook lies between us. . . .

The independent members of the Commonwealth do not always all agree on every subject. It is not a condition of their association that they should do so. On the contrary, the strength of our Commonwealth lies largely in the fact that it is a free association of free and independent states each responsible for ordering its own affairs but co-operating in the pursuit of common aims and purposes in world affairs.

Moreover, these differences may be transitory. In time they may be resolved. Our duty is to see them in perspective against the background of our long association. . . .

I hope—indeed I am confident—that in another 50 years we shall look back on the differences that exist between us now as mere matters of historical interest. For as time passes and one generation yields to another, human problems change and fade. Let us remember these truths. Let us therefore resolve to build, and not to destroy. Let us also remember always that weakness comes from division, and, in words familiar to you, strength from unity.

74
Edward Heath, Speech in Commons (1971). From Commonwealth to Common Market

Following World War II, Great Britain was closely associated with three areas, or power blocs—the United States, the Empire-Commonwealth, and Western Europe. During the 1950s and early 1960s, Britain's relations with each changed to her disadvantage. The dependent empire evaporated, beginning with Indian independence in 1947. Although most former colonies remained in the Commonwealth, it was not a force on which Britain could rely. Britain's "special relationship" with the United States was strained by the latter's denunciation of the 1956 Suez operation and the American assumption of Britain's support during the 1962 Cuban Missile Crisis. Britain increasingly appeared a junior partner. Finally, by the Treaty of Rome (1957), France, West Germany, Italy, and the Benelux nations formed the European Economic Community (EEC), a "Common Market," which Britain chose not to join. In 1962, Dean Acheson, the American secretary of state from 1949 to 1953, characterized the situation: "Great Britain has lost an empire and has not yet found a role."

In an attempt to find a role, Harold Macmillan, the Conservative prime minister from 1957 to 1963, announced in 1961 that Britain was applying belatedly for membership in the Common Market. This decision naturally alarmed the other Commonwealth nations, which feared the loss of their economic privileges in the British market. It also upset many in Britain. Some feared higher food prices. Others were simply repelled by the idea of becoming European and, as one member of Parliament argued, turning their backs on "a thousand years of history." Charles de Gaulle solved Britain's problem by vetoing her application in 1963. In Britain, however, the debate continued, and by 1966 both the Labour party of Harold Wilson and the Conservative party, now led by Edward Heath, supported entry into Europe in principle. Serious negotiations were resumed in July 1970 by Heath, the new prime minister; with De Gaulle out of the way, they proved successful. The historic debate to join the Common

Source: Parliamentary Debates (House of Commons), Fifth Series, Vol. 823 (1971), pp. 2076, 2202–2205, 2211–2212.

Market was concluded on October 18, 1971, by a brief speech by Heath.

Heath did not stress the economic rationale for membership. Although he believed that England's industry must have access to the larger European market, he viewed the decision as a political one. The Commonwealth had not become "a reality." The United States was preoccupied with "its relationships with other super Powers." Britain, a European nation, must seek its future within a "United Europe." Parliament, despite strong Labour objections, supported Heath, and Britain entered the Common Market on January 1, 1973.

Order read for resuming adjourned debate on Question [21st October]: That this House approves Her Majesty's Government's decision of principle to join the European Communities on the basis of the arrangements which have been negotiated. —[*Sir Alec Douglas-Home.*]

Question again proposed. . . . 9.31 p.m.

The Prime Minister (Mr. Edward Heath): I do not think that any Prime Minister has stood at this Box in time of peace and asked the House to take a positive decision of such importance as I am asking it to take tonight. I am well aware of the responsibility which rests on my shoulders for so doing. After 10 years of negotiation, after many years of discussion in this House and after 10 years of debate, the moment of decision for Parliament has come. The other House has already taken its vote and expressed its view—[HON. MEMBERS: "Backwoodsmen!"]; 451 frontwoodsmen have voted in favour of the Motion and, for the rest, 58. . . .

Earlier, the world was watching New York. They were waiting to see whether China was going to become a member of the Security Council and of the General Assembly. Tonight, the world is similarly watching Westminster, waiting to see whether we are going to decide that Western Europe should now move along the path to real unity—or whether the British Parliament, now given the choice, not for the first time but probably for the last time for many years to come, will reject the chance of creating a united Europe.

There can be absolutely no doubt of the world interest in this matter—of those physically watching and those waiting for the outcome. Nor can there be any doubt of the reasons why. It is natural that we in this House, in this long debate, have been largely concerned with the impact on our own country, but our decision tonight will vitally affect the balance of forces in the modern world for many years to come. . . .

The right hon. Gentleman [Mr. Callaghan] described the pursuit of a united Europe as an ideal which he respected. It inspired the founders of the European

Communities after the war. At that time we in Britain held back, conscious of our ties with the Commonwealth and of our relationship with the United States, both of which had been so strongly reinforced in war. We did not then see how we could fit that into the framework of European unity.

The Commonwealth has, since then, developed into an association of independent countries with now only a few island dependencies remaining. It is a unique association which we value, but the idea that it would become an effective economic or political, let alone military, *bloc* has never materialised. It has never become a reality. [*Interruption.*]

Our relationship with the United States is close, friendly and natural, but it is not unique. It is not fundamentally different from that of many other countries of Western Europe, except, again, for our natural ties of language and common law, tradition and history. The United States is now inevitably and increasingly concerned with its relationships with the other super Powers. This applies also in the economic field, because in the situation which I have described the United States is bound to find itself involved more and more with the large economic powers, Japan and the European Community.

This is a time of profound change. It is a time in which United States policy towards Soviet Russia and Soviet China, and in the trade and monetary field, is changing. It is a time when we must see how these problems can best be handled by Britain. . . .

When it comes to dealing with the major economic Powers in creating what has now to be a changed, if not a new, trading and financial policy, the strength of this country alone, or of any individual member of the Community, were it to act alone, is not enough to ensure a sensible or satisfactory outcome to the current monetary and trading discussions which, I believe, are bound to go on for some time.

We as a country are dangerously vulnerable to protectionist pressure if such a satisfactory outcome of a new financial and trading system is not achieved. But in Europe we can share and reinforce the strength and experience of the Community. We can work with partners whose interests are the same as ours. . . .

Surely we must consider the consequences of staying out. We cannot delude ourselves that an early chance would be given us to take the decision again. We should be denying ourselves and succeeding generations the opportunities which are available to us in so many spheres; opportunities which we ourselves in this country have to seize. We should be leaving so many aspects of matters affecting our daily lives to be settled outside our own influence. That surely cannot be acceptable to us. We should be denying to Europe, also—let us look outside these shores for a moment—its full potential, its opportunities of developing economically and politically, maintaining its security, and securing for all its people a higher standard of prosperity.

All the consequences of that for many millions of people in Europe must be recognised tonight in the decision the House is taking. In addition, many projects for the future of Europe have been long delayed. There has been great uncertainty, and tonight all that can be removed—[HON. MEMBERS: "No."] . . .

Throughout my political career, if I may add one personal remark, it is well known that I have had the vision of a Britain in a united Europe; a Britain which would be united economically to Europe and which would be able to influence decisions affecting our own future, and which would enjoy a better standard of life and a fuller life. I have worked for a Europe which will play an increasing part in meeting the needs of those parts of the world which still lie in the shadow of want. . . .

I want Britain as a member of a Europe which is united politically, and which will enjoy lasting peace and the greater security which would ensue.

Nor do I believe that the vision of Europe . . . is an unworthy vision, or an ignoble vision or an unworthy cause for which to have worked—[*Interruption.*] I have always made it absolutely plain to the British people that consent to this course would be given by Parliament—[HON. MEMBERS: "Resign."] Parliament is the Parliament of all the people.

When we came to the end of the negotions in 1963, after the veto had been imposed, the negotiator on behalf of India said:

When you left India some people wept. And when you leave Europe tonight some will weep. And there is no other people in the world of whom these things could be said.

That was a tribute from the Indian to the British. But tonight when this House endorses this Motion many millions of people right across the world will rejoice that we have taken our rightful place in a truly United Europe.

Question put:—

The House divided: Ayes 356, Noes 244.

75
Bernadette Devlin, Interview in *Playboy* (1972). Northern Ireland

England's Irish question, or Ireland's English question, appears to the world at large as the tragic outgrowth of unfulfilled nationalism and religious bigotry. This troublesome issue, bequeathed to the twentieth century by the failure of Gladstone's plans of Home Rule, was aggravated by Lloyd George's partition of Ireland in 1921. Southern Ireland, the Irish Free State, was granted responsible government within the British Commonwealth. In 1949, it became the Republic of Eire, free from all British control. Northern Ireland, or Ulster, chose, however, to remain a part of the United Kingdom. Its "Home Rule" parliament for domestic affairs, dominated by the Protestant Unionist party, continued systematically to discriminate against the Roman Catholic minority.

In 1967, the Catholic minority in Ulster launched a moderate civil rights movement. The initial concessions granted were too extreme for the Orangemen, or ultra-Protestants, led by Ian Paisley, and insufficient to satisfy the Roman Catholics. Attitudes hardened, violent demonstrations began, and in 1969 British troops were sent to maintain order. Gradually, the civil rights movement merged with the Irish Republican Army's determination to unite all of Ireland under the government of Eire in Dublin. One of the leading advocates of unification was Bernadette Devlin.

Devlin, a Roman Catholic, was, in 1969 at the age of 21, elected one of the twelve Northern Irish members of the House of Commons. She quickly established herself as a fiery debater. After serious disturbances in Londonderry, she spent time in prison for inciting to riot. To publicize Irish grievances, Devlin granted countless television and press interviews, like that in *Playboy* in 1972. Although she vigorously condemned British policy toward Ireland, she did not see Ireland's difficulties solely as a result of British political and religious oppression. Besides being an Irish nationalist, she was also a socialist, seeing "independent socialism" and the destruction of capitalism as essential if Ireland and other small nations were to be completely free.

Devlin's interview in *Playboy* and her earlier lecture tour of American cities with large Irish-American populations were in the established tradition of Irish appeals to the United States for support, a practice dating back to the Fenians of the 1860s.

Playboy: . . . What was it like growing up as a Catholic in Protestant Northern Ireland?

Devlin: Well, it was an education in more ways than one. I was born in Cookstown, in County Tyrone, a small farming community that's sort of a microcosm of Ulster. It was originally a plantation, settled by the Scots Presbyterians the British imported in the 17th Century to take over the land from us restless natives. To this day, the town is divided almost evenly between the descendants of the original Protestant settlers and the Catholics they subjugated; both groups are still segregated in the geographical areas of the town where their ancestors lived 300 years ago. And attitudes haven't changed much, either; the Protestants still have a sense of settler superiority and expect the Catholics to stay in their place and not get uppity, pretty much the way your own American colonists once viewed the Indians, or the way many white Southerners still feel about blacks. And, like the Indians and the blacks, we were poor, virtually disenfranchised and very angry. We still are. . . .

To understand the present struggle in Ireland, you must see it from the perspective of 800 years of invasion, oppression, exploitation and genocide. Irish history is written in Irish blood.

Playboy: Since that history seems to have a direct bearing on what's happening today, let's talk about it. When did the English first become involved in Ireland?

Devlin: It all began, ironically enough in light of what's happened since, when Pope Adrian IV, an Englishman, granted Ireland as an "inheritance" to the Norman king of England, Henry II, in 1154. Until then, there was no united Ireland as such, only a loose confederation of independent kingdoms, which united against Henry's invading armies and eventually drove them off. Over the next several hundred years, the English mounted sporadic, unsuccessful campaigns to conquer the island. Then, with the rise of the Tudors, a bloodier page was opened. Before this, the conflict between Ireland and England had had no religious overtones; both were Catholic powers fighting the kind of territorial war that was common in those days. But Henry VIII's break with Rome introduced the bitter note of religious antagonism, because the earls of Ireland remained loyal to the Pope. Their resistance was finally broken in 1601, under Elizabeth I. Protestantism became the official religion of all Ireland, and harsh penalties were imposed on any Irishman who refused to convert.

The vast landholdings of the Irish earls, comprising the richest farmland in Ireland, were seized and granted to English and Scots farmers, Protestants, of course. The original Irish inhabitants were driven into the woods and mountains by British troops. The seaport of Derry was renamed Londonderry, to be settled by London emigrants. For a while, Parliament debated whether the Irish would be transported to the New World as slaves or allowed to stay and work as serfs for the English. Although large numbers were transported, it was decided to keep the majority in Ireland as an agricultural labor force.

In 1638, the embittered Irish revolted against the British and the Protestant landlords, and fighting spread across the country; an Irish *Tet* offensive, you might call it. The situation grew so grave that Oliver Cromwell, the Puritan fanatic who had just beheaded his own king for alleged Catholic leanings, invaded Ireland and put city after city to the torch; in the town of Drogheda alone, he massacred more than 4000 people. After he had "pacified" Ireland, Cromwell accelerated the expropriation of Irish land and the importation of Protestant settlers. By 1660, the British had seized 12,000,000 out of 15,000,000 arable acres in Ireland.

After Cromwell's death, the Irish saw a vain glimmer of hope in the Stuart restoration. King James II was a secret Catholic and favorably disposed to the Irish. But then James was deposed and exiled by William of Orange, a staunch Dutch Protestant. James landed in Ireland to organize a war to regain his throne, and Irish Catholics rallied behind him; but after a bloody campaign, he was decisively defeated by the armies of King William at the Battle of the Boyne—July 1, 1690. That battle snuffed out the Irish Catholics' last real hope of freedom. From then on, Protestant hegemony over Ireland was total. The Orangemen still celebrate the Battle of the Boyne each year with huge parades. One of these, in 1969, triggered the rioting that led to the present crisis. Members of the Orange Order, a fascist group that effectively controlled Ulster until recently, used to recite an old toast on the anniversary of the Battle of the Boyne:

> To the glorious, pious and immortal memory of King William III, who saved us from Rogues and Roguery, Slaves and Slavery, Popes and Popery; and whoever denies this toast may he be slammed, crammed and jammed into the muzzle of the great gun of Athlone, and the gun fired into the Pope's belly, and the Pope into the Devil's belly, and the Devil into Hell, and the door locked and the key kept in an Orangeman's pocket.

In Northern Ireland, the Battle of the Boyne is still being fought. . . .

Playboy: As a professed believer in self-determination for all peoples, don't you grant the Northern Protestants the right to remain with Britain, if that's the desire of the majority?

Devlin: The partition of Ireland was no more acceptable to farseeing Irishmen that the secession of your own Southern states was to Abraham Lincoln. If you'd taken a plebiscite within the Confederacy in 1861, . . . you would have found that a majority of Southerners preferred to split off from the United States. Lincoln put the good of the entire country ahead of regional sectarianism, and this led to your Civil War. In Ireland, too, we had civil war—between the government of the new Irish Free State and the militant Republicans.

Playboy: A civil war won by the Irish leaders who accepted partition.

Devlin: Oh, they won, all right. And in the process, the hopes of the Irish people for social progress and human dignity were brutally crushed. The rulers of the Free State, who had the support of the Church and the Irish middle class—and, tacitly and ironically, of the British and the Unionists in the North— wanted no social revolution, only a nice tidy little bourgeois capitalist country, rigidly Roman Catholic and linked to Britain by preferential trade agreements. They ruthlessly suppressed the I.R.A. rebels, hundreds of whom were shot by their old comrades in arms. By the mid-Twenties, our revolution had been sold down the river and the Irish people, North and South, faced *two* enemies: the British and the Dublin government.

Playboy: Many people would contend that the leaders who eventually accepted partition were not traitors but realists. Wasn't partition preferable to another 10 or 15 years of armed struggle?

Devlin: Most historians believe the British would have caved in completely if the Irish negotiating team had just held on a little longer. The British public had suffered terribly in the first war; they were fed up with the mess in Ireland. Lloyd George knew his own political survival depended upon negotiating immediate British withdrawal. He would have been ready to surrender Ulster if the Irish had presented a united front. But, tragically, we played right into his hands, and the result was the loss of half our country, the continued exploitation of our people in the North and, ultimately, the institutionalization of a reactionary and corrupt capitalist regime in the South, which was just as rotten as the Protestant caste system in the North. . . .

Sure, we did get our own flag after partition, and that's about all we got. We didn't even get half a loaf; we lost the whole bakery. . . .

Playboy: Can you see no grounds for reconciliation with England? Or will your bitterness, violence and misery be handed down to the next generation?

Devlin: There's a solution to any human problem. In this case, I can actually see two solutions, short term and long term. For the short term, hostilities could cease tomorrow if the British would unconditionally release all internees and other political prisoners, declare an amnesty for all those currently charged with crimes against the state and withdraw all troops to their barracks with a specified date for total withdrawal from Northern Ireland.

Stormont and the whole Unionist state apparatus would have to be permanently dismantled, not just temporarily suspended as it is now, under Westminster's direct rule. All parties in Ireland, Protestant and Catholic, conservative and revolutionary, could then get together to determine conditions for the peaceful reunification of their country and the protection of minority rights. That would be a short-term solution for the immediate suffering and bloodshed. It's far from perfect and it might not work at all, given our hardened sectarian attitudes. . . .

The ultimate long-range solution for Ireland, which I realize won't come about overnight, is independent socialism. Until we have a society in which we solve our own economic and social problems and control our own destiny, the present problems of exploitation and injustice will remain. That's why I'm a committed socialist and why more and more of our people are turning toward socialism as the only viable alternative. We can't have true freedom without social justice; and in Ireland, we can't have either without socialism. It won't come today, tomorrow or the day after. But it will come. It *has* to come.

76

Margaret Thatcher, Speech to the Conservative Party Conference at Brighton (1980)

Margaret Hilda Thatcher (1925–) is Britain's most important political leader since Winston Churchill. Her political career, begun
with her election to Parliament in 1959, coincided with a growing
public conviction that government was incapable either of preventing Britain's decline or of coping effectively with her many
domestic problems. Successfully challenging Edward Heath for
party leadership in 1975, she led the Conservatives to victory in
the 1979 election. She became Britain's first woman prime minister and, in due time, the longest-serving prime minister
(1979–1990) since Lord Liverpool (1812–1827). Controversial and
abrasive, "the Iron Lady" had a definite goal, and she set out to
implement it with more energy and cold-blooded resolve than had
been seen since the Labour party's inauguration of the welfare
state after World War II.

The heart of Thatcherism, as can be seen from her speech to the
Conservative Party Conference in 1980, was the intention to reverse the tide of socialism and restore the self-sufficiency and enterprise of the British people. The power of labor unions should be
reduced. Nationalized industries should be privatized. Council
housing should be sold to the tenants. Monetary policy should be
used to reduce inflation, even at the cost of high interest rates and
unemployment. Early in her administration, many hoped and fewer
feared that the seeming political havoc she was creating would
cause her to lose her nerve and to effect a "U" turn, as had other
governments before. Speaking to her second annual party conference after becoming prime minister, she challenged the party
faithful, "You may turn if you want to. The lady's not for turning."

The fate of Thatcherism, and of Margaret Thatcher, without the
Falkland Islands War of 1982 remains uncertain. The popularity
she won by her stubborn wartime resolve and, probably more important, the ineptitude and internal divisions of the opposition parties gave her success in the 1983 and 1987 elections. Although
she enacted much of her domestic program, her imperious and

Source: Speech of Prime Minister Margaret Thatcher to the Annual Conference of the
Conservative Party, November 1980. Courtesy of the Conservative Party.

dictatorial manner offended and alienated many of her colleagues. Her poll (i.e., head) tax, reminiscent of that which produced the Peasants' Revolt of 1381, eroded public support. She also isolated herself by her reluctance to accept the integration of Britain into the European Community. Her resignation under fire in November 1990 and her succession by John Major have not diminished her achievement or her reputation as the dominant politician of Britain in recent decades. In 1992, she entered the House of Lords as Baroness Thatcher of Kesteven.

At our party conference last year I said that the task in which the Government were engaged—to change the national attitude of mind—was the most challenging to face any British Administration since the war. Challenge is exhilarating. This week we Conservatives have been taking stock, discussing the achievements, the setbacks and the work that lies ahead as we enter our second parliamentary year. . . .

There are many things to be done to set this nation on the road to recovery, and I do not mean economic recovery alone, but a new independence of spirit and zest for achievement.

It is sometimes said that because of our past we, as a people, expect too much and set our sights too high. That is not the way I see it. Rather it seems to me that throughout my life in politics our ambitions have steadily shrunk. Our response to disappointment has not been to lengthen our stride but to shorten the distance to be covered. But with confidence in ourselves and in our future what a nation we could be.

In its first seventeen months this Government have laid the foundations for recovery. . . . [T]here was a formidable barricade of obstacles that we had to sweep aside. For a start, in his first Budget Geoffrey Howe began to restore incentives to stimulate the abilities and inventive genius of our people. Prosperity comes not from grand conferences of economists but by countless acts of personal self-confidence and self-reliance. . . .

We have made the first crucial changes in trade union law to remove the worst abuses of the closed shop, to restrict picketing to the place of work of the parties in the dispute, and to encourage secret ballots. . . .

[We] have begun to break down the monopoly powers of nationalisation. . . . British Aerospace will soon be open to private investment. The monopoly of the Post Office and British Telecommunications is being diminished. The barriers to private generation of electricity for sale have been lifted. For the first time nationalised industries and public utilities can be investigated by the Monopolies Commission—a long overdue reform.

Free competition in road passenger transport promises travellers a better deal. Michael Heseltine has given to millions—yes, millions—of council tenants the right to buy their own homes.

It was Anthony Eden who chose for us the goal of "a property-owning democracy." But for all the time that I have been in public affairs that has been beyond the reach of so many, who were denied the right to the most basic ownership of all—the homes in which they live.

They wanted to buy. Many could afford to buy. But they happened to live under the jurisdiction of a Socialist council, which would not sell and did not believe in the independence that comes with ownership. . . .

The Left continues to refer with relish to the death of capitalism. Well, if this is the death of capitalism I must say that it is quite a way to go.

But all this will avail us little unless we achieve our prime economic objective—the defeat of inflation. Inflation destroys nations and societies as surely as invading armies do. Inflation is the parent of unemployment. It is the unseen robber of those who have saved.

No policy which puts at risk the defeat of inflation—however great its short-term attraction—can be right. Our policy for the defeat of inflation is, in fact, traditional. It existed long before Sterling M3 embellished the Bank of England Quarterly Bulletin, or "monetarism" became a convenient term of political invective.

But some people talk as if control of the money supply was a revolutionary policy. Yet it was an essential condition for the recovery of much of continental Europe. . . .

"Has Britain the courage and resolve to sustain the discipline for long enough to break through to success?"

Yes, Mr. Chairman, we have, and we shall. This Government are determined to stay with the policy and see it through to its conclusion. That is what marks this administration as one of the truly radical ministries of post-war Britain. . . .

Meanwhile we are not heedless of the hardships and worries that accompany the conquest of inflation.

Foremost among these is unemployment. Today our country has more than 2 million unemployed.

Now you can try to soften that figure in a dozen ways. . . .

But when all that has been said the fact remains that the level of unemployment in our country today is a human tragedy. Let me make it clear beyond doubt. I am profoundly concerned about unemployment. . . .

If I could press a button and genuinely solve the unemployment problem, do you think that I would not press that button this instant? Does anyone imagine that there is the smallest political gain in letting this unemployment continue, or that there is some obscure economic religion which demands this unemployment as part of its ritual? This Government are pursuing the only policy which gives any hope of bringing our people back to real and lasting employment. . . .

If spending money like water was the answer to our country's problems, we would have no problems now. If ever a nation has spent, spent, and spent again, ours has. Today that dream is over. All of that money has got us nowhere but it still has to come from somewhere. Those who urge us to relax the squeeze, to spend yet more money indiscriminately in the belief that it will help the unemployed and the small businessman are not being kind or compassionate or caring. They are not the friends of the unemployed or the small business. They are asking us to do again the very thing that caused the problems in the first place. . . .

I am accused of lecturing or preaching about this. I suppose it is a critic's way of saying "Well, we know it is true, but we have to carp at something." I do not care about that. But I do care about the future of free enterprise, the jobs and exports it provides and the independence it brings to our people. Independence? Yes, but let us be clear what we mean by that. Independence does not mean contracting out of all relationships with others. A nation can be free but it will not stay free for long if it has no friends and no alliances. Above all, it will not stay free if it cannot pay its own way in the world. By the same token, an individual needs to be part of a community and to feel that he is part of it. There is more to this than the chance to earn a living for himself and his family, essential though that is.

Of course, our vision and our aims go far beyond the complex arguments of economics, but unless we get the economy right we shall deny our people the opportunity to share that vision and to see beyond the narrow horizons of economic necessity. Without a healthy economy we cannot have a healthy society. Without a healthy society the economy will not stay healthy for long. . . .

If our people feel that they are part of a great nation and they are prepared to will the means to keep it great, a great nation we shall be, and shall remain. So, what can stop us from achieving this? What then stands in our way? The prospect of another winter of discontent? I suppose it might.

But I prefer to believe that certain lessons have been learnt from experience, that we are coming, slowly, painfully, to an autumn of understanding. And I hope that it will be followed by a winter of common sense. If it is not, we shall not be diverted from our course.

To those waiting with bated breath for that favourite media catchphrase, the "U" turn, I have only one thing to say. "You turn if you want to. The lady's not for turning."

77
The British Press (1982). The Falkland Islands War

In 1822, Thomas Babington Macaulay, commenting on the British constitution as well as the chambers of Parliament, stated that "the gallery in which the reporters sit has become a fourth estate of the realm." Certainly, *The Times* and such later papers as *The Manchester Guardian* sought a "cultured and earnest" audience and tried to influence public policy. The increase in democracy and literacy led, however, to an expansion of the national press. The key figure was Alfred Harmsworth (1865–1922), Viscount Northcliffe, who founded the *Daily Mail* in 1896, which appealed to a new lower-class readership with short, snappy articles catering to such puerile interests as murder and sports. Success bred competition, and Britain eventually came to possess numerous London-based national dailies. Appealing to different readerships and reflecting the competitive spirit of rival press barons, such as Rupert Murdoch (1931–) and Robert Maxwell (1923–1991), Fleet Street, the press center of London, provided a broad variety of opinions on the important issues of the day.

The most dramatic event of 1982 was the unexpected Falkland Islands (Islas Malvinas) War. Ownership of the islands, claimed both by Argentina and Britain, the latter in occupation since 1833, was disputed throughout the twentieth century. When negotiations failed to resolve the problem, largely because of the islanders' desire to remain British, General Leopoldo Galtieri, president of Argentina, seized the islands on April 2, 1982. Faced with her first major foreign policy crisis, Margaret Thatcher earned her title, the "Iron Lady." Within four days a large task force, including two aircraft carriers, began its 8000-mile voyage to the South Atlantic. Following intense naval conflict, highlighted by the sinking of an Argentinian cruiser, the *General Belgrano*, and HMS *Sheffield*, British troops landed on the islands on May 21. Hard fighting ensued, but on June 14, 1982, the Falklands were again British. Thatcher had vindicated the rule of law, but she also guaranteed her re-election in 1983.

Source: The Sun, May 21, 1982, p. 3, by permission; *The Daily Telegraph*, May 22, 1982, p. 14; *Daily Mirror*, May 22, 1982, p. 2, by permission; *Daily Mail*, May 22, 1982, p. 6, by permission of *Daily Mail* / Solo; and *The Guardian*, May 24, 1982, p. 14, by permission.

The war filled the British papers for weeks. Although they all had the same basic information, derived from official communiqués and a common press pool, their approaches varied, from the exultation of *The Sun,* which greeted the *Belgrano's* sinking with the headline "GOTCHA," to the embarrassment of *New Statesman,* a weekly which labeled the whole enterprise as "Mad Margaret and the Voyage of Dishonor." The following articles, printed at the time of the British invasion, reflect differing views. Nevertheless, despite the traditional differences between, say, *The Mirror,* a Labour tabloid, and *The Daily Telegraph,* solidly and stuffily Conservative, the press was surprisingly united. Reservations over responsibility for starting the war and the wisdom of further discussions paled before the commitment to support the troops. Furthermore, after years of frustration at home, the rediscovery of an imperial spirit struck many as a welcome diversion.

The Sun, May 21, 1982

Why We Must Go To War

Premier Margaret Thatcher told the nation yesterday why she had to fight for the Falklands. She said we had a just cause and had done everything to try to find a peaceful settlement. . . .

Mrs Thatcher admitted to MPs in the Commons that "difficult days" lie ahead after British forces have stormed ashore. She added: "The principles we are defending are fundamental to everything that this Parliament and this country stand for. *They are the principles of democracy and the rule of law."*

The Premier blamed the impending war on the Argentine junta's "obduracy, delay, deception and bad faith." . . .

The Premier addressed the grim-faced Commons after the Cabinet had considered a surprise "don't fight" plea by United Nations secretary-general Perez de Cuellar. She was clearly somewhat embarrassed by the well meaning, but untimely last-ditch effort. . . . Her robust "enough is enough" declaration earned her loud cheers from Tory MPs—but many bitter complaints from many Labour MPs.

Left-winger Tony Benn opened up a massive Labour split over the crisis. *He flatly rejected appeals from Party Leader Michael Foot and other Labour chiefs not to force an embarrassing vote against the Government at the end of the Commons emergency debate.* Cheered on by about three dozen left wingers, Mr Benn said he would lead a protest vote against Government policies. . . .

But Mr Foot won loud Tory cheers when he said the Opposition wished the troops: "God speed."

Daily Mail, May 22, 1982

The Principles We Are Fighting For

The battle has begun. Our troops are at this moment fighting the Argentine invaders on the Falkland Islands. There have been losses—on both sides—and there will inevitably be more. Such is the nature of war. We mourn our dead—and we shall remember them. As a civilized country we will not gloat at the suffering of the other side. But this is not a fight of our choosing.

The British are not, as a nation, warmongers, though, as many an aggressor has discovered to his cost, when called to it we can be a warlike people. We do not fight on the Falklands out of a sense of injured pride nor out of an inflated sense of national aggrandisement. That would indeed be jingoism and that is not the national mood.

We are there to protect great and abiding principles. We say aggression cannot be allowed to pay. We say that democracy is so precious that we will shed blood—and spill it—in order that it may be preserved. That is our heritage. Our hopes and prayers go with our men, conscious as we are, that they fight for a noble and an abiding cause.

The Daily Telegraph, May 22, 1982

Into Battle

The battle has been fierce. That much is clear. And only fools ignored the possibility that it could be so. . . .

We shall hear the argument again that the rights of 1,800 Falklanders, and the notion of a nation's sovereignty, are not worthy of defence. . . . Against such false arguments . . . we must prepare ourselves following our assault on the Falklands. Some of our friends abroad, particularly in the Common Market, may forsake us. . . . As for the Labour party, one need not lose all hope in its residual patriotism, though if there is no swift victory there will be much hand-wringing. . . .

This operation represents in a reassuring way the victory of nationhood. . . . Many disappointments in their recent history have not dimmed the British people's sense of what the hour calls for. If the Government had chosen appeasement, however . . . disguised, it would have displayed a grievous misjudgment of its own people. One test of statesmanship . . . is finding the right response to such national moods. The Government has now passed that test of courage. The courage of our Task Force, now engaged, has never been in doubt.

Daily Mirror, May 22, 1982

Pinning The Blame

Britain's case against Argentina, pinning the blame on the junta for ending negotiations and starting a war, is "clear and formidable."

Those are Mr Michael Foot's words and he is right. Not even those who believe fighting solves nothing would deny it. . . .

Britain offered concessions to the Argentines which went against the Prime Minister's promises to see that aggression would not pay. On the contrary, it would have paid well.

Had Argentina agreed to the British proposals, Mrs Thatcher would have had a hard time with her own MPs. But the junta was too stupid to see the advantages for them.

The Prime Minister says now that all our proposals have been withdrawn.

That is more dramatic than sensible. However long the day of the crisis, there will have to be talks at the end of it. . . .

In the meantime, it seems more men must die. That responsibility will lie clearly with what Mrs Thatcher called the junta's "obduracy, delay, deception and bad faith."

The Guardian, May 24, 1982

A Bridgehead to Thoughts of Peace

So far, so good. There is a bridgehead with an air strip and an array of Rapier missiles in place. . . . Fresh TV platoons of retired admirals and air marshals (there seem to be more of them than there are kelpers) sweep us swiftly forward. On to Port Stanley! . . .

But there are other, slightly less blithe ways of viewing events. . . . First (and this needs saying) the battle is not over yet. The odds may be better, but extreme perils remain. . . . A second note of caution—umbilically linked to the first—concerns the familiar anaesthetics of conflict. . . . Today, on the British side, we are moving towards 80 and on, alas, to the first 100 deaths. The Argentines must be close to 500. . . . And somehow . . . the break-point of "unacceptability" or "proportionality" recedes into the distance. Present casualties, says the MoD, are "acceptable in the circumstances." . . .

But surely, it will all be worth it in the end? When the Falklanders are free again, and the tinpot fascist dictator buried in shame, then a strong democratic nation will have fulfilled its obligation to world order and can proudly rejoice at an unpleasant job well done? Here lies a third, and most profound, note of caution. . . .

Apart from one strictly military aim, the British Government has presently scant notion about outcomes, peaceful or otherwise. Mrs. Thatcher has swept everything from sight. Wonky wheezes about American-guaranteed independence or peace for the return of Argentinian prisoners waft across a barren Whitehall landscape. . . . Rear Admiral Woodward knows what he is doing, and is doing it splendidly. But the politicians whose errors he may now briefly cloak in reflected glory seem as bereft of ideas as they were in the few desperate days when Argentine invasion was scheduled but unstoppable.

What Sandy Woodward achieves in the next few days is the foundation of what follows, the fabric of potential settlement or dragging decades. He cannot make an enduring peace. And his masters in Whitehall, who can make the peace, must now trace the connection between battlefields and fields where (next year, next century) sheep may safely graze.

78
Sir Garnet Wolseley, "Memo" (1881), and John Moore, Speech in Commons (1986). The Channel Tunnel

The channel tunnel, it has been asserted, is "less an engineering project than a state of mind." Through the better part of two centuries it has reflected the temper of Britain's diplomatic and military relations with the continent. Though the idea languished during the era of "splendid isolation," a protocol with France in 1876 allowed digging to begin. The project was soon aborted; Victoria found the idea "objectionable," and *The Times* warned of abandoning the safety of "the silver streak." The 1881 memo below of Sir Garnet Wolseley (1833–1913), later commander-in-chief of the army, typified Britain's fear and revulsion of any physical contact with France.

Plans for a tunnel were resurrected after the *Entente Cordiale* of 1904, but no decision could be reached prior to the outbreak of World War I. Economic arguments paled before the truism of the *News of the World:* the channel did "the work of two million conscripts." Although a tunnel was again considered between the

Source: Sir Garnet Wolseley, "The Channel Tunnel," 1881, in W. Turner Perkins, *Channel Tunnel,* Channel Tunnel Co., 1913, pp. 48, 51, 53–54; *Parliamentary Debates* (House of Commons), Sixth Series, Vol. 98 (1986), pp. 562–563, 566–567.

wars, serious discussion did not resume until the late 1950s, when a feasibility study was begun. Construction began in 1973, but two years later the Labour government of Harold Wilson canceled the project, ostensibly because of cost. Tony Benn, a radical socialist, stated the obvious—the tunnel had "become inextricably linked with the Common Market."

In the debate which followed, critics often used arguments reminiscent of those used in the past, reflecting an "earthy feeling that an island is an island and should not be violated." Barbara Castle, a Labour cabinet member, thought "the building of a tunnel would do something profound to the national attitude—and not certainly for the better." The Thatcher government resurrected the project, agreeing on January 20, 1986, without much enthusiasm, to proceed as long as no tax revenue was involved. Defenders of the "chunnel" and Europe 92 (the economic union of the European Community planned for that year) included John Moore, Thatcher's secretary of state for transport. In a speech in Commons on June 5, 1986, he stressed the future, the material benefits of direct rail service with France, and the need to confirm paper agreements with a more tangible commitment. In November 1990, Margaret Thatcher's resignation, at least in part due to her opposition to European economic integration, coincided with British and French workmen meeting and shaking hands 131 feet under the English Channel. The tangible symbol of Britain's future as a part of a united Europe had won, but many Britons still shared Palmerston's bewilderment that anyone could wish "to shorten a distance which we find already too short."

Sir Garnet Wolseley (1881)

The proposal to make a tunnel under the Channel may, I think, be fairly described as a measure intended to annihilate all the advantages we have hitherto enjoyed from the existence of the "silver streak," for to join England to the Continent by a permanent highway will be to place her under the unfortunate condition of having neighbours possessing great standing armies, a state of things which prevents any of the Continental Nations from disarming as long as any one of them refuses to follow suit. The construction of the tunnel would place us under those same conditions that have forced the Powers of Europe to submit to universal service. . . .

The advantages must be of immense importance indeed if they are to counterbalance the least risk to our national security. It is not the nation which has demanded this great change in our position; it is not the nation which has asked to become a part of the Continent, and to cease to be "a sea-girt isle." I confess I am at a loss to understand what we are to gain, except an immunity from sea-sickness when crossing the Channel. I am aware of sea-sickness being one of the most unpleasant and most trying of human ailments, but are we deliberately to make England less safe in order that tourists may not suffer form it during the $2\frac{1}{2}$ hours occupied in the Channel passage? . . .

A German having been asked lately by an Englishman why it was that his countrymen went on yearly drilling hundreds of thousands of men, who might be so much more usefully and profitably employed, replied: "You English, with your great wet ditch round you, know nothing of the horrors of invasion; we are well acquainted with them, and having no natural line of defence, like the seas which encompass your shores to protect us from attack, we infinitely prefer submitting even to the tyranny of our military system, to the immeasurable burden of universal service in the army, rather than run the risk of finding an army over-running our country, and having to undergo the sorrow, the pain, and the public and private humiliation which that would mean; of two evils we choose that which is a flea-bite compared to the killing poison of the cobra.". . .

I have heard it stated that this tunnel can be neutralized—held sacred—under a convention to be entered into with France and other Continental powers, and that it is ridiculous to imagine that any civilized power would ever, under any circumstances, disregard the terms of such an agreement. . . .

What is the nature of the treaty that a man of the great Napoleon's turn of mind and morality would respect or care anything for the moment he felt that the interests of his nation would be advanced by breaking it? Did the most solemn treaties save Genoa or Venice from his sword? What guarantee have we that another Napoleon may not again direct the destinies of France; and, supposing he did appear, should we know his intentions before he struck his blow?. . .

Dover held by an enemy in possession of the tunnel would place England at his mercy. Our fleet could do nothing to help us, and we have no army under present circumstances, nor are we ever likely to have an army capable of resisting the military strength of any of the great Continental Powers. It is essential that this fact, and fact it certainly is, should be known and realized by the nation. The flattering theory, imbibed in childhood from the history of Cressy, Poictiers, Agincourt, and of many more recent battles, that one Englishman is equal to any five foreigners, is doubtless very gratifying to the national vanity, but it is almost needless to say that our traditional valour does not, in these days of rifled arms, give us the advantages we formerly possessed over continental nations. There can be no doubt of the fact that whenever an enemy's army of about 150,000 trained soldiers is able to march on London, England will for ever afterwards cease to be a great nation. . . .

Surely, John Bull will not endanger his birthright, his liberty, his property, in fact all that man can hold most dear, whether he be a patriot or merely a selfish cosmopolitan, and whether this subject be regarded from a sentimental or from a material point of view, simply in order that men and women may cross to and fro between England and France without running the risk of sea-sickness.

Even now, when protected by our "silver streak," we suffer from periodical panics, which are as injurious to trade as they are undignified; this tunnel would render their recurrence much more frequent, thereby increasing the loss they occasion. The night does not follow the day more surely than will a vastly increased annual military expenditure follow upon the construction of the tunnel. Are we to be taxed additionally for these new military establishments in order to save a certain number of travellers and tourists of all nations from sea-sickness?

John Moore (1986)

Mr. Moore: It is with some trepidation, and not a little sense of occasion, that I come before the House today to move the Second Reading of the 1986 Channel Tunnel Bill. Hon. Members will know well the long history of Channel tunnel projects going back almost two centuries, and I will not dwell on them.

The process leading to the Bill that is before the House began over 18 months ago with a meeting in November 1984 between my predecessor, now the Secretary of State for the Environment, and his French counterpart, at the end of which they announced their agreement in principle to facilitate the construction of a fixed link by private promoters. . . .

The successful project—the twin rail tunnel of CTG-FM, now known as Eurotunnel—was announced at a meeting of Heads of Government on 20 January this year. . . .

Accordingly, on 12 February the Channel fixed link treaty was signed in Canterbury and on 14 March the concession agreement was concluded. Neither of these instruments—this is important—can take effect until the two Governments have the necessary powers to implement them. The purpose of the Channel Tunnel Bill is to give the British Government the powers they need. The purpose of today's debate is to establish the principle that there should be a Channel tunnel. Once the Bill has passed into law, the treaty can be ratified and the concession can come into effect. . . .

I begin therefore, with the national impact of these proposals, which I believe to be extensive, affecting not merely travellers, holidaymakers and business men, but manufacturers and traders throughout the country, our economy as a whole and, indeed, our attitudes as a nation.

Britain is a trading nation. One third of our gross domestic product is traded internationally—a very high proportion for a nation of our size. Last year our exports came to £78 billion, and they are an essential part of our livelihood. As has been said in previous debates, 60 per cent. of our exports go to western Europe—£46 billion worth.

Such a relationship to the world is two-edged. In the past it has brought us great wealth. But it places a premium upon competitiveness, initiative, and, most importantly, on the ability to adapt to change. It is only by adapting to change—in technical development, in new patterns of consumption, in new demands from consumers, in new industries—that a trading nation can prosper. We, much more than other countries which are self-sufficient, cannot avoid the challenge of change, the need to be out in front in new development, new methods, new products and new ways of delivering them to our customers.

Yet what has been the truth in Britain over the past half century? Has it not been that, far from welcoming and thriving on change, we have clung to what we have? While whole industries should have been finding new things to make and new ways to make them, thus expanding into new markets, instead they continued to do the old things in the old ways. They lost ground to those abroad with greater initiative. But the good news is that in recent years we have seen a remarkable change in attitudes and a new recognition of what the modern world requires, which has resulted in dramatic improvements in efficiency and productivity.

These important advances have laid the foundation for long-term improvement of the British economy. The Channel tunnel, coming now, when this crucial foundation has been laid, will provide an opportunity for our industry to expand and grow into one of the richest markets in the world. The Channel tunnel will give British business the opportunity to gain ever larger slices of this enormous market. That means more jobs for individuals, more profits for business, and more wealth and resources for the country as a whole. . . .

What effect will the tunnel have on our national attitudes? In the past, we were never afraid to venture abroad and never worried that contact with other countries would put our national identity at risk. But of late we seem to have grown fearful of change and timid in the face of challenge.

The truth is that our national identity is entirely secure. The unique qualities of British institutions, history and culture are recognised the world over. They are not threatened by contact with other European countries. Indeed, we are already part of Europe, connected in a multitude of ways, but physically less effectively connected than we could be. To improve the physical connection is plain good sense. It will offer unprecedented opportunities for business expansion, cultural enrichment and individual travel. It could stimulate a whole new era of endeavour and achievement for our country. It is in that light that the Channel tunnel becomes an opportunity, not a threat, and it is in that spirit that I commend the Bill to the House.

GABLER
KOMPAKT-LEXIKON
WERBEPRAXIS